Houston Symposium I

Psychology And Society:
In Search of Symbiosis

Edited by
Richard A. Kasschau
and
Frank S. Kessel
University of Houston

HOLT, RINEHART AND WINSTON
New York   Chicago   San Francisco   Dallas
Montreal   Toronto   London   Sydney

Library of Congress Cataloging in Publication Data

Houston Symposium, 1st, 1978.
Psychology and society.

Bibliography: p.
Includes index.
1. Psychology—United States.   2. Social problems.
3. Psychological research.   I. Kasschau, Richard A.
   II. Kessel, Frank S.   III. Title.
BF38.H66   1978   302   80-304
ISBN 0-03-053556-5

© 1980 by Holt, Rinehart and Winston
All rights reserved

Printed in the United States of America
0   1   2   3   038   9 8 7 6 5 4 3 2 1

In memory of
John F. MacNaughton

Copyright Acknowledgments

Appendix B first appeared as Miller, G. A. Psychology as a means of promoting human welfare. *American Psychologist*, 1969, 24, 1063–1075. Copyright 1969 by the American Psychological Association. Reprinted by permission.

Preface

On April 7 and 8, 1978, the department of psychology of the University of Houston initiated what is now an annual symposium series. Under the general title "Houston Symposium," each year's symposium will be entitled "Psychology and Society: . . . ," with the year's subject identified in the subtitle. The first symposium, then, is entitled "Psychology and Society: In Search of Symbiosis," and it represents an in-depth examination ten years after the fact of George A. Miller's controversial presidential address to the American Psychological Association (APA) in late summer 1969. Professor Miller raised a number of issues—seminal at the time they were offered—which have grown in importance in the intervening years.

We prevailed upon Professor Miller to chair our symposium and to react to six posthoc analyses of his 1969 address. In selecting our speakers we attempted to strike a balance between research and applications perspectives, between academic and other views, among various perspectives that were so important to the dynamics of society in the late sixties and certainly not less so now, and across some range of disciplinary perspectives. We were singularly successful in striking the various balances.

A review of the Table of Contents and the biographies included as an appendix to this volume will show that we invited a past president of the American Psychological Association, a former executive officer of the American Association for the Advancement of Science (AAAS), a vice-president of the Educational Testing Service, the then-current president of the American Educational Research Association, the chairman of the board of the Association for the Advancement of Psychology (AAP), a developmental psychologist with a remarkably balanced world view of the niche occupied by psychology as a discipline, and a scholar of international repute as an analyst of psychology's theoretical and philosophical foundations.

A little description of the dynamics of the symposium will help the reader. The speakers appeared in the order in which their papers are presented in this volume. The forum was a semicircle of easy chairs, with a podium and microphone facing chairs for 150—filled most of the time during the symposium's two days. Each speaker was allotted ninety minutes. Following an introduction by Miller, most speakers preceded their formal paper with ad lib comments ranging up to five minutes in duration. Some are relatively trivial, but others are focal points for some of the dynamics which became high points for the symposium. One example: When George Miller was about to begin his APA presidential address in 1969, the microphone was taken away from him by a dozen black graduate students who were pressing for a greater number of entry slots for black and other minority graduate students in the nation's psychology graduate programs. It developed during Miller's introduction of James Jackson (now chairman of the board of the AAP) that Jackson was one of those students. The exchange between the two at the Houston Symposium is the first meeting between the two since that day in 1969!

Such higher-level dynamics were operating continuously throughout the symposium, lending a very exciting, challenging, crisply analytic air to the proceedings. There are various flat points, to be sure, and after a couple of papers little discussion. Other times, however, discussions were started which moved back and forth across a wide range of issues raised by one or more of the speakers. The general caliber of exchanges among the participants in various discussions becomes a crucial element in appreciating the total impact and value of the symposium. The entire conference was recorded. We transcribed all the introductions, exchanges, and discussions, and as faithfully as possible we have attempted to preserve the spirit of pause and ponder, of give and take that became a kind of "seventh force" as the symposium proceeded.

Professor Miller's overall reaction was delayed until the beginning of the last portion of the symposium. He elected to analyze the papers briefly, focusing on what he considered to be the critical point of each paper. He then extended that critical point to the next logical question and redirected that question back to the person who had delivered the paper. For instance, since Professor Scriven evaluated psychology and gave it a rather low grade for successes in promoting human welfare, Miller challenged Scriven as to what psychology should instead be doing to "improve its grade." Each speaker—after Miller had finished—was given time to respond to the issue raised by Miller.

This presented a bit of a problem for us when casting the symposium in printed form, but our decision is to place Miller's comments as if they followed each paper immediately, since he clearly divided his comments into six portions. Thus this printed version presents his comments slightly out of order relative to the actual series of events, but gaining closure on some issues raised by each paper is easier to achieve with this format.

We did edit, but as lightly as possible to remove redundancies, broken thoughts where a nod of the head communicated a thought covertly, and even to remove occasional low-information content and redundant phrases with which we all seemed to be burdened.

There are—as already intimated—a number of dynamics (some stressful, some critical, some humorous) which pervaded the conference. Koch has an inimicable and penetrating sense of humor—nowhere better illustrated than in the exchange between him and a member of the audience when Koch mispronounced New Zealand as New England (he is now at Boston University) in the process of analyzing Miller's paper. The exchange speaks for itself, but illustrates the kinds of exchanges going on constantly during the symposium. We have included all of this dialogue as it occurred.

The only other major "tampering" with the sequential evolution of the conference concerns the discussion of Sigmund Koch's paper. The length of the opening statements on the first morning caused the symposium to run almost thirty minutes late—well into a scheduled lunch break. There was, as a result, no opportunity to discuss Professor Koch's paper immediately following its delivery. However, the speakers' inclination to address issues raised by Koch surfaced at the next opportunity—following Professor Scriven's paper early the first afternoon. It was unfortunate that Scriven could be with us only for the first of two days of the symposium, especially since time for discussing his paper was devoted to the preceding paper.

In order to "correct" these minor inconsistencies, we have moved the discussion following Scriven's paper so that it directly follows Koch's own paper. We have also given Professor Scriven an opportunity by telephone to respond to Professor Miller's challenge to him in the concluding discussion. Scriven's response—

given with no more time for organization of thought than the other speakers were offered—does follow Scriven's paper. Aside from these variances, we have remained faithful to the real-time sequence of events.

The initial introduction/anticipation of the conference's themes and issues composed by Professor Frank Kessel of the University of Houston does a good job of capturing the spirit of the times in the late sixties, but it also elegantly summarizes the major themes of Miller's paper for this symposium. After the fact, both Professors Miller and Kessel were extended an invitation to write a retrospective analysis of the symposium.

There are several people who helped us with Houston Symposium I whom I would like to recognize. One was Mary Carol Day, another was Jim Campion, both of whom helped in a number of ways. Frank Kessel was ever the voice of excellence, and in fact was the one responsible for our doing Houston Symposium I in April 1978 instead of April 1979 as I was quite inclined to do. Joy McCreary helped us with communications in no small way. And finally, our departmental chairperson, Ken Laughery, found the funds that were necessary and represented us to our upper-level administration. Without each of these people there would surely have been no symposium, let alone a series.

Houston Symposium II will address "Psychology's Second Century—Enduring Issues." But for now, let's get on with an examination of the relation between "Psychology and Society: In Search of Symbiosis."

Contents

Preface *Richard Kasschau* iii

Kasschau's Introduction of David Gottlieb	1
Welcoming Remarks *David Gottlieb*	2
Kasschau's Introduction of Frank Kessel	6

• PSYCHOLOGY AND SOCIETY: IN SEARCH OF SYMBIOSIS:
Introduction to the Symposium   *Frank S. Kessel*   7

Miller's Address	8
Issues and Questions	9
The Broader Context	10
Some Pre-Miller History	12
Some Post-Miller Developments and Observations	15
References	21
Kasschau's Introduction of George A. Miller	24
Miller's Opening Statement	25
PSYCHOLOGY AND ITS HUMAN CLIENTELE	27
Miller's Introduction of Koch	27
Koch's Opening Comments	28

• PSYCHOLOGY AND ITS HUMAN CLIENTELE:
Beneficiaries or Victims?   *Sigmund Koch*   30

Introduction	30
Some Deeper Problems in Dr. Miller's World View	36
The Varela "Paradigm"	37
Pupil-Contract versus Pupil-Contact in the Teaching of Reading	41
An Alternate View of Psychology	43
References	53
General Discussion of Koch's Paper	53
Question and Answer *Miller and Koch*	56

AN EVALUATION OF PSYCHOLOGY — 61

Miller's Introduction of Scriven — 61

- **AN EVALUATION OF PSYCHOLOGY**
  Michael Scriven   62

  The Report Card — 62
  The First Failure: The Ahistorical View — 64
  The Second Failure: Self-Scrutiny — 64
  The Third Failure: The Newtonian Fantasy — 69
  The Fourth Failure: The Value-Free Commitment — 73
  Conclusion — 77

General Discussion of Scriven's Paper — 77
Question and Answer *Miller and Scriven* — 79

TESTING—THE LIMITS OF SOCIAL RESPONSIBILITY — 83

Miller's Introduction of Williams — 83
Williams' Opening Statement — 84

- **TESTING—THE LIMITS OF SOCIAL RESPONSIBILITY**   E. Belvin Williams   86

  References — 96

General Discussion of Williams' Paper — 97
Question and Answer *Miller and Williams* — 98

PSYCHOLOGY IN ALL SORTS OF PLACES — 102

Miller's Introduction of White — 102
White's Opening Statement — 103

- **PSYCHOLOGY IN ALL SORTS OF PLACES**
  Sheldon H. White   105

  Historical Myths of Origin in Psychology — 106
  Revisiting the Dream Time — 110
  The Structure of Practice — 115
  How Psychology is Given Away — 120

viii   Contents

    On Giving   127
        References   130

General Discussion of White's Paper   131
Question and Answer *Miller and White*   137

PROMOTING HUMAN WELFARE THROUGH LEGISLATIVE ADVOCACY   *144*

Miller's Introduction of Jackson   144
Jackson's Opening Statement   145

- **PROMOTING HUMAN WELFARE THROUGH LEGISLATIVE ADVOCACY: A Proper Role for the Proper Science of Psychology?** *James S. Jackson*   **147**

    Legislation and Societal Needs   148
    Psychology and Societal Problems   150
        Defining Social Problems and Human Welfare   150
        Contributions of Scientific Psychology to the
        Amelioration of Social Problems   151
    Academic and Professional Psychology   154
    Psychology and the Legislative Process   157
        Models of Possible Involvement   157
        Activist/Collaborator Model   159
    Conclusion   159
        References   161

General Discussion of Jackson's Paper   163
Question and Answer *Miller and Jackson*   179

ACADEMIC SCIENCE AND THE FEDERAL GOVERNMENT   *184*

Miller's Introduction of Bevan   184
Bevan's Opening Statement   185

- **ACADEMIC SCIENCE AND THE FEDERAL GOVERNMENT: Less Wed, More Locked** *William Bevan*   **187**

Academic Science in the Late Seventies, or Life on a
Sinking Raft   189
   A New Deal for Basic Research?   189
   *Impediment to the Future of Research: Obsolete
   Equipment and Deteriorating Facilities*   193
   *Impediment to the Future of Research: Lack of
   New Blood*   195
   *Impediment to the Freedom and Responsibility
   of Scientists: The Federal Government's
   Penchant for Regulation*   198
Academic Science: Intellectual Playground or National
Resource?   202
The Politics of Professionalized Science   205
Where Do We Go From Here?   208
On the Nature of Policy   210
We Are the Government—You and I   211
   References   215

General Discussion of Bevan's Paper   217
Question and Answer *Miller and Bevan*   224

CONCLUSIONS   228

Miller's Closing Statement   228

- **AFTERTHOUGHTS** George A. Miller **229**
- **POSTSCRIPT TO THE SYMPOSIUM**
  Frank S. Kessel **234**

Science and Society   234
Psychology and Society   236
"Giving Psychology Away": Theory-and-Practice/
Basic-and-Applied   237
Psychology as "Science"   240
Educating Psychologists   241
Personal Styles and Qualities   243
Notes   246
   References   248

- **APPENDIX A   PSYCHOLOGY AS A MEANS
  OF PROMOTING HUMAN
  WELFARE** George A. Miller **249**

Role of the American Psychological Association 250
Revolutionary Potential of Psychology 253
Control of Behavior 256
Public Psychology: Two Paradigms 259
How to Give Psychology Away 262
   References 269

- **APPENDIX B   Author's Biographies**
*William Bevan   James S. Jackson
Sigmund Koch   George A. Miller
Michael Scriven   Sheldon H. White
E. Belvin Williams* **270**

Kasschau's Introduction of David Gottlieb

Ladies and gentlemen, it is a pleasure for me to start this two-day Houston Symposium. Our topic is to be "Psychology and Society: In Search of Symbiosis." We will be concerned with an analysis of Professor George Miller's presidential address to the American Psychological Association almost a decade ago in late summer 1969.

Before we get started, we would like to welcome formally our distinguished visitors from across the nation. The greetings of the university as we start this symposium will be delivered by the dean of our College of Social Sciences, David Gottlieb . . .

Welcoming Remarks

David Gottlieb

On behalf of Chancellor Barry Munitz, the faculty and students of the College of Social Sciences, I am delighted to welcome you to the Central Campus of the University of Houston. It is our hope that this symposium will be the first in a continuing series in which the focus shall be upon the fit between our academic disciplines and the workings of our society.

It is, of course, appropriate that this symposium, "Psychology and Society: In Search of Symbiosis," be held at this time and at this place. The University of Houston, Central Campus, is a major urban public institution. We would not and could not escape responsibility for a continuous exploration of the role which we might legitimately play in connecting with the needs, aspirations, and problems of our community, state, and nation. Timely because during the last several years this university has attracted an increasing number of faculty whose interests and concerns are with bridging between their disciplines, theory, methodology, and efforts of application and intervention. Such is most likely to be the case among social scientists because of the nature of our disciplines and the characteristics and attributes of our colleagues. As shown in the most recent Lipset-Ladd survey, social scientists, particularly sociologists and psychologists, are more likely than other academics to be liberal in political attitude, more action oriented, and more likely to believe in federal as well as state programs of social intervention and regulation.

I should point out, however, that it is my experience as dean that social scientists, particularly psychologists, are quite selective in their choice of regulation settings; they rarely respond in an enthusiastic manner when they are the subjects of such regulation and intervention.

A major purpose of this symposium is to revisit and reflect upon the comments made by Professor Miller in his 1969 APA presidential address. Hopefully, the experiences of the past will be considered as we go about the business of determining what should be the appropriate role for psychology and psychologists in the years to come.

The period from 1964 to 1968, which saw a series of attempts at social reform, followed by retrenchment, is unique in American political history. A deluge of legislation dealing with education, training, health care, housing, and numerous other areas affecting income and welfare, issued forth from the Congress. Then the flow ceased and some of the programs enacted during that period were repealed, scaled down, or delegated to state and local governments with few restrictions to ensure that the original purposes were carried out.

It may be of some value to attempt to understand the conditions which led to the rise and fall of social science reform efforts.

In summary: The 1960s were a period of the development of intellectual tools, particularly quantitative methods, more specifically, in the areas of economics and cost-benefit analysis. These tools were first used in the military and then later translated for social policy purposes.

The sixties were a period of unprecedented growth in college enrollments; huge boosts in graduate enrollments; and a massive increase in qualified, highly mobile, hungry researchers.

There was an overall faith in the government's ability to bring about social reform.

Further, there was consensus among social scientists as to the reasons for poverty, racism, unemployment, and learning. (Although Peter Rossi would challenge this conclusion by pointing out that it was not so much consensus as the fact that those social scientists involved in social policy were a highly selective group and not truly a representative sample.)

There was apparently a comfortable fit between the solutions proposed by social scientists and the kinds of legislative actions which Congress was prepared to pass. President Kennedy made the observation that while the problems were technically complex, they did not involve a conflict of ideology.

Social scientists were involved in policy issues, not only as researchers and expert consultants but as program/agency administrators.

The 1970s are clearly different. There is less faith in the federal government, brought about in part by Vietnam, Watergate, and a growing feeling that the huge bureaucracy cannot deal effectively with the dynamics of change. There are growing expressions of discontent about federal control and regulation. Interestingly, for the first time, I believe we have a phenomenon where university presidents join with private corporate presidents in order to resist the intrusion of the federal government.

Righted civil wrongs: Changes in laws and styles with regard to minorities have removed this question from among the more salient political concerns.

Thirdly, a breakdown in intellectual consensus as to how social problems should be handled. The *Bakke* case, for one, has created traumatic divisions between and among academics. Further, disagreement has emerged not only in the area of theory, but in program evaluation. Coleman, Jensen, Jenkins, Herenstein, Meadows, Kahn—the work and interpretations of each has managed to generate national attention and much highly publicized intellectual confrontation. Fourth, a less comfortable fit between that which is proposed by social scientists and that which policymakers are willing to endorse.

Finally, an inward retreat on the part of many social scientists. The reason or reasons for the shift to privatism are difficult to determine. Perhaps a growing awareness that problems are far more complex than initially thought; an increasing sentiment that the only real science is one that is value-free; perceptions of a lack of opportunity; that perhaps the academy does not reward those who move into applied-intervention efforts; that current theories and methodologies are not sufficient to deal with social problems; that, along with Moynihan, matters of social policy should be left with politicians, and social scientists would do better to concentrate upon program evaluation.

I do not pretend to have the empirical data necessary to answer the question, nor am I certain as to just how far-spread this selective apathy might be. Further, I am not convinced that the decline in action-oriented zeal is all that harmful to either the profession or those we seek to help. In retrospect, I believe that Professor Miller would concur that there are some parts of psychology that he would not want to give away, no matter the consumer demand.

Perhaps this less chaotic and kinetic period will allow us to raise and answer important questions in a more reasonable and systematic manner. The questions that need to be raised, I believe, are no different from those which might have been asked before: How can psychologists help raise the standards of admissible evidence? How can they enrich and deepen understanding of the complexity of problems and the unintended consequences of their actions? What role should psychology play? Perhaps we would agree with Peter Rossi that "social science and social scientists have not yet turned to the question of what is a good society and which social arrangements are to be preferred to others. I think we have reached the stage of maturity where we can turn again to these problems, for a completely value-free social science is a social science of little value."

Finally, I believe it would be appropriate for us to consider this statement by Henry J. Aaron of the Brookings Institution:

> How serviceable for the 70s and beyond are the faiths that motivated the reformers of the 1960s? The twin spectres of war and depression, both seemingly banished by government action, recede into the fog of past history, to be replaced in contemporary consciousness by another war

without valid purpose or tangible success, by economic and social dilemmas still poorly understood, and by a recognition that modes of government action suitable to the past may be inadequate today. Fear of nuclear catastrophe, initially a source of shared responsibility, has turned to dull awareness. The moods of the post depression and the postwar years, the sense that humanity must act to improve the world and secure it from disaster while time remains have ended. The mad sense of urgency will not be missed. Now, we can try again to solve many of the problems we tried to solve ten years ago, but as before and as always we must proceed with inadequate research. Nevertheless, sober attempts rationally to solve increasingly complèx problems may be advanced if we retain a bit of that sense of mutual obligation and community that flowed from economic catastrophe and the holocaust.

Again, I welcome you to this campus and I look forward to participating with you in this important symposium.

Kasschau's Introduction of Frank Kessel

Thank you, Dean Gottlieb. I hark back now to a comment I first heard an uncle of mine make some years ago about the wisdom of never volunteering in the Army. The gentleman who originally "volunteered" the topic that we're addressing here today has been prevailed upon to get us started with an introduction of the theme of the conference.

I give you Frank Kessel . . .

Psychology and Society: In Search of Symbiosis
Introduction to the Symposium

Frank S. Kessel
Department of Psychology
University of Houston

When I originally proposed the theme of this symposium, I knew, in some tacit way, that it might strike a responsive chord. Though harboring hopes I did not know that we would be fortunate to have such a distinguished group of participants. Nor did I know, or hope, that I would find myself preceding the symposium speakers, expected to present a thirty-minute introduction. After all, my tacit knowledge extended no further than the original two-page proposal, most of whose contents are printed on the symposium program anyway.

Be that as it may, my overall purpose will be to sketch a background in the form of issues and questions surrounding psychology-society relationships. I make no claims to completeness nor to a sketch in anything but selective, simplified strokes. But I trust that some sort of stage will be set for the symposium presentations. Specifically, I will use George Miller's (1969) APA address as a starting point, then attempt to place his address in its wider, contemporary context. I will then look backwards, giving a potted history of matters relating to the address, and finally, forward, tracing some developments from 1969 to the present.

In all of this I will be viewing the theme from a variety of perspectives, dabbling in the history, philosophy, sociology, and perhaps even psychology of science. For the dabbling I apologize; for drawing attention to these perspectives, I do not. As Gerald Holton (1975) has suggested, any particular "event" in science has a number of facets—in his analysis, nine in all. Considered in three major groups, these are first, the theories, data,

Paper prepared for *Houston Symposium I*, Houston, April 7–8, 1978.

techniques of public science—their logical and epistemological status, their historical development, their broader paradigmatic positions and underlying themata (Holton's specific interest); second, the personal, private aspects of science, especially in the context of discovery—what these are, their narrower and broader psychobiographical development; and third, within-science sociological conditions and influences, as well as broader cultural developments affecting and being affected by science. Though the "event" we are considering is as broad as psychological science itself, and though some of these perspectives are probably more pertinent than others, I'd like to suggest that they might serve as a fruitful, if largely implicit, framework for this introduction and for the symposium.

MILLER'S ADDRESS

Miller's starting premise is that, while psychologists have sought to apply their science to social problems and have had some success doing so, "we have been less effective than we might have been" (p. 1063). Why this should be so and what might be done about it, at a time when "vast social changes are in the making" (p. 1074), are the basic questions he addresses.

Miller first considers what role the APA should play in ensuring greater social relevance for scientific and professional activities. He examines the debate over whether psychologists should remain expert and "neutral" advisers or take more responsibility for determining public policy, as well as related arguments over whether the APA should play a more activist role in social policymaking. His conclusion is that "our real strength [in promoting human welfare] will come from our scientific knowledge, not from our national Association [which] can never play more than a supporting role" (p. 1065).

Miller moves on to a declaration that scientific psychology has great revolutionary potential. That potential does not rest, however, in providing new technological options or instrumental applications to specific practical problems, a model of "application" and of the link between science, technology, and society which Miller feels we mistakenly borrow from the natural sciences. "The real impact of psychology will be felt, not through the technical products it places in the hands of powerful men, but through its effects on the public at large, through a new and different public conception of what is humanly possible and what is humanly desirable" (p. 1066). "We should be trying to self-consciously analyze the general effect that our scientific psychology may have on popular psychology" (p. 1067).

From that populist perspective Miller looks critically at the notion of "behavior control," raising and reinforcing common concerns about who controls the controllers. He adds the thought that "behavior control could easily become a self-fulfilling prophecy" (p. 1069), again, through its impact on our shared views of ourselves. In any case, he argues the general case that "understanding and prediction are better goals for psychology than is control" (p. 1069).

"Public psychology" then becomes the focus, and Miller discusses "two alternative images of what the popular conception of human nature might become under the impact of scientific advances in psychology" (p. 1069). By his own admission, much of this is sketchy and schematic but, referring to the ideas of a Uruguayan engineer, Varela, Miller argues that the second of these images is one that seems to be supported by psychological evidence and, more important, is the image that psychology should seek to foster—an image or conception stressing individual differences, complexity of human motivation, the importance of people's personal perception or conception of events, and so on.

Miller finally considers how to give psychology away, acknowledging how difficult this might be and worrying the perennial worry of whether everything must be changed in order to change anything. He suggests several means of giving psychology away, arguing that "we are in serious need of psychologists who can apply our science to personal and social problems" (p. 1072), but also emphasizing that psychology's public should be seen as equal partners in the process. In response to those who might suggest "we should stay in our laboratories and do our own thing" (p. 1074), Miller emphasizes that we will, of course, seek to advance psychology and thereby human welfare "each in our own way"; but he concludes that "nothing would be more relevant to human welfare . . . than to discover how best to give psychology away" (p. 1074).

ISSUES AND QUESTIONS

Given the summary of Miller's paper, let me sketch, in question form, the kinds of issues implicated and to which, in one form or another, this symposium is addressed:

What are, or should be, psychology's social responsibilities? What status should "social relevance" have in determining its direction? Are there dangers in an unduly utilitarian view of psychology?

What should be the *psychologist's* social responsibilities qua psychologist, and how do these differ, if at all, from his/her responsibilities as a citizen?

What should be the role of the APA, and other professional societies, in meeting the discipline's social responsibilities?

What is the appropriate model for viewing relations between psychology and society? In what ways does and should scientific psychology affect and contribute to society? How do "basic" and "applied" psychology fit into this picture? What conception of "science" is implicit in "scientific psychology"?

What kinds of images of human nature does psychology project? Can we say which image it should project, and on what basis do we make such a claim?

Conversely, what is the public's image and understanding of psychology and should we be concerned about that? *Which* public are we referring to?

Finally, what are the implications of our view of psychology-society relations for the education of psychologists?

It should be apparent that, more or less explicitly, in greater or lesser detail, and with greater or lesser justification, Miller has taken a position on these questions. But rather than spell out, and in effect repeat, his position I'd prefer to move on to the context of his address, pausing long enough only to present one complicating question and one simplifying statement.

The complicating question is not dealt with by Miller but waits in the wings (close to Sigmund Koch's [1969] heart). *Which* (or *whose*) psychology are we talking about when we consider psychology-society issues? Is it meaningful to speak of a unified, single discipline; and if it isn't, how would recognition of the nature of the differences between different "areas" affect our view of the issues? Having stated the question, I conveniently choose to leave it in the wings.

The simplifying statement: For pedagogic purposes, I suggest that there is a "purist" position on the issues Miller has raised. This position rests on a strict distinction between "science" and "non-science," between science on the one hand and society or politics on the other. The "internal logic" (Haskins 1973) of science is what determines the conduct of scientists, and thus neither the discipline, the individual scientist, nor professional/scientific societies have any external, broader social responsibilities. To assert otherwise is to confound "is" and "ought" statements, to commit "the naturalistic fallacy" and to open the scientific door to "value judgments" and "subjectivity," and so on. Of course, I draw a caricature. Nevertheless, I suspect that some aspects of such a position remain in currency today (in undergraduate texts and even in graduate education?), sufficiently in currency at least for the "purist" position to serve as an instructive contrast to the views expressed by Miller and others.

THE BROADER CONTEXT

That Miller was part of a prevailing pattern is easy to demonstrate. He himself suggested that "the demand for social relevance that we have been voicing as psychologists is only one aspect of a general dissatisfaction with the current state of our society" (p. 1074). In psychology itself, Edward Walker (1969) had, a little earlier, devoted his presidential address to the Midwestern Psychological Association to the topic of "Experimental Psychology and Social Responsibility," arguing that "science cannot proceed as if the individual's roles as scientist and human being are completely separate" (p. 864). He concluded with a statement of four "social and political obligations," including "experimental psychology has the responsibility to interpret its basic research to society as a whole" (p. 867), and "experimental psychology must find a means of stepping up its attack on pressing social problems" (p. 868).

In his presidential address to the Eastern Psychological Association at almost the same time, Morton Deutsch (1969) spoke of "Socially Relevant Science," reflecting on decades of social psychological study of interpersonal conflict, and noting that he had been continuously concerned with "the interrelations among experimental research, theory and social policy" (p. 1076). Deutsch's address contains many a wise observation on that trinity, and I will have occasion to mention him again in discussing historical perspectives.

For the present it's instructive to note that these three presidential addresses all appeared in the 1969 volume of the *American Psychologist* (Deutsch in the pages immediately after Miller), and that the volume also contained Donald Campbell's (1969) paper on "Reforms as Experiments," a paper that signaled in singular fashion the launching of the evaluation movement in psychology. All in all, then, the 1969 *American Psychologist* was a vintage volume, suggesting that the field and the people in it were part of the *Zeitgeist*.

Psychologists were, of course, not the only folk affected. Nor was the *Zeitgeist* as calm and constructive as the surface of Miller's, Walker's and Deutsch's addresses might suggest. Scientists were intensely active on a variety of political fronts, within old and new professional societies, and elsewhere—campaigning against ABMs and against chemical and biological warfare, and, in a symbolic event, on March 4, 1969, calling a research strike at MIT. But, while fueled by the Vietnam War, these weren't purely political acts, for these matters were often tied to another set of issues, *viz.*, what was considered the widespread misuse of science and technology, and the related social and ethical responsibilities of the scientist (Brown 1971). There was talk of the "Faustian bargain" that American scientists had struck with their government, and argument against the "myth" that science, "basic" or otherwise, is above and beyond human affairs. One slogan of the day was, indeed, "Science for the People."

The *Zeitgeist* did, of course, add up to something more than a slogan and a day-long strike, and we live with its legacy. Nor was it confined to an activist, anti-establishment few. The clearest indication of that was another presidential address, this to the AAAS by Don Price (1969) nine months before Miller's. Price noted that science was under attack on two fronts: on the one side, a political reaction in the form of efforts in Washington to cut down on basic research appropriations and to reduce the scientific community's relative autonomy in decision-making on grant allocations; on the other, the rebellion against impersonal technological society, science no longer being considered the "beneficent instrument of progress" but identified as being at the root of the problem. (In a later paper, Holton [1976] talked of being caught between the "New Apollonians" and the "New Dionysians.")

Price took a phlegmatic attitude toward the political problems, calling them "a political discomfort." That matter will be taken up tomorrow by William Bevan who, as his title suggests, is anything but sanguine about federal funding. Price, for his part, felt that it was more important to consider implications of the challenge to science's centuries-old "comfortable assumption that it could pursue fundamental truth and at the same time contribute to human welfare and humane values" (p. 26). A flavor of Price's view of those implications will complete the context of Miller's address:

> As the first step toward a diagnosis of our problem, we must admit that, as scientists, we have not been very clear in the past as to the basic relation of science to politics. . . . We cannot dismiss the [rebels'] charge by repeating the old principle that political authorities determine policies on the basis of philosophical or moral values, and that scientific knowledge only tells us how best to carry out those policies—that is, tells us the best means to those ends. This reply will no longer do. . . . In America many scientists have been hypocritical on the issue; they use the old formula as a defense for public relations, even though they realize that science has, and must have, a profound influence on values, and are inclined to believe that science could provide the answers to policy questions, if politicians were not so stupid. It is high time that we become more critical—instead of hypocritical—in facing this fundamental issue. (p. 27)

SOME PRE-MILLER HISTORY

Critical awareness of science and the scientist's social responsibilities, calls for more relevant scientific work, and the seemingly contradictory concern for the abuses and dangers of science and technology—these were prominent features of the intellectual and social landscape in the late sixties. But they had not appeared *de novo*. Conflict and cooperation between science or philosophy and society can be traced almost as far back as one might choose. Galileo's encounter with the Church we know about, but did you know that he had previously offered his telescope to Venice for military use, the day thereafter receiving a salary raise and something similar to tenure? Did you know that Archimedes became a military consultant in the war of Syracuse against Rome? And did you know that Francis Bacon caught cold and died while tackling the applied problem of how to refrigerate poultry? (These gems, and more, can be culled from Schroeer's [1972] work entitled *Physics and Its Fifth Dimension: Society*.)

Dissatisfaction with science and particularly the role of scientific associations has also been in the air for a long while, at least for well over a century, often, as Arnold Thackray (1971) has demonstrated, in terms with a familiar ring. Perhaps partially because of such criticisms, scientific associations have not necessarily shied away from all social and political issues. Walker (1969), for example, cites the MPA's call for the Twelfth International Congress not to be held in Vienna in 1941 because, amongst other things, the Nazis had "confiscated the passport and available funds of Sigmund Freud" (p. 866).

Wars, weaponry, and sundry related matters figure prominently in the history of science-society relations. The impetus for the modern, social-responsibility-of-science movement came, of course, from the A-bomb, its repercussions and reverberations being felt within the community of physicists and beyond. This has become the paradigmatic, clear case of science's impact on the world and the role of scientists in attempting to influence and take responsibility for that impact. It is a case well known in general but one that always rewards a revisit for details; for example, to the relevant chapters (20 and 21) in Clark's (1971) biography of Einstein. "From regarding scientists as a group almost aloof from the rest of the world, [Einstein] began to consider them first as having responsibilities and rights on a level with the rest of men, and finally as a group whose exceptional position demanded the exercise of exceptional responsibilities" (p. 596). There follows the characteristically quotable quote (from 1948), Einstein arguing that it is "our solemn and transcendent duty to do all in our power in preventing these weapons from being used" and asking "what social aim could be closer to our hearts?" To pursue that aim, the Federation of Atomic Scientists had been formed, and its *Bulletin* first published, at the end of World War II.

What of psychology? In the person of David Krech and a dozen colleagues it too had started to take note of "the troubles and headaches of society" and to try to deal with "a variety of taboos and communication difficulties [that] seemed to separate the psychological laboratories and the field of social leadership and action" (Lippitt 1946, p. 1). Thus was born, at the APA meetings in 1936, SPSSI (The Society for the Psychological Study of Social Issues), its *Journal of Social Issues* appearing ten years later.

The Statement of Purpose in that first journal issue ran as follows: "The SPSSI is a group of several hundred social psychologists and allied social scientists with a particular interest in research on the psychological aspects of key social issues. . . . The Society believes it has the obligation to help get scientific knowledge into the bloodstream of applied social action by building as many bridges as possible between theory and practice in group, community, national, and international living." The statement then discusses the reciprocal responsibilities of the members of the society ("to communicate in a straightforward professional manner") and of applied social scientists ("to make us more aware of their key problems") and concludes that "at every step an enterprise such as this will have to be a cooperative one between the scientist and the actionist." Can we improve on that more than thirty years later?

What must immediately spring to mind is Kurt Lewin's phrase "action research." Lewin and his co-workers figure prominently in this history, and it is no surprise that their views can be found in many of the early and later pages of the *Journal*. In Volume 2, Lewin (1946) himself discusses "action research and minority problems," declaring that his interest is simply in "research which will help the practitioner" (p. 34). For him "research that produces nothing but books will not suffice," to which he promptly adds, "this by no means implies that the research needed is in any respect less scientific or 'lower' " (p. 35). Nor did he see any necessary contradiction between action/applied research and basic scientific interests. Hence, the adage "There's nothing as practical as a good theory." Lewin also suggests that on both "the practical and the scientific sides of the question" of intergroup relations "psychology, sociology, and cultural anthropology each have begun to realize that without the help of the other neither will be able to proceed very far" (p. 36). (Are we still beginning?) Finally, he suggests that "action, research and training [be considered] as a triangle that should be kept together for the sake of any of its corners" (p. 42).

That comprises the heart of the Lewinian credo, a credo that has an uncommonly contemporary ring. However, though the ring has sounded through the years, action research, at least in a strictly Lewinian form, can hardly be said to have flourished. In 1970 Nevitt Sanford was led to ask "whatever happened to action research?" and in 1968 Krech and Sanford complained of "the apparent shortage of social psychologists willing and able to work on major social problems," a shortage no doubt linked to the growth and predominance in the sixties of laboratory-based experimental social psychology (McGuire 1973).

Nonetheless, psychologists and other social scientists had been at the heart of a significant social and political event in 1954. The *Brown* desegregation case was as significant and symbolic for the social sciences as the Bomb had been for the physical sciences. It set in motion a stream of social science contact with educational and judicial policy matters that has yet to ebb, though it and its tributaries have taken various complicating turns. For the first time a social science brief was filed for, and had an apparently crucial impact on, a Supreme Court case. Not surprisingly, the brief was prepared by a special committee of SPSSI, a number of action researchers playing a prominent role in that preparation (Clark 1953). And research by persons like Morton Deutsch was central to the position taken in the brief: "Clearly our study of interracial housing had some immediately useful and significant social consequences. . . . It helped, along with much other research, to provide a supporting rationale for judicial decisions and legislation to bar segregation" (Deutsch 1969, p. 1079). (Note, however, Deutsch's admission that "this research did not contribute significantly to the ideas of social psychology" [p. 1079], principally because the study "was not formulated with a theoretical objective and we were not alert enough to appreciate fully the wider theoretical significance of some of our findings" [p. 1080]. To follow the credo of complementary and equally important action and scientific interests was, and is, no straightforward matter.)

If *Brown* was the significant event of the fifties, the War on Poverty was that and more in the sixties. In the design, lobbying for, and implementation of programs like Head Start, psychologists and other social scientists played a principle role and, in a sense, took up the Lewinian torch. Developmental psychologists, for example, rediscovering the activist spirit of those like Lawrence Frank who had initiated the child development movement in the twenties (Senn 1975), came to Capitol Hill strengthened by the happy coincidence of new ideas in their field with the ideological underpinnings of the social attack on poverty. These were optimistic, heady days (Caldwell 1974), no one much inclined to spell out what we did not know and which expectations were unrealistic.

But as the social climate changed and as the decade drew to a close the bubble burst. The National Impact Study of Head Start appeared (Smith & Bissell 1970), with apparently less than encouraging findings, the word went out that compensatory education had failed, and related words brought back psychology's bugaboo about the genetic basis of racial and ethnic differences. From the other side of the fence came the charge that "early intervention [was] the social science base of institutional racism" (Baratz & Baratz 1970). The "difference-deficit" debate was born (Cole & Bruner 1971), while many who had been involved took a critical look at the War on Poverty not for what it said about the poor but about social science's ideological underpinnings, about the professionalization of reform practices, and so on (Guttentag 1970a, 1970b). So, precisely at the point where Miller and others were calling for greater involvement and responsibility history had produced a more sobering picture. Perhaps Miller had this in mind when he acknowledged that "giving psychology away will be no simple task" (1969, p. 1070), although those who had been in action on the poverty-war front might have considered that an understatement. The complexities of any relationship between psychology and society, at least on the larger political stage, had become more than apparent by the end of the sixties.

SOME POST-MILLER DEVELOPMENTS AND OBSERVATIONS

In many respects the events of the early seventies were merely a continuation of earlier trends. The political picture was hardly more peaceful, the ecology movement gathered momentum, and the general disquiet about science and technology was given even greater expression by Holton's (1976) "New Dionysians," the Charles Reichs and Theodore Roszaks. And while the surface of the times is quieter now, I think it would be a mistake to see any marked discontinuity between then and now.

In the scientific world itself, as the decade has gone by, the "purist" view of science-society relations has been progressively displaced in both practice and theory. For example, scientific professional societies have become more socially aware and active. Many, in the natural sciences as much as elsewhere, have adopted or proposed codes of professional conduct, and within associations numerous official and ad hoc groups have emerged to deal with science-and-society issues. The clearest illustration of this trend came in the form of the AAAS Committee on Scientific Freedom and Responsibility which filed its report in mid-1975 (Edsall 1975). That committee considered the wide range of ethical problems faced by scientists today and advocated that the AAAS should no longer take a relatively neutral stand on such issues. The committee also examined the role of professional societies as "protectors of the public interest" and urged that, "in matters directly related to the professional competence of members of the society . . . the societies can and should play a much more active role than they have in the past" (Edsall 1975, p. 691). Many societies have indeed adopted such an activist role, much as Thackray predicted in 1971 in his analysis of the evolution of scientific societies.

One result of this reorientation in existing societies and of the formation of new organizations has been the emergence of "public-interest science"—scientists acting in the public interest, often in concert with citizens' groups, through appropriate channels and deploying appropriate political strategies. And they do so, not in an ad hoc way in their spare time as private citizens, but on an organized, full-time professional basis. Noting that "a substantial number of good young scientists have made career commitments to public-interest science," Martin Perl and his colleagues in a 1974 overview of the field in *Physics Today* discussed its growth since the mid-sixties and predicted its continued contribution even in a more placid, post-Watergate world.

That the seventies have brought continued concern over science-society relations in other respects could be illustrated in a variety of ways. I should simply like to refer to a series of essays bearing the title "Science and Its Public: The Changing Relationship" first appearing in the Summer 1974 issue of *Daedalus* and then published in 1976 as a volume in the series of Boston Studies in the Philosophy of Science (Holton & Blanpied 1976). In his introduction to the Boston Studies volume Blanpied observes:

> By the mid-70's the virulence of these attacks [on science] had largely abated; however, there remained as a potentially positive residue the perception that the relationship between science and its public was in a state of flux. Thus, although it is now generally agreed that science and technology will continue to play a central role in contemporary society,

> there is a widespread recognition of the fact that many if not most of the earlier tacit assumptions that were made about their relationships to other important societal institutions can, and indeed must, be subject to searching critical examination. (p. xiii)

And in their foreword, Cohen and Wartofsky (longtime editors of the series) suggest that

> philosophers [of science] should be interested as much in the changing social situations of science and of scientists as in the changing empirical findings and explanatory conceptions. . . . Moreover, the historical development of scientific perceptions of nature is linked . . . by the development of perceptions of science itself. Perceptions of science [in turn] are located not only in the self-awareness of scientists but also in the critical awareness of their fellow human beings. . . . Tacit or plain, the public view of science must not be evaded. (p. v)

Mention of the philosophy of science brings me to several brief points. First, the "purist" view of science-society relations is based in part on the positivist view of science that insisted, amongst other things, on the clear and rigid demarcation between science and its application, between facts and values, between observation statements, theoretical statements, and value judgments. Second, as Sigmund Koch (1964) and many others have repeatedly pointed out, to the extent that psychology still seeks to hew its "science" out of that positivist piece of wood, it works with nothing more than a fossil. Third, developments in the philosophy and history of science over the last ten to fifteen years merely reinforce that conclusion. To anyone who wishes to maintain that science is, or should be, free of value judgments, I simply commend Michael Scriven's (1966) paper on "Value Claims in the Social Sciences." And although, as Koch (1976) has contended, we psychologists may have made more of Thomas Kuhn than we should have, the general implications of his work in this context are consistent with the demise of the "purist" position.

Finally, then, to post-Miller developments in psychology itself. Here again we can find continuity in many of the earlier themes and continuing interest in points Miller had raised. At the scientific-association level the APA has demonstrated its concern with matters broadly social in a variety of ways, ranging from a revised, extended Code of Ethics to its recent decision (hotly debated as it was) not to hold its meetings in states failing to ratify the ERA. And if the term "social-interest science" is not encountered much, "relevance" certainly is. (One comment on that state of affairs refers to "relevance-chic"; Meehl's [1972] discussion of "second-order relevance" is both witty and wise.) In any case, psychologists concerned about families, daycare and the like, and serving on a body such as the Carnegie Council on Children (Keniston 1977) are, for example, certainly engaged in "public-interest science." James Jackson talking here about "legislative advocacy" in the promotion of human welfare is another such straw in the wind.

Of the long-standing points of contact (gentle and otherwise) between psychology and society, testing, IQ, and the like remain very much in the spotlight. As Sheldon White (1976) has demonstrated, and as he will discuss tomorrow, intelligence testing represents a complicated compact between psychology and society that needs to be viewed in broad historical and sociological terms. The *Larry P.* trial in California (*APA Monitor* 1977, 1978) highlights the issues involved, the plaintiffs contending that IQ tests are inherently biased culturally and racially and hence result in unconstitutional discrimination. That thorny rose (if it is a thing of beauty at all) I leave to Belvin Williams to pluck. It does represent, however, yet another instance of social science evidence in court, a matter that continues to be scrutinized by legal scholars and others (cf. *Educational Forum*, March 1977). Was Kojak in particular, and TV violence in general, "responsible" for Ronnie Zamoro's behavior? And what might all this imply about the public's view and understanding of psychology? Better than most, William Bevan (1976) has argued that that view and understanding, and their implications, need to be urgently addressed.

From the public's image of psychology to psychology's image of Man, and Man's related image of Man—here too, a perennial set of issues. For example, Jerome Bruner's (1976) Herbert Spencer Lecture at Oxford bore that very title, "Psychology and the Image of Man." In it he bemoaned the fact that scientific psychology's initial scientistic self-definition has had such a protracted, negative impact, leading it away from central matters of "mind, intention, and culture." (On another occasion, Bruner [1957] had spoken of psychology's "methodolatry.") Referring at one point to Fritz Heider, Bruner concludes: "In making man comprehensible to himself, we start with man's knowledge of himself, his intricate sense of what he is like. Unless we begin from a better systematic description of that, we will fail" (p. 6).

But, as Bruner acknowledges, over the last decade or so we have witnessed "the cognitive revolution," and we now hear much of the organism as an "active, goal-seeking, information processor." There has been movement elsewhere. In social psychology, persons like William McGuire (1973) urge a radical departure from the experimental paradigm, paramount in the sixties, toward a paradigm involving "multiple and bidirectional causality among social variables." Thanks to Michael Cole and others (Cole & Scribner 1974), psychologists can no longer easily avoid consideration of the cultural context. And in developmental psychology, Urie Bronfenbrenner (1977), sounding Lewinian themes, persuasively pushes for examination of "the ecology of development," believing that part of the payoff will be in building a two-way bridge between science and policy. He and others reintroduce Brunswik's notion of "ecological validity" and "representative design," thereby reinforcing the impression that the European expatriates (Lewin, Heider, Brunswik) may be coming to their due day in the sunshine.

Movement there is. But some final, critical observations are in order. A "cognitive revolution" perhaps, but that revolution must still find space for affect, personality, and individual differences. Also, as pointed out by Verbrugge and McCarrell (1977, p. 531), interested as they are in metaphor comprehension, cognitive and psycholinguistic research has tended to focus on "the formal proposition." That, in turn, "has shaped the way we define the problems of expression, comprehension, and representation" (p. 531), leading us to downplay, if not ignore, the figurative, the imaginative, the poetic in language and cognition. But indications are that this sort of imbalance is going to be corrected and, as a result, a more faithful and rounded image of human capabilities and sensibilities drawn.

More important perhaps are the implications of recent writings in the area of policy and evaluation. The new wave of social science's links to society is certainly breaking over this area (MacRae 1976; Shannon 1973) and there may be a tendency to be carried along on a technocratic tide, along the lines of: "Given high-powered tools of systems and multivariate analysis, policy and evaluation research can be both effective and efficient." As happened in the sixties, however, this wave could turn into a wipeout if some philosophical and pragmatic complications are not duly attended to.

First: A new form of "methodolatory" will not do any better than the old. Note that Donald Campbell (1974), in his Kurt Lewin Memorial Award address, has stressed "qualitative knowing in action research," urging recognition of the qualitative, judgmental grounding of quantitative methods and intelligent use of "the methods of the humanities" in evaluation research.

Second: Note the implications of a multidimensional, multivariate scheme of things. Reviewing twenty years of study of aptitude treatment interactions and speaking of "going beyond the two disciplines of scientific psychology," Lee Cronbach expresses "pessimism about our predominant norms and strategies. . . . Interactions are not confined to the first order; the dimensions of the situation and of the person enter into complex interactions. . . . Once we attend to interactions, we enter a hall of mirrors extending to infinity" (1975, p. 163). He goes on to talk about the need for "interpretation in context," leading me to the observation (1978) that contextualism as an emerging "root metaphor" in contemporary psychology has some complicating implications for all aspects of giving psychology away.

Third: Herein may lie part of the fundamental reason for the state of affairs described by Cohen and Garet in their review of applied research efforts in reforming educational policy: "Methodological sophistication has not in the least reduced substantive disagreement over the meaning of research results. . . . In fact, it seems plain that applied research on the effects of schooling is more complex and difficult to interpret now than it was a decade ago. Improving applied research has produced paradoxical results: Knowledge which is better by any scientific standard, [but] no more authoritative by any political standard, and often more mystifying by any reasonable public standard" (1975, p. 33). No wonder, as Cohen and Weiss (1977) point out elsewhere, some judges are showing signs of irritation and impatience with social science evidence.

Where does this leave us? For one thing, as Cohen and Weiss (1977) themselves have done, analyzing and reanalyzing the nature of the reciprocal relations between theory and research and policy and practice. As a minimum, acknowledging that those relations are more complex than a classical "engineering" model allows, and especially, striving to acknowledge that complexity in the process of educating psychologists. As William Bevan (1976) and others have suggested (Haskins 1973), that process and our related conceptions of professional roles, responsibilities, and rewards demand attention. Says Bevan: "There has been . . . a progressive distortion of values in the education of many young scientists. They have been increasingly led to believe that the only career in science that can be truly fulfilling is original laboratory research in the university setting" (p. 490), and, I would add, educationally prepared for that career only. Society—and in a symbiotic way, psychology—needs "skillful integrators and interpreters of science," "scientifically or technically knowledgeable legislative staff officers," and "scientists qualified to work with large-scale, multi-faceted social systems." Reminding you of the slight complication of "*which* psychology?" I happily pass on to George Miller and the other symposium participants the question of how academic education and psychology's career structure will have to be modified to meet such needs. My tacit knowledge has now certainly been exhausted.

References

Exhibit A: IQ Trial. *APA Monitor,* 1977, *8* (12), 4–5.
Exhibit B: IQ Trial. *APA Monitor,* 1978, *9* (1), 15–18.
Baratz, S. S., & Baratz, J. C. Early childhood intervention: The social science base of institutional racism. *Harvard Educational Review,* 1970, *40,* 29–50.
Bevan, W. The sound of the wind that's blowing. *American Psychologist,* 1976, *31,* 481–491.
Bronfenbrenner, U. Toward an experimental ecology of human development. *American Psychologist,* 1977, *32,* 513–531.
Brown, M. *The social responsibility of the scientist.* New York: The Free Press, 1971.
Bruner, J. S. Mechanism riding high. Review of K. W. Spence, *Behavior theory and conditioning. Contemporary Psychology,* 1957, *2,* 155–157.
Bruner, J. S. Psychology and the image of man. *The Times Literary Supplement,* December 17, 1976.
Caldwell, B. M. A decade of early intervention: What we have learned. *American Journal of Orthopsychiatry,* 1974, *44,* 491–496.
Campbell, D. T. Reforms as experiments. *American Psychologist,* 1969, *24,* 409–429.
Campbell, D. T. Qualitative knowing in action research. Kurt Lewin Memorial Address, SPSSI, Meeting of APA, New Orleans, September 1974.
Clark, K. B. The background: The role of social scientists. *Journal of Social Issues,* 1953, *9,* 2–74.
Clark, R. B. *Einstein: The life and times.* New York: World, 1971.
Cohen, D. K., & Garet, M. S. Reforming educational policy with applied research. *Harvard Educational Review,* 1975, *45,* 17–43.
Cohen, D. K., & Weiss, J. A. Social science and social policy: Schools and race. *The Educational Forum,* 1977, *41,* 393–413.
Cole, M., & Bruner, J. S. Cultural differences and inferences about psychological processes. *American Psychologist,* 1971, *26,* 867–876.
Cole, M., & Scribner, S. *Culture and thought.* New York: Wiley, 1974.
Cronbach, L. J. Beyond the two disciplines of scientific psychology. *American Psychologist,* 1975, *30,* 116–127.
Deutsch, M. Socially relevant science: Reflections on some studies of interpersonal conflict. *American Psychologist,* 1969, *24,* 1076–1092.
Edsall, J. T. Scientific freedom and responsibility: Report of AAAS Committee. *Science,* 1975, *188,* 687–693.
Guttentag, M. Introduction to "The poor: Impact on research and theory." *Journal of Social Issues,* 1970, *26* (2), 1–14. (a)
Guttentag, M. The insolence of office. *Journal of Social Issues,* 1970, *26* (3), 11–18. (b)
Haskins, C. P. Science and social purpose. In J. A. Shannon (Ed.), *Science and the evolution of public policy.* New York: The Rockefeller University Press, 1973.
Holton, G. On the role of themata in scientific thought, *Science,* 1975, *188,* 328–334.

References

Holton, G. On being caught between Dionysians and Appollonians. In G. Holton and W. A. Blanpied (Eds.), *Science and its public: The changing relationship*. Dordrecht: D. Reidel, 1976.

Holton, G., & Blanpied, W. A. (Eds.), *Science and its public: The changing relationship*. Dordrecht: D. Reidel, 1976.

Jensen, A. How much can we boost IQ and scholastic achievement? *Harvard Educational Review*, 1969, *39*, 1–123.

Keniston, K. *All our children: The American family under pressure*. New York: Harcourt Brace Jovanovich, 1977.

Kessel, F. S. Contextualism: Its coming-of-age in contemporary psychology. 1978 (in preparation).

Koch, S. Psychology and emerging conceptions of knowledge as unitary. In T. W. Wann (Ed.), *Behaviorism and phenomenology: Contrasting bases for modern psychology*. Chicago: University of Chicago Press, 1964.

Koch, S. Psychology cannot be a coherent science. *Psychology Today*, 1969, *3* (4), p. 14ff.

Koch, S. Language communities, search calls, and the psychological studies. In W. J. Arnold (Ed.), *Nebraska Symposium on Motivation 1975*. Lincoln: University of Nebraska Press, 1976.

Krech, D., & Sanford, N. From David Krech and Nevitt Sanford. . . *Journal of Social Issues*, 1968, *24*, iii–vi.

Lewin, K. Action research and minority problems. *Journal of Social Issues*, 1946, *2*, 34–46.

Lippitt, R. Preface. *Journal of Social Issues*, 1946, *2*, 1.

MacRae, D. *The social function of social science*. New Haven, Conn.: Yale University Press, 1976.

McGuire, W. J. The Yin and Yang of progress in social psychology: Seven Koan. *Journal of Personality and Social Psychology*, 1973, *26*, 446–456.

Meehl, P. E. Second-order relevance. *American Psychologist*, 1972, *27*, 932–940.

Miller, G. A. Psychology as a means of promoting human welfare. *American Psychologist*, 1969, *24*, 1063–1075.

Perl, M., Primack, J., & von Hippel, F. Public-interest science: An overview. *Physics Today*, June 1974, 23–31.

Price, D. K. Purists and politicians. *Science*, 1969, *163*, 25–31.

Sanford, N. Whatever happened to action research? *Journal of Social Issues*, 1970, *26* (4), 3–23.

Schroeer, D. *Physics and its fifth dimension: Society*. Reading, Mass.: Addison-Wesley, 1972.

Scriven, M. Value claims in the social sciences. Publication #123 of the Social Science Education Consortium, March 1966.

Senn, M. J. E. Insights on the child development movement in the United States. *Monographs of the Society for Research in Child Development*, 1975, *40* (Serial No. 161).

Shannon, J. A. (Ed.). *Science and the evolution of public policy*. New York: The Rockefeller University Press. 1973.

Smith, M. S., & Bissell, J. S. Report analysis: The impact of Head Start. *Harvard Educational Review*, 1970, *40*, 51–104.

Thackray, A. Reflections on the decline of science in America and on some of its causes. *Science*, 1971, *173*, 27–31.

Verbrugge, R. R., & McCarrell, N. S. Metaphoric comprehension: Studies in reminding and resembling. *Cognitive Psychology*, 1977, *9*, 494–533.

Walker, E. L. Experimental psychology and social responsibility. *American Psychologist*, 1969, *24*, 862–868.

White, S. H. Social implications of IQ. In S. H. White (Ed.), *Human development in today's world*. Boston: Little, Brown, 1976.

Kasschau's Introduction of George A. Miller

Thank you, Frank. I had not counted on two such elegant, high-powered introductions and statement-of-theme messages this morning. As a result we're running a bit behind before we even get started. So let me not dally on a lengthy introduction of our moderator.

As I noted earlier, we'll be focusing over these next two days on an analysis of the substance and impact of Professor Miller's presidential address to the American Psychological Association back in 1969. Although his influence has reached far and wide across the world of psychology, Professor Miller himself spent most of his early career in the Boston area—specifically Cambridge—first at Harvard, then MIT, and back again. Now he is at Rockefeller University, where he has been since 1967.

It might seem unfair to line up six recognized psychologists to "analyze" Professor Miller's address, but Dr. Miller has served as president of both the Eastern Psychological Association and the APA, so he must clearly be prepared for abuse! And, in fact, we are going to give the gentleman "equal time" to defend himself. Our moderator for today and tomorrow is Professor George A. Miller . . .

Miller's Opening Statement

Thank you, Dr. Kasschau. Ladies and gentlemen, it's an honor to be here, and a special honor to serve as moderator of this symposium. I assume that the role of a moderator is to say something when everyone else falls silent; with the prolific group that the University of Houston has assembled here for this occasion, I assume my duties will be reasonably light.

Now, before introducing the first speaker, I want to thank Dr. Kessel for giving a very fair and balanced picture of the situation in 1969 and my attempt to contribute to it. My own memory of those times are as being very turbulent. Not just in the APA or on the campuses, but in almost every aspect of our national life, I was grateful for his attempt to recapture some of that stirring. The speech that he outlined for you was given as a result of two years of presiding over the meetings of the board of directors of the American Psychological Association in which I discovered for the first time what psychology really is on a national scale, and the kinds of things that most psychologists are really concerned with.

The board was torn at every meeting, by issues presented to it, by particular members, by pressure groups, by special interest groups within the organization, by anti-special interest groups within the organization. Over and again we debated and argued about and questioned what the APA as a professional organization should be doing about these issues. Was it really just a scientific organization that ought to do its science and shut up? Many of the members believed that was the case and they did not want their dues dollars, which were large even in those days, to be devoted to promoting social causes with which they were not identified. On the other hand there was a very vocal component—small, but vocal—that was saying that the world is unjust, that psychology should not even implicitly endorse the inequitable distribution of privilege in our society, and that we should become active. As those issues raged back and forth, people in the privacy of the boardroom said some very strong things.

Those were questions that couldn't be ignored, and there I was trying to provide some kind of leadership for the American Psychological Association. I was very poorly prepared for leadership, coming as I did from the sheltered academic environments of the laboratories at Harvard and MIT. In fact, I was on the verge of resigning from the APA at just the time I was elected president!

I remember when word came that I had been nominated. I looked at all the clinicians and social psychologists and really competent people on the ballot and thought, Why should I go through the humiliation of losing an election? Art Melton can do it year after year, but why should I? I went into Jerry Bruner's office, just a couple of doors away, and said, "Jerry, they've nominated me to run for president of the APA. Should I run or not?" He looked at me and said, "George Miller, who are you to turn down being president of the APA?" I didn't know who I was to turn that down, so I left my name in the pot, feeling quite sure nothing would come of it, and lo and behold I was elected president.

Well, my . . . Perhaps the only qualification I had for leadership in that time was that I had so little to unlearn. I was forced to take positions on many issues that I had never before thought seriously about. After two years of learning in the School of Hard Knocks, I tried to reach some sort of a reasonable compromise that I could live with. I wanted to share what I felt I had learned with my psychological colleagues.

In preparing to come here I have reread what I said then, reread in a calmer, less pressed atmosphere, and I was struck and a bit surprised by the populist line that I took. It was a naive thing in many respects, but I think what rescued it and rescued me was that it was hopeful. I'm going to be listening especially for that note of hope here today and tomorrow, because if we lose hope on these issues there's very little future for us. I want to see how or in what form that hope has survived the intervening decade. How, now that we've all had more time to think about the problems that exploded on us fifteen, ten years ago, how now do we hope to use psychology for the promotion of human welfare?

Psychology and Its Human Clientele

Miller's Introduction of Koch

Our first speaker in this symposium is Professor Sigmund Koch of Boston University. Professor Koch is well known for his penetrating analyses of psychological theories and for his valiant attempts to get our leading theorists to formulate their ideas in such a way that a serious student could compare and contrast them.

When you hear that Sig Koch is going to comment on something you've done, you begin to tremble. I've seldom heard him say a generous thing. But personally I've always admired, and on occasion been inspired by, his willingness as a hardheaded person to face the consequences of the possibility that truth is not the only value that a scientist must respect.

I could recite his professional history and major accomplishments for you, but those matters are well set forth for you to read in the program of the symposium (Appendix B of this volume). So I won't take valuable time away from him, time that we could spend better listening to his views on "Psychology and Its Human Clientele: Beneficiaries or Victims?" Dr. Koch. . .

Koch's Opening Comments

Thank you for that gracious introduction, Professor Miller. I have good news for Professor Miller: I'm at a total disadvantage today in that I have a rather strange biological rhythm such that I work at night and sleep during the day. This is precisely the point at which I would have been in bed for a half hour on my normal diurnal rhythm and so I'm a pushover today. Moreover, I came prepared to be generous and hopeful—even though the richness of the natural language is such that there are always different possible interpretations of the generous and the hopeful.

When I was invited to participate, I accepted with alacrity because I thought I had actually already written a suitable paper for this symposium in 1967. There is a sense in which I have been writing in answer to Dr. Miller's suggestions for about twenty-five years, but there was indeed a particular paper that I wrote for popular presentation in 1967 in response to a wild-blue-yonder, joyous thing that was going on at that time. A very fat issue of the *American Psychologist* had just been published, devoted to the Social Sciences and Congress. The premise of the issue was that 1967 marked the year in which the promise of the social sciences for human welfare had finally been acknowledged by society and government in a large way. The theme was "This is the take-off year," and the paper I wrote then was addressed to the testimony that had been rendered by prominent social scientists at two congressional hearings. Senate committees were taking expert testimony on two bills. One, which had been introduced by Senator Harris, proposed the formation of a National Social Science Foundation. The other, a rather weird bill, called the Full Opportunity and Social Accounting Bill, was introduced by our current Vice President, then-Senator Mondale.

I wrote that article with glee because in those days I wasn't quite so generous as I am now, and it seemed to me that the testimony rendered by the prominent social scientists who appeared at these hearings was scandalous. I mean *scandalous*. It would be difficult to imagine a more feckless, foot-in-the-mouth representation of the interests of a special interest group than that generated by the people who testified. I hope to have an opportunity to read some choice quotations, should an appropriate context arise during the course of our discussions. In my 1967 paper I predicted that both of these bills would fail—which they did. I had an operative of mine, who's highly placed in government, try to track down the subsequent history of those bills, and even that proved very difficult to do. Apparently, the ludicrous is as subject to repression as the painful!

After agreeing to participate in this symposium, I reread Professor Miller's 1969 presidential address. It seemed to me to raise issues of such a fundamental sort that I abandoned the easy strategy of responding with my 1967 article. What follows, then, is a new paper, or at least mainly new. (I do have a few modules that I transport from one paper to another, as most academics do.) Professor Miller's paper reactivated in me an old interest in literary criticism. In a sense my essay is a totally impersonal response to Miller's paper because I'm approaching it as, let us say, a twenty-first century historian might approach a cultural artifact. I am viewing it as a datum deposited by the *Zeitgeist*, as a kind of intellectual ambiance that existed at some time in history.

I had already inferred that a man as intelligent as Professor Miller would, by normal processes of growth and maturation, have come out with a somewhat modulated version of his position by 1978, and he has just indicated this to have been the case. Though I am happy that my prediction has been verified, I still think it important to examine his original position.

Finally, may I note that Miller's will be the first presidential address in the history of the APA to be subjected to the analytic tools of the new criticism in English literature.

Before I commence, I should also like to note that I've never heard so comprehensive, judicious, and indeed dashing a "theme-definition" as was presented by Professor Kessel. I want to thank him for that statement.

Psychology and Its Human Clientele:
Beneficiaries or Victims?

Sigmund Koch
Boston University

INTRODUCTION

In 1930, one of the most rigorous English literary critics of the century, F. R. Leavis, was eager to show in an essay on D. H. Lawrence, whose novels he much respected, that there are worse things in this world than Lawrence's admitted extravagances in his treatment of certain psychological topics. To illustrate, he quotes the following passage by another author:

> Is it too unattainable a social ideal to believe that every man, woman and child should be trained about his own organism as thoroughly as the last boy was trained about the clock? We could very quickly teach children enough anatomy to give them a thorough working notion of their body, nervous system, heart, lungs, liver, kidneys, glands, sex apparatus. . . .
> Next we should teach the rudiments of hygiene (what may be called "mental hygiene"), show them in the simplest kind of terms how infantile unverbalised behaviour arises, and how it is carried over into adult life; teach them about fear, love, and anger reactions, work out with them how the individual behaves in depressions. Teach them what exhibition behaviour is like, how easy seclusion behaviour develops, about invalidism and other nascent psychoses. Teach them first to spot these reaction patterns in others, and then, most important of all, how to spot them in themselves by watching and tabulating their own behaviour. What boy or girl taught in this way could not check his own behaviour three or four times a month? "For days I have fought with my parents—two or three times in the last week I have been depressed and have tried to find excuses for not going to school and doing my work." . . . Or once more, "I find that I am going with girls much less than I used to and that I have begun to gang up with boys in the neighbourhood."
> Having taught individuals to observe their own behaviour in this way, as they observe the behaviour of others, can't we next teach them

what to do when their records show that they are getting into jams? In other words, give them the essentials of corrective hygiene. For example: "All my work has slowed down. I am lacking in pep, don't care whether I go to see anybody or not; I have been leading a humdrum existence, things haven't gone right at home. I guess I'll talk to my physician. He will probably tell me I had better pack up and go for a week's fishing or hunting, and that when I come back I'd better change things around a bit and try to do some interesting jobs, get some hobbies going that I have been flirting with for a long time, and to reach some satisfactory decision about my sex life which has been bothering me lately."

I would give this training before the fourteenth year, since at this age the great mass of our population gives up its schooling. Can young children get all this? I am hopeful of it. My business experience has opened my eyes to how simply things can be put to the public—how in homely words nearly all the worth-while truths of science can be set forth.

Among Leavis's comments, he points out that:

> Dr. Watson, of course, is an extreme instance, but he has great influence in America, and it is not for proposals like the above that he is regarded in England as a crank. They merely represent in a pronounced form certain tendencies that are general in the West. . . . Civilised life is certainly threatened with impoverishment by education based on crude and defective psychology, by standardisation at a low level, and by the inculcation of a cheap and shallow emotional code. (Leavis 1930)

Little did Leavis know at this time that, far from Watson's continuing to be looked upon as a "crank" in England, a second behaviorist revolution—deeming itself more sophisticated than Watson's but in no wise embarrassed by his priority—would be staged twenty years later among Oxford philosophers!

When I arrived in England in 1952 to commence a Fulbright year, I was amazed to discover that British psychologists were beginning a frenetic love affair with Hullian theory, especially in that this was precisely the juncture at which Hull's influence had begun its rapid decline in America. That circumstance, incidentally, was not a little embarrassing to me, for I had just completed a massive critique of Hull (Koch 1954) which did nothing to mitigate the erosion of his influence.

Dr. Miller's (1969) invitation that psychology be given away was fulsomely realized long before he had issued it. Is this not the psychological—nay, the psychologist—century? Who, these days, would consort with a friend, lover, relative—even dog, cat, or horse— who was not a psychologist? Who, in recent decades, has eluded teachers, preachers, friends, parents, bosses, colleagues, brokers, bankers, salesmen, air hostesses, who do not *treat* one rather than ply their respective crafts in the scientifically unillumined modes of olden times?

Throughout this century (and before), psychology *has* been under gracious dissemination—whether in school, bar, office, or bedroom; whether by book, magazine, electronic propagation, or word of mouth— to a voracious consumership. People everywhere have been given, gratis, revolutionary reconceptions of the nature of man—reams, truckloads of them— all based on cogent and valid *scientific* evidence. They have been analogized, even hypostasized, as cockroaches, dogs, monkeys, and especially rats; as telephone exchanges, computers, or colligations of billions of the latter; as configured systems of protons, electrons, neutrons, and neutrinos, or as epiphenomena of direct current distributions in electrolytes, or as code-bearing macromolecules; as products of insufficient prophylaxis, or of neurobiotaxis, homeostatics, conditioning, reinforcement contingencies, cognitive maps, cell assemblies, TOTE hierarchies, or computer programming lists; as empty intersection areas between S's and R's, topologically differentiated Jordan curves, collections of exponential functions, or schematic sowbugs; as cybernetic mechanisms, information-processing entities, or finite automata; as utilities optimizers, game strategists, pleasure-principle protagonists; as mutual voyeurs, ego titillators, or masturbators; as collectivities of traits, attitudes, dispositions, instincts, or factors; as reactors, agents, achievers, self-realizers, autonomy maximizers; as id-ego-superego structures, orgone receptacles, plastic-phallus copulators, vibrator cohabitators; as elements of group mind, filings in social force fields, cooperating or competing or reinforcement bartering socii.

These are but a few of the revolutionary conceptions freely available in the public domain—and mankind has listened reverently. No matter if sometimes the mind of the eager apprehender will spin a bit. The revolutions are sufficiently graded in difficulty to make at least a few accessible to everyone. "Everyman" has been well served! And indeed, each ardent seeker of a theory of himself will do everything possible to conform his person to the theories that come his way (for the truly diligent, that *could be* all of them), even if he understands them not at all. "Everyman" is grateful!

In his 1969 paper, Dr. Miller does seem a bit vacillatory as to where the great thrust of psychological philanthropy should be localized. He does, in all fairness, seem to favor a conception of man as self-therapist rather than patient. But his somewhat inconsonant emphasis on the need for augmenting our cadre of human and social *engineers* seems to leave a place for problem-oriented troubleshooters. If this indeed be "giving psychology away," it can be said that at this prosier level of dealing with particular personal problems (if they ever *are* particular), psychology has been distributed with immense abandon, even if a bit less cheaply. Who among us has not been psychoanalyzed, encounterized, non-directive counselorized, professionally humanized, Tao-or-Zen or transcendental meditationalized, reality or sexuality therapized, biofeedbackized, behavior modified, drug cathecticized, transorbitally leucotomized, lobotomized; or merely tranquilized and/or shocked; massaged and/or Rolfed; group nudified and/or "crotch-eyeballified"?

In short, I fear that by 1969, when Dr. Miller was making his invitation, he was calling for a policy that had been under massive and explosively cumulating implementation ever since that glorious moment in the history of civilization when psychology discovered itself to be a science. Lest any perverse hypothesis be formed that Dr. Miller's invitation *turned off* this policy in the years after it was made, may I refer the potential contrarian to the following culling of titles of books reviewed in the fat December 1977 issue of *Contemporary Psychology: Attachment Behavior; Schizophrenia: The Sacred Symbol of Psychiatry; Increasing Leadership Effectiveness; Stay Slim for Good; Stop Smoking for Good; Take It Off and Keep It Off: A Behavioral Program for Weight Loss and Healthy Living; Permanent Weight Control; Alternatives to Alcohol Abuse; Take Charge: A Personal Guide to Behaviour Modification; Learning to Use Extrasensory Perception; Marital Communication and Decision Making; Hypnosis and Behavior Therapy; The Naked Therapist: A Collection of Embarrassments; Human Sexuality in Four Perspectives; Androgyny: Toward a New Theory of Sexuality; The Intensive Group Experience: A Guide; Interpersonal Living: The Skills/Contract Approach to Human-Relations Training in Groups; The Powerholders; Psychosexual Problems: Psychotherapy, Counseling and Behavior Modification; Psychology of Women: Behavior in a Biosocial Context; Exploring Sex Differences; Barred from School: Two Million Children; Marriage and Alternatives: Exploring Intimate Relationships; Beyond Intellectual Sexism: A New Woman, A New Reality; Learning to Teach: A Decision-Making System; In Search of Identity; Children and Television; Drug Education: Results and Recommendations; The First Encounter: The Beginnings in Psychotherapy; Korotkyi psykhologichnyi slovnyk* (Short Dictionary of Psychology in the Ukrainian); *Psychology and Consumer Affairs; Psychology of Sport: The Behavior, Motivation, Personality, and Performance of Athletes; Love and Hate on the Tennis Court: How Hidden Emotions Affect Your Game; Death, Society, and Human Experience; Mutual Criticism; Behavioral Psychology for Teachers.* I would estimate that of the 110 (or so) books reviewed in this issue of *Contemporary Psychology*, perhaps twenty-five could be thought addressed to a technically or professionally qualified audience. Let us be generous about the matter and set the "giveaway" ratio as 4 to 1. If *any* man has a basis for complaint, it surely cannot be Everyman!

Leavis's appalled demur to Watson is but one ripple in a flow of critical concern with the massive dehumanizing impact of certain aspects of science and technology that has extended throughout the century. This phenomenon (whether its manifestations be phrased as the simplification of sensibility, homogenization of taste, attenuation of the capacity for experience, or in some other way) has formed the basis for that continuing chorus of pain in which every sensitive critic of twentieth-century culture—whether he be writer, artist, humanist-scholar, or scientist—has participated. One can doubt that there has been a period in history in which the style and message of its intellectuals have been so uniformly rejective.

Of one thing we can be sure: However the symptoms of dehumanization be phrased, they are certainly in the first instance psychological symptoms. Coarsening of discrimination, simplification of sensibility, homogenization of taste, whatever their far-flung dependencies, are matters which certainly seem relevant to psychological concern. One would expect that psychologists and social scientists would be more deeply concerned with such trends than members of any other group in the community of scholarship. Have they been? Far from it. Though some secret part of many psychologists must surely be troubled by these trends, few have given this part of themselves a hearing.

But that is not all. There are some—mainly outside psychology—who would maintain that modern psychology, far from developing a counterstress to the dehumanization process, had itself contributed to it. Such diagnoses have not been uncommon in the past four or five decades. Though the details of the argument vary widely, the pattern is familiar: Psychology has projected to the world a simplistic and demeaning image of man (as we have seen, a generous phethora of such!); modern man, rendered especially vulnerable to the authority of science by the many social and historical factors which have exacerbated his need for security, embraces these images and happily compresses himself to them. A seemingly absurd argument, and one often made by absurd people! But it is disturbingly true that some form of it is often made as well by minds who are among the most brilliant and intellectually responsible of our time: literary, philosophical, *and* scientific. *Could* such an argument, when properly spelled out and qualified, contain a germ of truth? Even a germ of such truth would entail a terrible responsibility.

Apparently, Dr. Miller senses some of the horror that critics seek to convey by such attributions as "dehumanization." In his paper there is strong evidence of unrest over one common presupposition of many of the "images of man" in wide currency—namely, their definition of man as *object*. Along with Kingsley Davis, Dr. Miller does not wish to treat human beings as "pure instrumentality." He "agree[s] with Davis that behavioral and social sciences cannot be applied to people and institutions in the same way physical and biological sciences are applied to objects and organisms." Nor does he claim to like the notion of *control* as a goal for the applied psychological enterprise. He would "prefer to speak of understanding and prediction" as the major routes towards implementation of the psychological "revolution." Moreover, the "heart of the psychological revolution will be a new and scientfically based conception of man as an individual and as a social creature." Indeed, this revolution is not altogether "pie in the sky," it is "already upon us" and its furtherance requires us not merely to "strengthen its scientific base, but we must also try to communicate it to our students and to the public." Furthermore, the "enrichment of public psychology by scientific psychology constitutes the most direct and important application of our science to the promotion of human welfare."

I am agreeably impressed by aspects of Dr. Miller's paper, both in the letter and in the spirit, but more so in spirit than letter. What is attractive about the spirit is a certain tentativeness, humility, even irresoluteness of the sort that betokens deep perturbation over the tendency of our dicipline. But these very qualities of spirit tend to cloud the contours of letter. Then, too, Dr. Miller's mood oscillations are engaging but do not enhance univocality: When he renders judgments that he labels "optimistic," I sense a weaker registration of conviction (and a stronger one that he is in course of a presidential address) than when he counterposes his doubts and reservations. In short, this is a difficult paper to deal justly with but, to my mind, is sufficiently fraught with dangerous profession-centered simplisms and autisms to merit analysis even at the risk of some injustice.

Take Dr. Miller's abrogation of "control" as the objective of the psychological enterprise: I am delighted to find him saying that "changing behavior is pointless in the absence of any coherent plan for how it should be changed." And he is on solid ground when he suggests that detailed reinforcement-contingencies demonstrated in animal behavior studies may prove but tenuously extrapolatable to the human case. But it is worrisome to find that his "concern has nothing to do with the validity of these ideas." I am impressed when he advocates the principle of "habeas mentem" and adds that if "we really did have a new scientific way to control human behavior, it would be highly immoral to let it fall into the hands of some small group of men, even if they were psychologists." But I flag a bit when the ground for rejection becomes "there is a better way to advertise psychology" in that "reinforcement is only one of many important ideas that we have to offer."

The succubus of *control* is not, however, easily exorcized! After "giving psychology away" in the form of a new "paradigm" for the conduct of social life, we find Miller discovering the need for scads of human and social "engineers"—for "many more psychological technologists who can apply our science to the personal and social problems of the general public." Though this psychotechnological troubleshooting is to be mitigated by shaping it to "the *perceived* needs of the people who receive it," it is nevertheless to include such matters as teaching supervisors "how to write a job description and how to evaluate the abilities and personalities of those who fill the job"; also, "perhaps we should teach him the art of persuasion, or the time and place for positive reinforcement." Moreover, why not pass on the "many obvious and useful suggestions that we could make" to *non*-psychologists, as, for instance, "principles governing the design and evaluation of programmed materials," psychometrics, interview methods, etc. Indeed, the "techniques involved are not some esoteric branch of witchcraft . . . reserved for those with Ph.D.'s in psychology. When the ideas are made sufficiently concrete and explicit, the scientific foundations of psychology can be grasped by sixth-grade children." As a matter of fact, "if we pychologists are ready for it, we may be able to contribute a coherent and workable philosophy, based on the science of psychology."

I will note only in passing the striking similarity of Dr. Miller's tone (and argument-line) to that of Watson. But are we not here in the ambiance of a Russellian "type"-paradox? *Control* has been abjured. We do not impose our *own* solutions on the personal and social problems that we address. We allow the subject to suffer his problem, define it (though for *that* he'll probably need our expert help), and even decide it (though, there too, we're certainly on the ready). All we as psychologists do is provide the "scientifically valid" technology—based on the latest Ph.D. dissertation and saturated with the authority of Science—which will convey the inept lout to a solution. We refrain from controlling the subject; we control the subject's control of the subject. "We are," in the words of Dr. Miller, "proposing to tamper with the adaptive process itself." Did I say "subject"? Or are we already in the presence of an "object"?

And similarly, Dr. Miller fails to see that the revolutionary reconception of the nature of man that he will be gallantly offering the world—whether in the guise of paradigm 2 or paradigm 42—will, by the very rhetoric of its proclaimed "scientific validity," its linkage with the iconology of science, have the force of making, remaking, steering the development of its beneficiaries. Did I say "beneficiaries"? Or are we already in the presence of "victims"?

SOME DEEPER PROBLEMS IN DR. MILLER'S WORLD VIEW

There are some assumptions built into Dr. Miller's conception of the human applicability of psychology which are deeply revelatory of the superficiality, ahistoricism, and, indeed, hubris of the modern psychological enterprise. These assumptions—or at least the cognitive scotomata that foster them—will emerge from an analysis of Dr. Miller's *central* examples of actual or potential gifts that scientific psychology can make to the world. I am prepared to argue that *every one* of Dr. Miller's illustrative "gifts" is either (1) of dubious efficacy, utility, or truth value; or (2) *not* uniquely attributable to the exercise of psychological method or to the power of the technical psychological imagination; or (3) *not* uncontestable by alternate analyses or insights (sometimes a large plurality of such) that have emerged in the rangy history of observation and cerebration essayed by humanists and other scientifically illiterate citizens. I will scrutinize, however, only two major examples: his Varela-based paradigm "of the social nature of man," and his speculations on the import of what might be called the "pupil-contract" approach to the teaching of reading developed by Ashton-Warner. Because of the complexity of the issues raised by these examples, my discussion will necessarily be a glancing one.

The Varela "Paradigm"

The Varela conception of man—which is "based on psychological research" and is to bring about the brave new world that Miller would like to foster—is developed in contrast to "a set of assumptions on which our social institutions are presently based." It is necessary that I quote Miller's précis of these two paradigms.

The Current Social Paradigm.

All men are created equal. Most behavior is motivated by economic competition, and conflict is inevitable. One truth underlies all controversy, and unreasonableness is best countered by facts and logic. When something goes wrong, someone is to blame, and every effort must be made to establish his guilt so that he can be punished. The guilty person is responsible for his own misbehavior and for his own rehabilitation. His teachers and supervisors are too busy to become experts in social science; their role is to devise solutions and see to it that their students or subordinates do what they are told.

Varela's "Revolution."

There are large individual differences among people, both in ability and personality. Human motivation is complex and no one ever acts as he does for any single reason, but, in general, positive incentives are more effective than threats or punishments. Conflict is no more inevitable than disease and can be resolved or, still better, prevented. Time and resources for resolving social problems are strictly limited. When something goes wrong, how a person perceives the situation is more important to him than the "true facts," and he cannot reason about the situation until his irrational feelings have been toned down. Social problems are solved by correcting causes, not symptons, and this can be done more effectively in groups than individually. Teachers and supervisors must be experts in social science because they are responsible for the co-operation and individual improvement of their students or subordinates.

It would require a ten-year seminar to disentangle the skein of intellectual grotesqueries contained in this contrast. Looking first at the second paradigm (the Varela-Miller universe), it can be said that not a single one of the beliefs there set forth is historically recent, nor was "psychological research" required for its discovery. Cognate views emerge from many strands (some of multi-millenial length) within the humanities and, in the broadest sense, the social studies (e.g., social philosophy, philosophy of history, etc.). And there are cognate strands within social doctrines associated with major world religions. The history of utopian thought alone will provide a hypersufficient basis for every one of these ideas, and the history of utopian *experimentation*, even if restricted alone to the some two hundred utopian communities established in this country during the nineteenth century, has involved the embodiment of such ideas in multiply permuted combinations. Moreover, it is in these humanistic and practical contexts that such ideas and their cognates have received their most powerful and subtle formulations. It is dubious that the psychological research has strengthened or clarified these "insights."

In the very same breath, I must add that not a single component of this paradigm is non-problematic (whether as formulated, or on the presumption of the best conceivable fomulation), and not a single component, in all probability, will ever achieve pre-emptive or totally general warrant. Finally, looking at these word-strings as given, some are truistic or even tautologous, and some are plain silly. Let us consider these statements one at a time, and point merely to the most obvious objections or qualifications that a non-psychologist human of average critical intelligence would raise.

That "there are large individual differences . . . both in ability and personality" is a truism to which few demurs have been registered in the history of the world *except* by psychologists afflicted with rampant environmentalism. Fortunately, with the demise of classical behaviorism, this quaint disease has largely disappeared, but it must be added that in the opinion of many, the psychology of individual differences has had a scandalously deleterious impact on human welfare throughout the century.

That "human motivation is complex and no one reacts as he does for any single reason" is a truism few persons who have led normal lives could have doubted, but has been brought under question only by the rhetoric of certain of the simplistic drive theories that dominated certain areas of psychology over a wide time-swath in this century. It is, however, the humanist—and especially the more exalted masters of such forms as drama and the novel—who has documented the complexity, indeed, the antinomal character of human motivation at the most profound and subtle levels, and has massively conveyed and evidenced a human truth to which psychologists have given little heed: namely, that the complexity of human motivation can be such as to render the *meanings* of action inherently ambiguous and unrecapturable, that man (when conceived as agent, not object) can never finally adjudicate the question of self-sincerity, or attain final and cosy confidence in his appraisals of others.

Are "positive incentives . . . more effective than threats of punishment"? Mankind did not wait upon psychologists to perceive that often this is so. Often it is not so. I doubt that psychologists can define the differential conditions for selecting and applying the one technology of influence as against the other with any greater nicety than ordinary mortals of perspicacity and sensitivity. In this century, modal practice has certainly moved towards a preference for use of positive incentives in many of the institutions which seek to guide and influence human beings. But it is possible to argue that there have been intervals and contexts in this century in which permissiveness has been practiced to a fault.

The assertion that "conflict is no more inevitable than disease" is both false and silly. Of course, modality judgments (in the philosophers' sense) are notoriously dangerous. Yet the distinguished microbiologist and pathologist Dr. René Dubos in fact believes that disease is here to stay. And *conflict*—in some ample subset of its infinitude of forms—is not *merely* inevitable; it is a definitive condition of life in the absence of which no experience or action could have meaning, structure, or value. That particular conflicts "can be resolved" and even "prevented" is news to no sentient creature.

How "a person perceives the situation" *has* to be more important to him than the "true facts" if only for the reason that consensual truth cannot be persuasive upon one who, by hypothesis, is no party to the consensus. Of course, there *have* been "cosmic eye" theories of truth throughout the history of epistemology, but side by side with these have been theories stressing the perspectival and observer-dependent character of "truth." That a person "cannot reason about the situation until his irrational feelings have been toned down" is my candidate for a niche in a Hall of Fame dedicated to the housing of tautologies. On a kinder interpretation, this word-string can be seen as registering the view that emotion or affect distorts reason—a view which is assertable but, in my opinion, unless considerably qualified and specified, wrong.

As for the insight that "social problems are solved by correcting causes, not symptoms"—it can be said that the lexical constraints upon "cause" and "symptom" are such that the correction of a symptom *cannot* entail the correction of its cause. Are "social problems" solved "more effectively in groups than individually"? A sane, even if scientifically illiterate, response would have to be: that depends on cases.

The final element of the "paradigm" ("Teachers and supervisors must be experts in social science because," etc., etc.) has the weird property of being contraindicated by every preceding assertion, on the assumption that the asserter is a social scientist.

If we turn now to the initial paradigm, the bad one, the contrast case descriptive of current social dynamics which must be replaced, it can be said that not a single component is determinately more anemic in truth value, or necessarily more counterproductive in its bearing on social life, than is its putative contrary in the second paradigm. I quail before the project of a sentence-by-sentence analysis. Let us be content with a sample.

In relation to the first sentence ("All men are created equal"), the presumption is apparently that such an assertion is disconfirmed by modern differential psychology. But, of course, the literal fact of variance has no bearing on such a statement when read in the light of its historical and normative context. It is embarrassing to have to point out that for several hundred years it has been evident to most humans, however psychologically misinformed, that it is "equality of rights" that such a statement predicates of man, and not equality of ability, hair color, nose shape, personality, or any other psychic or physical trait. The widely prevalent (and indeed, persuasive) reading is, of course, that there is a range of rights, considerations, entitlements, which all human beings can claim by virtue of their membership, *as such*, in the human race. Under law and God. It should be news to no one that there is a large and respectable body of literature—within social philosophy, law, ethics, theology—addressed to the identification, specification, and adjudication of these rights, a vital task, even if resistant in principle to full and final resolution.

Few reasonable men believe that "one truth underlies all controversy," but one would be hard put to find a reasonable man who does *not* believe that "one truth" underlies *some* controversy. What is implicit here is a regrettable belief, widespread among behavioral scientists and among do-gooders of fuzzily egalitarian proclivity, that "truth" is an epiphenomenon of a vested interest. The view that "unreasonableness" is *not* "best countered by facts and logic" can be seen as reflecting another pseudo-sophisticated stereotype within the behavioral science Weltanschauung. Committed or tendentious persons *may*, in fact, be refractory to "facts and logic." Changes of attitude and belief *may*, in fact, be more easily facilitated by therapy, bribery, flattery, and other extra-rational modalities of persuasion than by rational means. Whether even *this* will be so will depend on person and context. But note that what is considered naughty in this plank of the paradigm is the view that unreasonableness is "best" countered by "facts and logic." Certainly there is a wide swath of mankind— inclusive of the community of all genuine scientists and all genuine scholars (in contradistinction to the pseudo case) who believe that the best antidote to unreason is reason, in any normative sense of the word "best."

Note the statements concerning "guilt" and "responsibility." I shirk differentiated analysis of the pattern of assumptions from which the proscription of such beliefs (e. g., that the "guilty person is responsible for his own misbehavior and for his own rehabilitation") issues. But I would certainly rather read Dostoevsky on guilt, responsibility, and rehabilitation than Miller, or even than Freud. I would rather read Kant on these matters than Watson, Skinner, or even the most able management theorist or the most streamlined penologist.

I apologize for this painfully literal analysis. It is even in some respects unfair. Mr. Varela may indeed be a superb manager. But so was Robert Owen, in his management, at the very beginning of the industrial revolution, of the factory, schools, and associated community, at New Lanark—and *he* was able to set his utopian microcosm into effective operation without the help of a single scientific finding from industrial, social, or general psychology.

As for Dr. Miller, it must be acknowledged that the context of his presentation permitted him but the barest adumbration of his two paradigms, and that he modestly indicates that "no doubt other psychologists would draw the picture somewhat differently." But Dr. Miller addresses a large and grave issue when he proposes to promote human welfare by giving psychology away, and the potential recipient has a right to expect that even illustrative tidbits of the beneficences to be vouchsafed by this general policy make sense. We psychologists have held forth to humanity some of the most grandiose promissory notes ever issued by a field of scholarship. What we have thus far delivered is miles and miles of half-meaningful prose which has conveyed quarter-truths and eighth-truths and untruths concerning the human condition in a sordid patois of tarnished scientific imagery. Our "gift" has been a progressive obfuscation of what man already knows about his own condition.

Pupil-Contract versus Pupil-Contact in the Teaching of Reading

Dr. Miller's second major illustration of the kind of gift that mankind can expect from psychology is the approach to the teaching of reading developed by Ashton-Warner. In brief, this is a "contract" approach such that the child is asked what words he wants. The "children ask for . . . words that are bound up with their own loves and fears. She [i.e., Ashton-Warner] writes each child's word on a large card and gives it to him. . . . And he learns to read them almost immediately. It is *his* word, and each morning he retrieves his own words from the pile collected each night by the teacher. . . . Given this start, children begin to write, using their own words, and from there the teaching of reading follows naturally. Under this regimen, a word is not an imposed task to be learned with reinforcements borrowed from some external source of motivation. Learning the word is itself reinforcing." Dr. Miller proceeds to link this method with White's conception of "competence motivation," which suggests the "use" of "psychology to give people skills that will satisfy their urge to feel more effective." He is enthusiastic over the possibility that "some might want to learn more about the science that helped them increase their competence." In other words, "competence motivation" is a good thing for the world and a good thing for psychology, which, in turn, entails more good news for the world. It is the thin end of a wedge which will insert psychology right into the action—we will be in a position to "do something practical for nurses, policemen, prison guards, salesmen—for people in many different walks of life."

May I first note the curious fact that the Ashton-Warner example is an obvious counter-example. It flies in the face of Dr. Miller's thesis that scientific psychology has profound resources of knowledge to give away. The seminal method that he proposes to give to the world was discovered right in that world *not* by a psychologist but—as he himself records—" by an inspired teacher in a small New Zealand school."*

There is, however, a plexus of deeper issues here; I can only scratch their surface. John Stuart Mill was subjected to an extraordinarily pressureful and hyper-disciplined education by his father, James, who assumed the role of tutor when his son was a virtual infant. The story is told in detail in J. S. Mill's autobiography, and the tale is more or less of an archetype of the genesis of a child prodigy. As we further learn in Mill's autobiography, he went through a period of deep and sustained melancholia as a young man, and it is easy to discern a relation between this and the mode of his early education. Many writers have pitied Mill for the severity of his training, but Raymond Williams has pointed out that it did, after all, eventuate in a very fine mind and a very fine person. It clearly would not be sensible to universalize upon such an educational model. But are we to create the conditions that would disenfranchise the very possibility of such exceptional modes of education? Shall we not be permitted to have *occasional* prodigies like Mill?

The institution of the English public school has been characterized by a degree of discipline and pressure that verges, in the opinion of many who have been exposed to it, on brutality. Some of its products, like George Orwell, have expended much of their adult psychic energies on the effort to recover from their school experiences. Yet this system has had a very high success ratio in turning out persons of exceptional intellectual altitude, refinement, and cultural literacy.

Despite the harsh rigors of their early educations, a John Stuart Mill and a George Orwell have not, one can guess, had to depend on extrinsic motivation for the functioning and development of their rather high-order linguistic skills. It can only be assumed that even within the pressureful context of their early training, intrinsic motivation soon came to their aid! It is well to note, also, that the intrinsic interest ("grab-value," "value-property saturation") of certain ranges of intellectual material can only

---

* *Ad Lib* by Professor Koch

Koch: May I first note the curious fact that the Ashton-Warner example is an obvious counter-example. It flies in the face of Dr. Miller's thesis that scientific psychology has profound resources of knowledge to give away. The seminal method that he proposes to give to the world was discovered right in that world *not* by a psychologist but—as he himself records—"by an inspired teacher in a small New England school."

There is, however, a plexus of . . . pardon?

Audience: New Zealand.

Koch: New Zealand. Didn't I say New Zealand?

Audience: You said "New England."

Koch: New England?

Audience: You said "New England," and he said "New Zealand."

Koch: There *are* no inspired teachers in New England! Very, very definitely New *Zealand!*

become evident on the assumption that the material is encountered. It is unlikely that pupils who learn reading on a contract basis will stipulate words from Homer, or even Virgil.

What I have said is certainly not to be interpreted as a rejection of the Ashton-Warner method. It could well be a method of choice for some persons in some contexts. As a generalized pattern for the human race to be implemented by all schools tomorrow on the say-so of "scientific psychology" it must be adjudged highly questionable.

Dr. Miller could have found better examples from ordinary human experience of the importance of—and even the developmental conditions of—"competence motivation." To suggest that scientific psychology has a larger or deeper range of insights into the conditions which promote particular competences (or the illusion thereof) than what is already known by sensitive and intelligent teachers in every field— or by summit-level possessors and practitioners of every complex skill in the human gamut— is simply counterfactual.

AN ALTERNATE VIEW OF PSYCHOLOGY

So much for an analysis of Dr. Miller's highly philanthropic proposals of 1969. I, too, am a philanthropist. In sum, I believe that the most charitable thing we can do is not to give psychology away, but to take it back. Such a program of reverse philanthropy, however, would require the efforts of a far larger work force than we now have for at least the next century. And even that effort would fail, for Dr. Miller's "revolution" is already in place. Modern man now *wishes* to be an object; it is deeply reassuring to think oneself mendable, calibratable, lubricatable, and refinishable like any other machine. Our victims are so convinced that they are beneficiaries that they would no doubt reconvince us.

Views as to the applicational potentialities of psychology, the promise of the field (if any) for human welfare, depend, of course, on one's positive conception of psychology. Mine is a modest one, but so radically different from the currently regnant conception of the field that it is difficult to convey it in brief compass. I shall try.

For some years I have argued that psychology has been misconceived, whether as a science or any kind of coherent discipline devoted to the empirical study of man. That psychology *can* be an integral discipline is the nineteenth century myth that motivated its baptism as an independent science—a myth which can be shown to be exactly that, both by a priori and empirico-historical consideration (cf. Koch 1971).

On an a priori basis, nothing so awesome as the total domain comprised by the functioning of all organisms (not to mention persons) could possibly be the *subject matter* of a coherent discipline. If *theoretical* integration be the objective, it should be considered that such a condition has never been attained by any large subdivision of inquiry—including physics. When the details of psychology's one-hundred-year *history* are consulted, the patent tendency is towards theoretical and substantive fractionation (and increasing insularity among the "specialties"), not integration. Almost forty years ago, Heinrich Klüver was enthusiastically looking forward to the "impending dismemberment of psychology." No prediction ever made by a psychologist has been so fulsomely confirmed! As for the larger quasi-theoretical "paradigms" of psychology, history shows that the hard knowledge accrued in one generation typically disenfranchises the regnant analytical frameworks of the last.

My position suggests that the *non-cohesiveness* of psychology finally be acknowledged by replacing it with some such locution as "the psychological studies." The psychological studies, if they are really to address the historically constituted objectives of psychological thought, must range over an immense and disorderly spectrum of human activity and experience. If significant knowledge is the desideratum, problems must be approached with humility, methods must be contextual and flexible, and anticipations of synoptic breakthrough held in check. Moreover, the conceptual ordering devices, technical languages ("paradigms," if you prefer) open to the various psychological studies are—like all human modes of cognitive organization—perspectival, sensibility-dependent relative to the inquirer, and often non-commensurable. Such conceptual incommensurabilities will often obtain not only between contentually different psychological studies but between perspectivally different orderings of the "same" domain. Characteristically, psychological events are multiply-determined, ambiguous in their human meaning, polymorphous, contextually environed or embedded in complex and vaguely bounded ways, evanescent, and labile in the extreme. This entails some obvious constraints upon the task of the inquirer and limits upon the knowledge he can hope to unearth. Different *theorists* will—relative to their different analytical purposes, predictive or practical aims, perceptual sensitivities, metaphor-forming capacities, pre-existing discrimination repertoires—make asystematically different perceptual cuts upon the same domain. They will identify variables of markedly different grain and meaning contour, selected and linked on different principles of grouping. The cuts, variables, concepts, that is, will in all likelihood establish different universes of discourse, even if loose ones.

Corollary to such considerations, it should be emphasized that "paradigms," theories, models (or whatever one's label for conceptual ordering devices) can never prove *pre-emptive* or preclusive of alternate organizations. That is so for any field of inquiry, but conspicuously so in relation to the psychological and social studies. The presumption on the part of their promulgators that the gappy, sensibility-dependent, and often arbitrary paradigms of psychology *do* encapsulate pre-emptive truths is no mere cognitive blunder. Nor can it be written off as an innocuous excess of enthusiasm. It raises a grave moral issue reflective of a widespread moral bankruptcy within psychology. In the psychologial studies, the attribution to any paradigm of a pre-emptive finality has the force of telling human beings precisely what they are, of fixing their essence, defining their ultimate worth, potential, meaning; cauterizing away that quality of ambiguity, mystery, search, that makes progress through a biography an adventure. That, incidentally, is one strong reason why the success of any such "revolutionary" reconception of the nature of man as Dr. Miller invites would have to be adjudged a calamity. Freud's tendency to view dissidents and critics in *symptomatic* terms—and to resolve disagreement by excommunication—is no circumscribed failing, but indeed renders problematic the character of his entire effort, not only morally but cognitively. One is tempted to laugh off the ludicrous prescriptionism of self-anointed visionaries like Watson, Skinner, and even certain infinitely confident prophets of the theory of finite automata—but their actual impact on history is no laughing matter.

Because of the immense range of the psychological studies, different areas of study will not only require different (and contextually apposite) methods, but will bear affinities to different members of the broad groupings of inquiry as historically conceived. Fields like sensory and biological psychology may certainly be regarded as solidly within the family of the biological and, in some reaches, natural sciences. But psychologists must finally accept the circumstance that extensive and important sectors of psychological study require modes of inquiry rather more like those of the humanities than the sciences. And among these I would include areas traditionally considered "fundamental"—like perception, cognition, motivation, and learning, *as well as* such more obviously rarefied fields as social psychology, psychopathology, personology, aesthetics, and the analysis of "creativity."

Much of what I have proposed is grounded on an analysis, on which I have been working for twenty years, of the functioning of lexical units in natural and technical languages (cf. Koch 1961, 1964, 1973, and especially, 1976). The work suggests a sensible alternative to the absurdities of the definitional schemata of logical positivism and operationalism, and leads, I think, to fresh insights into problems of inquiry and of knowledge. This analysis shows that definition of abstract, general, or referentially "rich" concepts upon any delimited base of "epistemic simples" (such as a putative class of "physical thing predicates" or of verifying "operations") simply does not work. Such reductive definitional schemata confound symptom and meaning: if taken seriously they denude the universe of everything worth talking, or indeed thinking, about.

Analysis of the conditions of actual communication will show that effective definition is essentially a perceptual *training process*. The definer seeks to guide the addressee towards perception of the intended property, relation, or system thereof. If the referent is a subtle, delicately contoured, or embedded one (which it often is), such guidance may be very difficult indeed. The addressee may not possess pre-existing discriminations requisite to perceiving "the point." The event manifolds which "carry" the referent may be too fleeting, complex, or variable for ready segregation of the constancy in question. In the ideal case, definition would be a form of ostension via a perceptual display that exhibits the referent in its purest, least masked, most sharply contoured form. Scientific experiment may be interpreted in that light. It is often difficult to approximate the ideal form. Verbal definitions, though limited by their surrogate character, depend for their efficacy on the definer's skill at mobilizing relevant components of the addressee's discrimination repertoire. And whether (and with what precision) the communication actually takes place will depend on the fineness and nicety of the discriminations within the addressee's repertoire. Definition is thus sensibility-dependent and probabilistic: Nothing says that the intended property or relation will be noted—or brought into comparable resolution—by all addressees.

This analysis suggests that all definition is *real definition*: A definition tags and preserves the discrimination of *something* within the world flux—however embedded or intricately contoured that something may be. Moreover, *what* is tagged is no more stable than the discriminal activities and powers of appliers of the term. Processes of *metaphor*—i.e., the perception in new settings of relational characters which overlap (or are similar to) the characters tagged by an "old term"—are ubiquitous in language use. Though metaphor can lead to debased usages when the discrimination is less differentiated than a previously established use (or overlaps it only vaguely), in *creative* uses of language the meaning of a word can be sharpened and enriched by attaching it to contexts in which the original relational characters are more purely or richly exhibited. Man has the capacity for effortful perceptual search for subtle overlaps that can refine and extend established meanings. When such efforts towards creative metaphor are successful, then *knowledge* has been extended!

This perceptual theory of definition has many consequences—including certain of the judgments made in earlier paragraphs of this précis of my conception of psychology. But I have yet to underline one obvious set.

It should already be apparent that this account stresses the continuity between precise, differentiated, and subtle discriminations upon the human universe within the resources of natural language and *technical* knowledge—even of the most abstruse character. It emphasizes the circumstance that the so-called technical languages—whether of science, the psychological and social studies, or the "hard" humanities—develop as differentiations from natural language, and always continue to depend on their embedding context in natural language for their interpretation and use. Particulate and nice *description* is no lowly or easy task: it is in fact the very basis—indeed, the flesh—of all non-spurious knowledge.

There is a strong sense in which psychology was already "established" before it commenced as a science. Once we appreciate the vast resources of psychological knowledge coded in the natural language, and internalized in the sensibilities of those who use it well, it should become a paramount matter of intellectual responsibility for those who explore the human condition to ensure that this knowledge not be degraded, distorted, or obliterated in their technical conceptualizations. Such a responsibility cannot be met by experientially impoverished or functionally illiterate persons. Since the task of the psychological studies is not to *supplant* the cognitive achievements stabilized within the natural language, but to refine and extend that knowledge, it is incumbent upon its inquirers that they have *extraordinary* capacities for discriminating upon the inner and outer world, and for the precise and supple mapping of language to their discriminations. Indeed, the requirements for such capacities are so stringent as to render problematic the very idea of a massively populated profession. And *meaningful* pursuit of the widely varied psychological studies will demand of the inquirers in each area rich and specialized sensibilities relevant to the particular phenomenal domain at issue. This means that the psychological studies taken together require a work force of more heterogeneous character (relative to the backgrounds and skills of its members) than does any other currently institutionalized branch of inquiry.

Some psychologists will no doubt be appalled by the conclusion that psychology, over a broad range of its proper concerns, must involve modes of inquiry rather more like those of the humanities than the sciences. Perhaps they will feel that humanistic knowledge is "soft" knowledge based on soft intellectual disciplines, while scientific knowledge and research discipline are hard. But musicology is hard (in several senses), as are classics, comparative philology, biblical archeology, and responsible forms of literary criticism. And philosophy—even logic and the philosophy of science—is typically assigned to the humanities.

Perhaps they will have qualms to the effect that scientific methods (whatever these may be) guarantee the cumulative advance of knowledge, while humanistic insight does not cumulate. This question of cumulativeness is, of course, an intricate one which cannot be dispatched in passing. But no epistemologist or historian of science any longer believes that scientific knowledge moves in a linear and continuous progression, and it is dubious that any competent student of science in this century ever did. It did not wait upon Thomas Kuhn to stress the discontinuities and divigations in the temporal trajectory of science; such of his masters as Alexander Koyré, George Sarton, and, of course, Conant, were sharply apprised of such matters. Cumulation means literally a "heaping up," and the heaping up of knowledge is as characteristic of the so-called humanities as it is of the sciences. It may be thought that in science this heaping up has a special force: that of a progressive refinement, differentiation, and specificity of knowledge (at least in the long run), and, indeed, this may be one of the differentiae between science in the strict sense and the humanities. But it must be carefully asked whether this happy property of scientific knowledge is conferred upon it by the magic of scientific methods per se or by characteristics of the world domains addressed by the established sciences which render these methods applicable and fertile.

Only in the pages of *Popular Mechanics* (if there) do we any longer see vestiges of a "cosmic-eye" view of science as a *durch-und-durch* impersonal and objective enterprise. Scientific inquiry and its outcome are now seen to be sensibility-dependent and perspectival in much the sense heretofore seen as definitive of humanistic modes of knowing. There are subtle differences in the degree of the transmissibility of the knowledge achievable in the sciences as against the humanities, the univocality and scope of the formulations that can be attained, and, perhaps the multiplicity of significant perspectives from which the characteristic phenomena of each may be approached at any given time. But there *is* cumulation in the humanities, and it is easy to explicate the sense in which this is so.

Take, for example, the polymorphous, tenuous, ramified, and "open-horizon" concept of love—human love. The history of the humanities presents us with not a few savorers and explicators of this rather intricate context of human phenomenology, each approaching that context with his or her own special angle of vision, sensibility, sensitivity range. Plato has told us something about love; so have Shakespeare, Joyce, and Lawrence Durrell, to pick out three other inquirers almost at random. No one would consider the special perspectives of each of these men comparably profound, but no one would consider their perspectives as non-differential and non-preclusive in important respects. These four explorers have left behind four sets of spectacles through which differential modalities, contours, textures, and involvements of love may be viewed. The opportunity each of us now has to view love through each of these sets of spectacles does not mean that—by some magic of conceptual optics—they can be combined into one set of integrating spectacles, but it certainly does mean that the availability of the *four*, as against any given one, *enriches* our sense, our understanding of love. *This* is a form of cumulation, and a precious one.

Certain other circumstances should be noted. Shakespeare's theory of love does not refine the Platonic theory. Nor does Joyce refine or in some sense "improve upon" these two illustrious predecessors, and, most assuredly, Durrell does not represent some kind of "advance" upon the findings of his three predecessors. It is just that these four explorers perceive their bounded, yet inexhaustible, domain *differently*. Does it therefore follow that each is uninfluenced by his predecessors or that the perspectives and "findings" of each are genetically independent of those of his predecessors? I do not think so. The sensibility of each explorer has been enriched by the discriminations registered in the artifacts bearing the imprint of his predecessors; he can thus be helped to arrive at his angle of search, of vision, by the discriminations of his intellectual forebears. That, too, is cumulation—and in a more subtle sense than mere "heaping up."

It is my contention that much of psychological inquiry and knowledge must, in principle, have characteristics rather more akin to such features of humanistic scholarship as I have just tried to convey than to scientific research, even when the conception of scientific research is liberalized—as it has been by Polanyi, Bronowski, and others—in such a way as to punctuate its continuities with humanistic and all other forms of knowledge seeking.

Relative to the aspirations of psychologists who wish to hoist man to a new and revolutionary conception of himself on the petard of a science that can be rendered fully intelligible to "sixth-grade children," the notion of the psychological studies just reviewed will be seen to entail but modest promises to the human race. The psychological studies, when significantly conceived, will be seen as immensely challenging, immensely difficult, and very possibly in some ranges entirely refractory areas of *scholarship*. As is the case in other serious and dignified fields of scholarship, knowledge exceeding in precision and differentiation what the human race already knows will be won only by the ardent and creative efforts of relevantly equipped and sensitive persons who proceed with a minimum of public-relations fanfare. Psychology has been flagrantly and vulgarly oversold. In my view, it will find its dignity only to the extent that it retracts the feckless promises, pseudo-conceptualizations, and corrupt technologies it has flung out upon the world, and succeeds in reestablishing authentic continuity with the Western scholarly tradition.

My view proposes a relation of partnership between the psychological studies and the human race, rather than patronizing handouts of counterfeit knowledge, or even the variant of the latter implicit in Mr. Miller's policy of palsy, "on-the-line" troubleshooting. The partnership that I propose would see the best efforts towards specifying man's inner universe (and his condition) of the most sensitive and prehensile minds in history as *already* part of the *tissue* of psychology. It would see those efforts as criterial in respect to the assessment of "new" psychological knowledge.

In this connection, I have devised a classificatory test (Koch 1976) for conceptual frameworks (or more pretentiously, "theories") in the psychological studies—a test which I believe to provide a central criterion in so-called issues of "theory choice" or even in absolute judgments of significance. This handy epistemological device can, if you will, be seen as a kind of consumer protection law in relation to the marketing of psychological wares. My perceptual theory of definition—which sees so-called empirical definition as *real* definition—entails that the knowledge coded in natural language and internalized in human sensibility gives us a kind of ontology of the human universe. On this basis, it becomes possible roughly to distinguish three kinds of theories or conceptual frameworks within the human studies: some that are *ontology-distorting*, some that are *ontology-respecting*, and some that are *ontology-revealing*. My theory of definition permits me to call any technical framework which obliterates or does not permit us in some way to "recapture" the network of epistemically rich concepts in the range of natural language bearing on its domain, *ontology-distorting*. A frame which merely "respects" such distinctions but does not (by processes of metaphor, etc., as I have analyzed them) permit the sharpening, extension, supplementation, or enrichment of natural language knowledge is *ontology-respecting*. A frame which *does* permit such sharpening, supplementation, or enrichment of the natural-language knowledge is *ontology-revealing*. At any given time it is, I think, possible to find within the gamut of the psychological studies conspicuous instances of frameworks within each of these categories. Regrettably, however, a frequency distribution of the frameworks currently comprising the substance of the psychological studies, as conventionally conceived, would be savagely skewed towards the ontology-distorting category.

My sense of partnership means also that we must relate to gifted humanists, artists, scientists, possessors of special skills and forms of connoisseurship in every field (not excluding managers, political leaders, planners—yes, and salesmen, nurses, and automobile mechanics, too) as allies and collaborators. We can expect no "technical" insight, or more refined insight than nontechnical mankind already has, into complex and subtle and humanly important pheonomena until we address those phenomena. We do *not* address such phenomena when we inferentially recompose them from the activities of rats, college sophomores, or even computers. In every human area we must use high-order, refined, and relevantly specialized sensibility as a probe into the structure and dynamics of its own operations. In every field individuals of summit-level attainment must be assumed not only to generate the most interesting phenomena for study but must be assumed to know (in some sense of that slippery word) most about those phenomena. We should not be inhibited by the stereotypic belief that ownership of a process or skill disqualifies the owner as an explicator thereof. Though we must presume an ultimate core of ineffability in respect to all "tacit knowledge," we may also presume that the boundaries of what is tacit at any given time are larger than that core, and can be made to recede. The history of reflexive awareness is not, after all, a totally barren one. *Our* role as investigators must be to facilitate a recession of the tacit. To this we bring some slender but actual resources—at the minimum, a deep sense, derived from our own past failures, of the complexity of those factors of which action (or experience) is a function, and a bit of wisdom, similarly derived, about the criteria for an informative analysis. On this view of partnership, in which the target phenomena are located in other persons, it should be stressed that those persons are more properly to be construed as co-investigators than as subjects.

What does my conception of psychology say about the currently institutionalized implemental areas: the so-called applied fields which render formal services to our human clientele? It says, somewhat trivially but wholly confidently, that any analogy of their status to that of an applied natural science is obfuscatory, and remains so even when bearing in mind that the division between pure and applied science is nowhere a well-defined one. Further than this, it says that the various psychological studies of implemental cast would have to be addressed one at a time. To take one large case: My theory of definition suggests there to be severe and *principled* constraints to fullness and univocality of communication within such fields as clinical psychology or psychopathology (cf. Koch 1976). I suspect, for instance, that not only do no two psychoanalysts *do* psychoanalysis in the same way (a fact granted by virtually everyone) but that no two of them "speak" psychoanalysis in sufficiently similar ways to warrant the conclusion that they hold the "same" theory. Yet the various theories or conceptual frames within clinical psychology do loosely influence the professional sensibilities of their followerships, and feed and guide their therapeutic practices, but differently so for each member. Clinical work is necessarily an *art* which must tap the resources of the entire person. It is well that clinical training involve broad exposure to the differentiated and subtle knowledge of the human condition embedded in the humanities (I would exclude only the one known as "humanistic psychology"), and perhaps even a soupçon of involvement in extra-academic and extra-professional life.

Not all human predicaments are resolvable, not even in principle. An ounce of mitigation is therefore preferable to a pseudo-solution weighing a ton. My modest conception of psychology can have, at best, only small and slow mitigative consequences.

Throughout the writing of this paper, I have been obsessed by an image of gauges: billions of them reproducing at bacterial speed and threatening the residual space in the ecosystem. Hundreds of gauges are protruding from the orifices and integuments of each inhabitant of the world. The rational biped who used to stride through the world in quest of experience has become the sedentary reader of gauges and oscilloscope displays which monitor his condition. Do I feel elated or depressed? What does my electronic sphygmomanometer say? Better peep at my portable biofeedback module and get a fix on my brainwaves, too. And why not make an early appointment with my psychiatric team for a good going over? Better remind them to send me over to Neurology for a CAT scan.

The same interposition of gauges between events and our apprehension of them qualifies our reading of the social world. What is happening out there in the society at large, the body politic, the economy, or just merely in our own micro-world (whether it be General Motors or Blowing Rock State Teachers College) is totally obscured by a miasma of gauges, computer readouts, sociometric indicators, surveys. Reality is not merely displaced—indeed, rendered superfluous—by these instruments, but the surrogate reality is rendered even more perversely chaotic and unpredictable than the initial one by virtue of the "self-fulfilling-prophecy" impact of *each* reading. The trouble is compounded by the fact that most of these scale-faced beings are merely mock-ups, sans sensors.

The behavioral and social sciences have set a generous fraction of these instruments in place. Is it not time to relent? It will be painful while these quills are being retracted, but is it not possible that we gauge-bearing porcupines can yet rediscover our humanity?

References

Koch, S. Clark L. Hull. Section 1 of *Modern learning theory*. New York: Appleton-Century-Crofts, 1954. Pp. 1-176.

Koch, S. Psychological science versus the science-humanism antinomy: Intimations of a significant science of man. *American Psychologist*, 1961, *16*, 629–639.

Koch, S. Psychology and emerging conceptions of knowledge as unitary. In T.W. Wann (Ed.), *Behaviorism and phenomenology: Contrasting bases for modern psychology*. Chicago: University of Chicago Press, 1964. Pp. 1–45.

Koch, S. Reflections on the state of psychology. *Social Research*, Winter 1971, *38*, (4), 669–709.

Koch, S. Theory and experiment in psychology. *Social Research*, Winter 1973, *40*, (4), 691–707.

Koch, S. Language communities, search cells, and the psychological studies. In W.J. Arnold (Ed.), *Nebraska Symposium on Motivation, 1975*. Lincoln: University of Nebraska Press, 1976. Pp. 477–559.

Leavis F.R. *D.H. Lawrence*. Cambridge, Eng.: The Minority Press, 1930.

Miller, G.A. Psychology as a means of promoting human welfare. *American Psychologist*, 1969, *24*, 1063–1075.

General Discussion of Koch's Paper*

Miller: ... There must be somebody who can put in a good word for psychology.

White: I'm very strongly inclined to put in a good word for psychology.

Miller: Can you get close to the (microphone) uh ...

White: Yeah, I'm very strongly inclined to put in a good word for psychology. I don't want to give my presentation tomorrow today, but I think what I'd rather do right now is react to the

---

* Since there had been no time for discussion immediately after Koch's paper, this discussion actually took place later in the day after Scriven's presentation.

talk of the morning [Koch's] rather than the talk we just heard. Because I think the notion of taking psychology back struck everyone as an interesting idea.

I think I would thoroughly agree that psychology is being given away in great quantity. I think it's very gratifying to have the kind of evidence that was put forth, those wonderful lists this morning, which clearly showed something being given away. Furthermore I thoroughly agree that psychology ought to become, and in fact is now becoming, more humanistic in many forms. And that's all to the good. But I think I'm very suspicious of a humanistic psychology that ridicules and downplays human efforts to work with issues like behavior modification, crotch-and-eyeball therapy, nude group groping, and on and on . . . those lists. The ideal that was being conveyed is that that kind of communication of psychology is not valid or is inferior. But I think that a humanistic psychology ought to respect, let's say, the fact that the humans who both give and receive those things attach value to them. And I think you'd have to ask yourself a lot of questions before you judge exactly what the value is supposed to be.

Someone with whom I studied, Gustav Bergmann—not one of the broadest of people by any means—once said a tremendously broad thing that impressed me. He used to say, "Everybody has a point." Well, I suspect that crotch-and-eyeball therapy has a point and I suspect that behavior modification has a point. It may not be as sophisticated a point as one would want and it may be ridiculous—in fact, a lot of that stuff is ridiculous—but I'm not really sure. Maybe if you're going to try to get a social system to absorb psychology, you have to do some ridiculous things. People have to creep before they can walk. Just because you've learned . . . let's say you've become a connoisseur of wine, I don't think you should ban beer very quickly. That's my remark for psychology.

Koch: Speak up for wine!

It is difficult for me at this level of fatigue to give the kind of eloquent and obviously complete and final answer that I'd like to, but I think that my position has been misinterpreted in a number of ways, possibly as a result of my tendency to make somewhat large, dashing generalizations in a quasi-humorous way.

When I say I think psychology should be taken back, I don't mean that in an absolutely literal sense. I would hope that was clear from the context. But I'd like to address this specific point with respect to crotch-eyeballing. That is one of the more—shall we say, uh, what?—Byzantine or bizarre or baroque things that psychologists have advocated during this "crawling" period. I do not disrespect the solace that human beings derive from *anything*, whatever my view of the quality of the solace or the weirdness of its agency.

I do, however, very much agree with Michael Scriven that psychology and the social sciences are not value free. I have a much more ornate way of saying this than I think even Scriven (though I know his full analysis to be more complex than what he was able to say today); I've been talking about this matter for years. And I think I can present an analysis that shows—by having, let us say, the people who do feel things like crotch-eyeballing are valuable look over my shoulder—I think I can exhibit to such people (and successfully have on actual occasions) the simplisms and the counterproductive impact on their own sense of themselves and, indeed, perhaps on their own functioning, of such approaches. And I believe I can do this with at least comparable authority to that of virtually any "dustbowl" empiricist who might believe otherwise.

I would refer this audience to a paper of mine called "The Image of Man Implicit in Encounter Groups" published in *The American Scholar* [1973] and, in varying forms in several other sources. The mere fact that I talked about encounter groups made this (apparently) the most widely read article I've ever written! I don't think it deserves to be the most widely read article I've ever written, but there it is—which again says something about what psychology has done in the line of sensitizing people to certain kinds of interests.

I am not an elitist; I am not looking down my adequately long nose at people who do have a sense of alienation or a sense of insecurity or are in deep distress, and who latch on to many of the things that we have sold them. Nor do I look down in some ultimately dismissive way at the people who have been doing the "crawling" and have been offering their wares. But I would say that within any field of scholarship, whether scientific or humanistic, there is need at every point in history for the activities of the second-order kind of person—the analyst, the critic, the watchdog type of person—and I think that the utility of such critiques, in fact, will always depend on the extent to which one can make them plausible, and in some sense liberating, to both the people who have been affected by the "contributions" in question and to the people who actually do the work. I do want to be understood

White: on this point. You don't have to accept my contention that I can succeed in doing this, but just grant me the fact that I have that intent.
Okay?

White: Okay.
May I pursue you on another point, or do you want to open this up, George?

Miller: Well, we've exhausted Professor Scriven's time, there is coffee available, and you will have the podium tomorrow, so all right.

Koch: May I address just one . . . just get this off my mind? Two sentences in relation to something you [Miller] said?

Miller: Two sentences?

Koch: Two sentences. Okay? Really, *two* sentences.
Just a correction. You implied that I said that psychology is simply not a science, etc., etc. I want to make a strong correction here. I said that if we talk about the psychological studies we have to look at them case by case, context by context; and that there are indeed large sub-areas of psychology—and incidentally, in my estimation among the most productive and interesting sub-areas of psychology, especially during the past twenty-five years—which can definitely be ordered to the biological and natural sciences, and I took sensory psychology as an example and biological psychology in its more general sense as an example.

Miller: I take comfort in that. And now I'd like to take comfort in a cup of coffee.

Question and Answer: Miller and Koch*

Miller: With respect to Professor Koch, I do agree with the neo-Wundtian position that he espoused on experimentation. I find myself, more and more—as I get into interest in the psychology of language—having more and more difficulty

---

* Composed from exchanges occurring at the end of the second day as Miller analyzed each paper and redirected a question to each member of the symposium.

doing what I would regard, or would have regarded in my psychophysical days or my physiological psychology days, as bona fide experiments. However, I think that as a psychologist I bring to some of these humanistic questions a different way of approaching them. In doing linguistics, for example, I don't rely solely on my own intuitions about the language, but I look for ways to pool intuitions of others. I think that simulation is a way to test the coherence of a set of ideas. It's a somewhat different approach than most humanists would take to their problems. It's not an experimental approach. It wouldn't be ruled out by Kant, Herbart, or Wundt on that basis.

I think you can even do such things as measure reaction times in naturalistic situations if you do it unobtrusively and often get interesting ideas about what's going on from that. And above all we can collect naturalistic data, data that we see occurring around us, and use it, as someone said, "as a text" that we can apply, not just the traditional methods of analysis to, but some of our own methods of analysis. Perhaps even resorting occasionally to a test of statistical significance to validate our results. Now, I think of those as extensions of the traditional methods that are used in humanistic studies, and I think they are still well in the spirit of what Sig was advocating.

But I wondered . . . how to say this . . . I do agree that the value to mankind of Psychology with a capital P is going to be a function of the strength of psychology with a small p, and therefore I agree that this is a good way to strengthen some of the most interesting aspects of psychological studies—psychology with a small p. But what didn't come across to me in your remarks were your recommendations for the best way for us to supply the psychological services that society is now demanding of us, and I don't think either you or I would be satisfied with a program to take psychology back and just not supply it. I mean, for whatever reason, we are stuck with that, and I would like to draw you out on that question.

Koch: Well, I must say that was a moderate, sotto voce, dignified, charming response, Mr. Miller.
White: Generous.
Koch: Despite your best efforts, you're a charming, friendly man.

I'm delighted to learn that Mr. Miller is slightly chastened, as against the optimism conveyed by his—1969, was it?—presidential address. I would remind Mr. Miller, however, that one of his central emphases in that talk was that psychology is potentially a "revolutionary" science; that, in fact, the revolution was under way; and what was at issue was a revolutionary reconception of man, which he then was sufficiently indiscreet—modestly, but actually—to illustrate. I attempted an analysis of the proposals that he made with respect to a paradigm, presumably descriptive of current arrangements of social life, and another paradigm that would—admittedly in some vague way—presage a new and liberated world order based on scientific evidence. I tried to show that there was no determinate way, either in terms of psychological evidence or scientific evidence or hermeneutic analysis, of saying that the one paradigm consisted of statements of greater efficacy (relative to the requirements of the human condition) than the other paradigm. My analysis also tried to show that with respect to each element of *each* paradigm there had long been a *range* of defensible, particular, differentiated positions in the history of the humanities. Therefore, I found Miller's claims to be over-optimistic, and his illustrations of the profound knowledge that psychology had to give away, worthless. And Mr. Miller has not addressed *that* in detail. But I think he'd be willing to admit at this phase that the slight chastening of attitude to which he has confessed would involve at least a modification of his optimism with regard to those particular proposals.

Over and above that, I think we come out extraordinarily well. He agrees with my so-called neo-Wundtian position with respect to experimentation. I didn't ever christen it a neo-Wundtian position myself, but I'm not insulted by the nomenclature. I hope that what I've said is not as dull as the ten volumes of Wundt's *Völkerpsychologie*, and, if given ten volumes, I think Mr. Miller would be even more chastened, but that we'll leave be. [*laughter*]

Now, he says that currently in his work on the psychology of language, he's apprised of the fact that he's not doing bona fide experimental work that can be made to adhere to any of the simpleminded paradigms which try to convey what the nature, let us say, of the analytical methods of physics might be. And I'm glad to hear him say that. I'm sure he's correct.

He says, however, that he brings a different perspective than the humanist, in that he is willing to try out a range of methods that are not necessarily at the command of the humanist. From this point of view there is no disagreement whatsoever. My conception of the psychological studies is not that each one of the many psychological studies that can be distinguished is identical to what a humanist does, but rather that any description of what the inquirer is doing in most of them would come out more like the description of what a humanist is doing by virtue of his objectives, the kinds of evidence available to him, the way in which he processes meanings, constancies, regularities in his data, and so on. Such a description would more closely resemble a description of humanistic method than the rather simplified and fallacious descriptions of what physical scientists do that we as psychologists claim to have been following in our so-called scientific work. So there is no disagreement there whatsoever, and if Mr. Miller ever were sufficiently interested in reading my comments on the psychological studies in more extended form—I had only about ten minutes in which to talk about them—even the tiny, apparent trace of disagreement would probably disappear.

I have no objection to the use of statistical methods where they are appropriate in connection with the psychological studies. I have no objection to people who want to play with simulation methods, etc. I would, of course, point out that much of the work done in the humanities has been influenced by analytic methods coming from the same sources (which are outside of psychology, actually) as those that have provided psychology with these analytic methods. And indeed, I would criticize a great deal of the current work in the humanities—a great deal of the work that has been done in the humanities in the twentieth century, as a matter of fact—because of a tendency for the humanities to be pervaded by a kind of dilute scientism which in effect transforms what the humanist is doing into a highly incompetent form of quasi-social science. But that's a complicated issue, and I just throw that out as an aside.

Now, Mr. Miller would like to have my recommendations for the best way to provide psychological services. And here again I'll obviously have to be very brief and I'll simply say one pregnant, but no doubt opaque, thing which Mr. Miller can dwell on and unpack as aggressively or unaggressively as he might choose. I would say that the best way to provide psychological services would be to provide, where relevant, *human beings* (as consultants, as therapists, etc., etc.) in any context involving human welfare: to provide psychologists as human beings who may—or indeed may not—be *disciplined connoisseurs* of certain ranges of human action and experience. The point here is that we do the world a great injustice if we provide a core of "technicians" who really have very little to offer or, indeed, have counterproductive wares to offer under the cloak of scientific impeccability.

Which brings me to my last point: namely, that there's been a great deal of talk about the central metaphor of giving psychology away. Now, I'd like to point out that psychology, because it bears or seems to bear on our human problems, is of deep interest to mankind. It is, therefore, automatically given away. There's no way not to give it away. If it gets published, it gets given away. It is my contention that psychology has been given away with increasing largesse since that glorious moment in the history of scholarship in which it was institutionalized as a coherent, scientific field.

In my opinion, much of what has been given away has indeed had a reducing and demeaning impact on man's image of himself. This I have tried to demonstrate in terms of my funny lists of multifarious images of man that psychology has purveyed. And I think that Mr. Miller's own attempt at a kind of image—his revolutionary reconception of society—hasn't helped the situation very much.

Therefore, I would like to conclude by saying that I think the significant psychology that resides in the sensibilities of our *competent* people certainly should be made available to society, is available to society, and will continue to be available to society. And my own objection to this would not influence those circumstances one whit, but I do not object. I want to make that very clear.

When I say psychology should be taken back rather than given away, that is a figure of speech known as hyperbole. I am pointing to the fact that very, very much, an enormous percentage of what we have given away, is extraordinarily shabby and has had a most unhappy influence on human welfare. And many of my other colleagues seem to have at least inadvertently proved this in the following way: When they address what psychology at the present time should contribute, what psychology *at the present time* is called upon to give to mankind, they almost characteristically suggest the taking back of psychology's *past* "gifts" that have led to disastrous consequences.

I think that's as far as I want to go. I think that we are close together actually.

Miller: That may be bad. . . . Maybe we'd better fight! . . .

An Evaluation of Psychology

Miller's Introduction of Scriven

Our next speaker, Professor Michael Scriven, is a philosopher with strong interests in psychology; interests that led him to become a professor of education, as well as a professor of philosophy. In my encounters with Dr. Scriven in the past I've found him to be a man who simply bubbles with interesting and challenging ideas—at least some of which are good! He was one of the earliest contributors to the current activity (or even hyperactivity) focusing on educational evaluation. He introduced such terms as "formative and summative evaluation," "meta-evaluation," "goal-free evaluation," and a lot of others. He's presently a University Professor at the University of San Francisco and director of the Evaluation Center. Today Professor Scriven is going to apply his long experience in problems of evaluation to "An Evaluation of Psychology."

An Evaluation of Psychology

Michael Scriven
University of San Francisco

THE REPORT CARD

The time for kindness and generosity has been used up by Professor Koch. I assumed that I could count on him to clear the ground, of Miller and anyone else nearby, and I am proceeding to tackle the issues from a slightly different point of view. Psychology should, one might argue, be evaluated along three dimensions—in terms of its ethical standards, its practical contributions, and its intellectual importance. The conventional distinction between applied and pure science seems to me less useful and less clear than that between practical and intellectual; both of these may have social effects. On each of these dimensions we might evaluate it either in terms of how well it did compared to what other behavioral and social sciences *have* actually achieved, or compared to what psychology itself *might* reasonably have done given its resources and age. Those frameworks lead to very different results. And of course they will yield somewhat different grades depending on who does the grading. I have only the credentials of long interest as an independent observer. My very first publication was a critique of group dynamics; my first text (co-authored) was in psychology; I served under Gary Boring's editorship on the reviewing staff for *Contemporary Psychology*, worked with Fred Skinner when the first teaching machines were built, learnt from Paul Meehl about psychotherapy outcome and process designs, and from Herb Simon about the General Problem Solver, spoke at the second Nebraska motivational symposium, cohabited with two echelons of the Stanford Think Tank, and served on the APA Board of Social and Ethical Responsibility. None of that produces validity, but if you add in some long arguments with Sig Koch and Carl Rogers, Bettelheim and Ellis and Brunswik and Kohlberg, Rollo May and Erich Fromm and Donald Campbell, then you have the next best thing to validity, which is *durability*. That is really the only credential I can offer as support of what follows. I wouldn't even claim credibility, just durability, except insofar as I produce a few reasons for the ratings—but we'll start with the grades themselves.

First the good news. Compared to the other behavioral sciences, one would have to say that psychology has been above average, even if not truly outstanding. Let us say a B+ on ethics, where very considerable and worthwhile efforts have been made in meeting and enforcing professional standards in the clinical and testing field, and in examining considerations of social responsibility of the profession. Perhaps a B on practical payoffs; they have not been impressive, but the competition from economics, sociology, and political science is so pathetic that the B comes easily enough. In the intellectual dimension I think we can justify a B+, though a slightly backhanded one since most of the progress has consisted in discovering that the simpler and the sexier theories don't work.

Turning now to a rating of the performance of psychology against what we conventionally call "absolute standards" but which are better described as reasonable achievements and criteria, the news is not so good. Here it is helpful to distinguish between a grade for the performance to date, i.e., for the time-integral of the achievement so far, and for the present level of performance. Remember that we now ignore the comparison with other behavioral sciences. Ethical concerns were near zero for so long that the present status of C+ is not enough to pull the overall performance above a D. Practical payoffs have been enriched lately by the activities of non-academic psychologists and were always mainly due to the efforts of low-status non-academic types like industrial psychologists working on ergonomic problems or—for all its excesses and errors—testing types. Overall, they have never been very impressive, but are now, perhaps mainly because of the work on clinical prediction formulae, at the C+ level.

In a moment we'll look more closely at the reasons for these grades, but first let's complete the listing. On the intellectual dimension, the great achievements have been the success—limited though it was—of early behaviorism, the fascination of depth psychology, the vast contributions of qualitative and quantitative methodology—contributions which have given us most of the tools we need for investigation of psychological phenomena—and most recently the work in cognitive psychology. This is not, by itself, too bad a record. But there is another aspect of the matter which cuts the grade down badly. Psychology has failed many of the intellectual challenges that it faced—failed badly, indeed frequently grotesquely. For although the failure has been on some of its greatest challenges, I would say that on four out of the five most important that I can identify it has failed. Of course an honorable failure is almost the equivalent of success in science, that is, if the failure is due to the fact that the phenomena are intransigent, and that's not the fault of the scientist. But these have been dishonorable failures, failures which can be explained only in terms of scientific incompetence. For this reason I have to award another D. Three Ds out of three. It is not impressive. One would have to say that psychology has flunked. Not straight Fs to be sure, but grades with which even an undergraduate cannot graduate.

THE FIRST FAILURE: THE AHISTORICAL VIEW

Let's look at the reasons for this somber judgment—a mere pronouncement so far. Perhaps I can indicate the line of reasoning most clearly with an example or two. If I had to pick out one intellectual discovery by psychologists in the twentieth century that deserved an award for its significance, I'd nominate Harry Harlow's discovery that he made in a casual moment in his study in Wisconsin one afternoon, that the word "love" did not occur in the index of any of the psychology texts that were then available. Now he did something about it. He began that long series of studies from which we learned various interesting things—at least about chimpanzees. However, Freud had previously mentioned the term, and in fact set out quite a good deal of material on the subject. What had happened, however, in Freud's discussion and those of others—although distinctly interesting and hence picking up some points on the intellectual dimension—did not compare in importance to Harlow's discovery. For Harlow's discovery was the discovery that psychology had abandoned its past. The discovery of the Sahara desert must always stand as more important than the creation of an oasis in it, and that was what we found there.

There were other deserts in psychology. I remember my amazement in finding no entry or reference in the index of the last edition of the *Encyclopedia of Educational Research* to moral education or ethical training, or even to morals or ethics . . . which one might casually think had something to do with education. We have, indeed, irrigated a little of that desert in recent years—largely thanks to Larry Kohlberg's work—but not very much of it. Now it was not that no good work had been done in that area. Hartshorne and May's brilliant study from Columbia dates from 1928— one of the great landmarks in social science research. The problem was that as with Freud on love, the climate had changed. The desert has spread, and that is the great disgrace of psychology. It has been a creature of fickle fashion, ruled by the crude urge for novelty—not the model of patient, cumulative science. True enough of many subjects. Many of the fascinating fields in physics, for example, have been made into deserts by the march of the great accelerators, the modish push to particle work. But unforgivable in psychology because psychology is the subject which studies such tendencies, which should be well if not fully armed against them. So the first great disgrace is the failure to remember its own history, to respect the accumulation of learning; more simply put, the failure of psychology to cultivate the territory it claimed.

THE SECOND FAILURE: SELF-SCRUTINY

The second disgrace is the failure to apply to itself the standards of science which are taught in every introductory course. In the heyday of individual differences, where were the psychologists who trumpeted the sexism within psychology as evidenced by the ratio of appointments and promotions to Ph.D.s and publications, or of rank to research grants or positions of power?

When it came to dealing with controversy, what happened to the standards of evidence that were proclaimed every Monday, Wednesday, and Friday at 10 A.M.? They were not to be found in the behavior of psychologists reacting to the claims of documentation for parapsychology coming from Duke—with the notable exception of a few genuine scientists like Paul Meehl. More recently, the reactions of academic psychologists to the humanistic/holistic approach have been similar. The Jensen controversy shows that even the lesson of Galileo is still not learnt: Suggestions of censorship or ostracism or sanctions came crowding forth as if the Inquisition had died in vain.

When it comes to applying the standards of scientific proof to one's own brand of psychotherapy, what do we find? Good-bye proof, hello hucksters! Half a dozen decent studies in three-quarters of a century and a thousand articles. When I mentioned in the American Psychological Association's *Monitor* that I thought psychologists did not meet FDA standards for drugs and that incoming patients should in all conscience be handed a card stating this, a deluge of correspondence ensued in which senior psychologists painstakingly constructed and proudly exhibited every fallacy known to freshmen, such as "I know I'm effective—hundreds of my patients come in sick, take a couple of years treatment, and go out cured." Why don't we treat *that* as professional incompetence? If they double-charged a patient, the Standards Committee would step in—but simple intellectual ineptitude in the psychotherapist's capacity to think about therapy—no, that's nothing to do with the Standards Committee!

When the relatively simple general procedures of the scientific investigation of psychological phenomena have been laid out in class, in what proportion of those classes do we find them routinely applied to that same class in order to find out how to improve it? Or even applied by the chair of the psychology department in order to make personnel decisions? The proportion would have been nearly zero five years ago. Today it is more substantial—but only because of *administrative* fiat, originating from *legislative* pressure, not because of a sense of scientific propriety, internally generated.

Let us turn to the spoils system in psychology, more honorifically referred to as research funding. The hallowed core of this process is the so-called peer review system. By those not getting funded, it was often described less favorably as the Old Boys' Club. No one with even a B.A. in psychology could deny the possibility of shared bias, halo effect, and group dynamics effects on the value judgments of the small committees that, in effect, handed out all these funds, hundreds of millions of dollars in the aggregate. How large were these effects? Nothing could be simpler than to apply the kindergarten type of experimental design required to yield an answer. It was never done—as far as I have ever been able to tell—until after I started making it an issue when I got on an NSF associate director's advisory board. The pigs had got their snouts in the trough and everyone else could be counted on either to keep quiet so as not to jeopardize their chances, or to be dismissed as crying sour grapes. Of course, it's generally regarded as socially maladroit to refer to the distinguished scientists receiving funding from federal agencies or large foundations as pigs with their snouts in the trough. But the description is in fact rather on the moderate side—one should probably say *male chauvinist* pigs and not just pigs. The argument for the porcine metaphor is simple. The difference between pigs and people is that people can reason explicitly and by use of that reason have developed both science and ethics. A person with scientific commitment would regard trough-feeding as an important subject for scientific research. A person with ethical standards would know that distribution of wealth is something to which basic principles of justice should apply. If an entity feeding at the trough *neither* studies that feeding behavior scientifically *nor* seeks to assess it ethically, how can one suppose it to be human?

It should scarcely surprise you to hear that when we finally did get the same proposals refereed by two panels working independently, the results came out very differently. In short, interjudge reliability of the revered system is poor. Which means the validity is poor for that reason alone. But it may be poor for other reasons, which might make the process a farce even if consistency between panels did occur. Senator Proxmire raised questions about geographical and perhaps historical bias. They are good questions and quite easily investigated. Because of this threat from *Congress*, the trough to which the *agencies* go, NSF started a few little nibbles at these problems. Feeble, perfunctory, defensive—but a start. No credit to psychology, of course. The impetus didn't come from psychology, though fortunately a competent psychologist is now running the shop and is functioning with at least the basic tools required for this kind of investigation. I remember my last discussion with his predecessor. No need to evaluate the peer review procedure, he said, since it is self-correcting: If people aren't really competent, their papers won't be published, and they'll be dropped from the selection process. Admittedly he was a physicist, but where were the social scientists to laugh at him? Busy on their panels, of course.

What I am saying is that the scientific imperative in psychology is self-scrutiny, not because of some philosophical need for narcissism but for the much better reasons that it comes with the territory and that it leads to improvement. Psychology begins at home, but no one noticed that it didn't. How many times has one heard it said that psychologists' children are the worst-behaved on faculty row? But how often has a psychologist looked at the question of whether the children of child psychologists have more or less behavior problems than a matched group of historians? Of course, one can be a good preacher without being a good person—but it would be very *encouraging* to discover that the kids of psychologists were a *little* better than average. It would still be possible that the psychologists' theories were correct even if they couldn't apply them. I'm talking about ethics a good deal in this paper, but I'm no great model for ethics—I didn't even get my paper done in time for Dr. Miller and the other symposiasts to see it in advance. I'd probably be a *better* teacher if I were a better exemplar. You will have noticed that we began looking at the intellectual failures of psychology and that that has led us quite quickly into considerations of practical payoffs and also of ethics. That is because intellectual studies grow out of, are abstractions from, practical requirements; and ethical standards are—or should be—the ultimate result of practical studies of social life. Our three dimensions are not ultimately, but only conveniently, separable.

Let us now look at psychology's success in increasing its practical payoff, rather than just checking on its own reliability. Let's restrict ourselves for a moment to the problem of increasing the payoff for the fixed sum of money that the funding agencies have available in a given year. This is probably what generates most of psychological science. It therefore seems like an obvious target for payoff oriented research. We could, for example, consider the relative efficacy—that is, reliability/validity/cost—of various ways of running the peer review system. For example, should we use a preliminary screening process involving brief outlines of potentially detailed proposals; or should we go to full proposals immediately? It is well known in contractor circles that using the latter procedure will quite often generate, say, a hundred proposals which cost several thousand dollars each to write, which are then fed into a review process whose true cost (including panelist and staff costs, overhead, oversight review by OMB, GAO, CBO, AA, etc.) is some tens of thousands, in order to compete for a pot of half a million, which is less than the total cost of the competition. A more fatuous effort would be hard to find. The two-tier approach radically improves the cost-effectiveness of the process—even if it does not lower validity much. To put the matter bluntly, a joint effort by the professional associations could get this nonsense stopped in a year; but in fifty years that joint effort has not occurred and I do not recall hearing that the president of the American Psychological Association has ever tried to get it started.

Other gross wastes of taxpayers' money are involved in the procurement process, for example in the excessive use of contracts instead of grants (usually done in the name of *saving* taxpayers' money), in the failure to develop systematic track records for grant applicants, the failure to use reasonably defensible forms and procedures for panelists to screen proposals, the failure to train project monitors adequately, the absurd delays and hidden agendas and lack of appeal procedures against "forms clearance" (i.e. the approval of questionnaires). All of these lead to good psychologists not applying or to bad psychologists using hopeless designs because they avoid the hassles; in short, they lead to bad science driving out good. But psychologists have—as do most scientists—a conception of such matters as being outside their purview, as being mere administrative concerns. For that reason, I flunk them on both ethics and intellect. There is no need for the primatologists to abandon lovable gorillas and spend all their time on reforming intolerable bureaucrats. That is what the division of labor is for—to avoid such choices. But there is no excuse at all for them not to spend one hour a month selecting delegates who will do this, writing supporting or critical letters to their own representatives and journals, or reading reports on such matters which not only provide their sustenance and their image and their social obligations—as they do for any scientist—but in the case of the psychologist also happen to be relevant to their training and often their subject matter.

The whole discussion of pure and applied research, of relevance, of basic and policy orientations, all that seems to me far too remote from the kind of failure that characterizes much—I think most—of psychology today. Why get into the question of what courses an accountant should teach—pure or applied—if he consistently fails to add up his own expense account? There is *some* limit to the independence of teaching and practice; at *some* level physicians have to be able to diagnose themselves, psychiatrists cannot be *catatonic*, priests can't *blackmail* those who confess to them, psychologists must *suspect* bias in all-male panels reviewing papers identifiably authored by women.

We have talked about two great intellectual failures of psychology, each of which develops into a failure of practical payoff and an ethical failure. The first was the failure to treat the domain of psychology seriously and systematically, as illustrated by the elision of past research from texts and references, plus the failure to replace it or improve on it or even comment on it despite its intellectual and practical importance. In short, a failure to do the scientific job. I'm not a scholarly historian, and indeed I was always rather sceptical about the payoffs from history of psychology until I heard the then professor of psychology at Oxford announce (in 1951) that one of the most pressing problems in the science of perception at that time was to work out how people come to see the world the right way up although the retinal image is inverted. It was then sixty years since that "problem" had been definitely resolved—by exposure as a pseudo-problem—and I wondered how much time he had wasted reinventing the wheel. I now serve on the editorial board of *The Journal of the History of the Behavioral Sciences* and find comparable experiences—essentially as a reviewer of the philosophical content—documented in every issue. Yet how many departments of psychology require and treat a course in the history of the subject just as a data base for the avoidance of conceptual errors?

While the first sin is failing to follow the minimum standards of what cannot be treated as the defined criterion of the sciences, their cumulative nature, the second sin we discussed is the failure to apply the standards of psychology to the study of psychology itself. Looking in the mirror is surely an essential step for improving one's appearance, a minimum proof of sincere interest. What a remarkable laboratory for a science course the psychology classroom is! It might not be too bad a practice to forbid psychologists from using any exogenous demonstrations or a separate laboratory. If all the students learnt was some understanding of the learning process in which they are so deeply embedded for many years, and if in so doing they learnt to look at themselves as scientists, they might become better psychologists than most of those we have graduated so far. It might also be interesting to see whether the enthusiasm for this process of self-appraisal in the student and teacher roles could be stimulated to match the enthusiasm for the off-campus baths of self-appraisal via other-appraisal that the encounter groups provide. It would be interesting to see if that effect could be combined with the standards of scientific appraisal. Self-study and self-reference are very rich fields for psychology in the classroom. As an example of the limits of self-reference, I offer the following which I first set as a complete final exam: "Is this a good final exam?" A more conventional one would be "Was this a good course?" (Hint; try a reductio proof of a negative answer.)

THE THIRD FAILURE: THE NEWTONIAN FANTASY

The third great failure of psychology was its failure to break free of the Newtonian fantasy, the fantasy that underlying overt behavior, thought, or phenomenology there lies a theoretical structure which awaits discovery and will yield precision, prediction, and power. I have argued against this for a long time, but now it just seems better to poke fun at it, doing the poking with a good strong stick labeled The Three Body Problem. Since the Newtonian synthesis cannot provide a solution to the problem of predicting the behavior of a universe containing just *three* bodies operating under just *one* force—that of gravity— even if we assume the bodies are *perfectly spherical and homogeneous*, and that the force of gravity is *precisely* an inverse square force—then why in the name of analogy should we think for one minute that the behavior of thousands of millions of heterogeneous humans interacting with each other and with a substantially unpredictable environment via forces that—whatever they are—are *demonstrably* not as simple as gravity, should be generally predictable, explicable, or otherwise reducible to a simple structure? But the search for the Newtonian chimera still pervades a great part of the conceptual/intellectual activities of psychologists and of other social scientists. Given the history of failure alone, even without any deep understanding of what happens to applied math when it has to face even well-behaved irreversible changes such as fatigue in metals, the quest is not only foolish but self-indulgent.

Let me give you an alternative model for psychology, which we can call the One-Way Toll model or OWT. It will show you why I avoid the term "applied" and prefer the term "practical." For "applied" presupposes something to be applied and it is just one of the many symptoms of the Newtonian disease that many people simply can't conceive of practical research that doesn't involve applying a theory. For example, one often hears it said that one can't have a procedure for evaluating or improving teaching unless one has a theory of learning. One might as well tell a consumer that they can't have a procedure for evaluating apples unless they have a theory of apple-growing.

The One-Way Toll model is a model of how to make huge contributions to human welfare without a theory of human behavior at all. A few years ago the toll bridges in the San Francisco Bay area as elsewhere in the country were converted from picking up twenty-five cents in each direction to picking up fifty cents in one direction. This change has the following effects, roughly speaking:

1. It eliminates half the payroll costs
2. It eliminates half the booth maintenance
3. It eliminates half the time costs for commuters of the delay at the booths during rush hours
4. It eliminates half the gasoline loss, emissions increase, and wear and tear on the cars
5. It eliminates half the psychic and physiological costs of tension in the usual traffic jam for commuters.

The *first* of these amounts to a million dollars per annum in the Bay Area alone. If the idea had been thought of during construction, a few hundred thousand more would have been saved in booth construction and roadbed widening costs. Now here's a really valuable idea, and one that involves behavior management. I'm not suggesting that it *is* an example of practical psychology—it was a suggestion untouched by psychology—just that it's a useful model. At first sight, it appears to be purely practical, to have little intellectual content. But that, as the Zen masters say, *is* the intellectual content. It is *precisely* what is significant about this model. It is not "applied" anything; it is straight problem-solving. Perhaps a total of a million and a half dollars a year in one area, perhaps fifteen or twenty million in the United States, fifty million in the world, conservatively. Enough to save the lives of a hundred thousand or two hundred thousand people by feeding them or giving them medical care. This much *every year*. That's not a bad achievement without a theory of learning or traffic or toll booths. It should inspire us.

Now I want to add two facts about this case history that will tell you, louder than I can shout, how badly hooked on theories we are. First, I tell you that—although I was in the Bay Area at the time of the OWT reorganization—neither I nor anyone I know can tell you the name of the person who thought up OWT when it was implemented. Second, I tell you that shortly after it *was* implemented, a traffic engineer wrote to Herb Caen—the most widely read columnist in the area—and pointed out that he had suggested this same arrangement in a letter to Herb Caen twenty years earlier and that Herb Caen had published and commended the suggestion. We had thrown away perhaps $20 million in our area, perhaps hundreds of millions in toto, by ignoring that suggestion. And we ignored it because we are theory junkies. We expect the panoply and the trumpets of a theory of a new movement before we listen—and then we turn our cynical attention to the suggestion, often to refute it. But something like OWT is below the threshold of attention, below the radar of our recognition. No one now remembers who produced it, the first or the second time. Yet how many psychologists or even movements within psychology have produced as much simple practical payoff? I doubt if the Skinner box improved even pharmaceutical research that much; it certainly had less effect on child-rearing. And what movements in psychotherapy have had that sized effect? None—unless you suppose that in their absence, people would have received far less help from whatever surrogates they sought. The evidence as I read it today makes that extremely unlikely.

That doesn't mean that *all* the theory-oriented or theory-presupposing work in psychology has been wasted. The first few years in pursuit of a new model is worthwhile. That would justify about 5 or 10 percent of the effort. The rest was wasted. We got into the rut of theory-hunting, chasing the Newtonian dream, seeing ourselves as scientists *only* because we did that, or our leaders did it. So for decades the work on the white rats went on because it was thought that this followed the model of approaching the final goal of a science of human behavior via the behavior of simpler and more manipulable organisms, in much the way that Galileo approached the study of falling bodies via the study of bodies rolling down an inclined plane. But this was just fantasy. Galileo had a proof of the essential similarity of the two cases. *We* had ample evidence of their crucial differences, e.g., with respect to symbol manipulation. There's no point in studying A as a way to understand B unless you can *now* establish a close relation of one to the other. The fact that both A and B *learn* doesn't mean that the way each learns is the same; it doesn't even slightly support the idea that there are non-trivial laws of learning underlying both. We became rat junkies because we were theory junkies, but if we ever looked carefully at the supposed justification for using rats to get to theories, it would have evaporated instantly.

What we should have been doing was looking at practical problems and trying to solve *them*, being open to the possibility that we would have to develop a theory to do the solving. Instead, we applied the model of classical physics despite its demonstrable irrelevance, going after a theory with no connection to practical problems. And wasted our time and our society's resources. Classical physics worked well because astronomy involves extremely simple systems. When you look at the physics of complex systems, for example, turbulent-flow hydrodynamics, then you very quickly turn to the wind-tunnel or the bubble tunnel and start empirical testing of inventive designs. That's what science should have been doing, and of course a few psychologists like Pressey *were* doing just that. Like the OWT inventor, we forgot them until a theorist—if Fred Skinner will pardon the expression (and perhaps "ideologist" is better)—rediscovered them.

Is the OWT model really feasible for psychology? It may be useful to look at another example, one that involves less technology and more straight behavioral management—and has an ethical dimension as well. Let us call this the IQ model. IQ does not here refer to the Stanford-Binet but to Integrated Queue. You've noticed that neat system they now use at airline and bank counters in which each of the service ports is fed from the head of a single line, what the British call a queue. All those terrible injustices of not being served until after someone who arrived later, all the risks of missing a flight because the person ahead of you is booking a round-the-world tour for next Christmas, all eliminated by a simple and effective idea! Please note that the OWT and the IQ models do not involve a tricky trade-off of costs and benefits. The cost of instituting them is negligible. That is one of their greatest attractions as models.

Are such models really applicable to psychology? Of course they are. Pressey is one example, but let me take another. Paul Diderich's work is in this excellent tradition. To begin with, few people know his name, the first condition for being an example. When Diderich began his work as director of freshman composition at the University of Chicago, he became interested in the interjudge reliability of the essay grading that he was doing and that was going on under his supervision. Note the second point: the self-scrutiny. Discovering abysmally low correlations there, well below .50, he then asked what the test-retest reliability was. It turned out to be only slightly over .50. So far, interesting—perhaps even important—but not very creative. What distinguished Diderich from the pack was that he then began years of work devoted to the problem of improving the reliability *and* validity (not "at the expense of the validity") of essay grading. And he succeeded. The procedures he developed can validly yield an interrater reliability of over .8. Hence—a third key point—not only science but justice was served. Today we use his procedures in many large-scale composition evaluation efforts around the world. So even psychology can aspire—though it rarely does—to the success of the OWT and IQ models.

In passing, I want to explain why I used the ambiguous acronym IQ. It is to remind you of the origins of that durable concept. The original IQ test was devised as a measure of *intelligence as that term was currently used* by teachers familiar with individual students, and it was devised with two requirements in mind. First, that it should provide a faster route to determination of intelligence than awaiting the results of months of interaction. Second, that the measure should be more accurate than the ratings of any individual teacher. It meets those requirements. Whether intelligence as used by all of us is important is not something that the IQ test assumes. More could be said of course, but the IQ test is not a bad model for psychology, not even despite but because of its present disfavor. The trouble with IQ was bad intellectual interpretation by psychologists, not (by and large) bad measurement—though there was indeed a small amount of cultural bias in the test items. The poor thinking led to poor practice and to injustice—the usual sequence.

So the OWT and IQ models are not inappropriate. They are atheoretical. They are high yield. They are the right models for a complex field. Of course, they are seen as overtly or covertly deeply insulting by those with theoretical aspirations in or for psychology. Such people are correct to see these models as implicitly insulting. The models can indeed be laughed at. But they can laugh back, all the way to the bank. The minute one stops laughing and starts thinking, one begins to see not only promising areas for this kind of research, but the importance of treating the practical as the intellectual. To paraphrase Lewin, there's nothing as theoretically important as a good practice.

Harking back to our earlier discussion of peer review systems, for example, one can immediately think of promising procedures that might generate better results. One of these is the "wild-card" approach. Each panelist gets one vote which can be used to guarantee support for a proposal that cannot achieve majority support. In this way we might avoid some of the worst effects of fashion swings in psychology. Another procedure with the same intent is the "maverick fund," a 10 percent set-aside that is to be allocated only by consideration of payoff, not the probability of getting it (above a very low threshold of "minimum plausibility.") Doing follow-ups on these procedures and on panelist recommendations and rejections to get an estimate of accuracy is obvious payoff territory. And so on.

A more traditional and respectable example is the literature of clinical versus statistical prediction. Notice its practical importance; its bearing on the legitimacy of professional fees, an ethical issue; its crucial self-reference; and its intellectual importance in stimulating reconceptualization of the role and power of the clinician and the clerk. It came out of no theory, but it cut a hundred theories off at the ankles. It came out of no opposition to theorizing, but it led to a much better conception of theorizing.

THE FOURTH FAILURE: THE VALUE-FREE COMMITMENT

We now come to a fourth failure of the intellectual efforts of psychology, the great fiasco of the value-free commitment. Now if there is one thing worse than the arguments for value-free science it is the arguments for abandoning it put forward by most of the SPSSI types that explicitly and vehemently reject that position. I am never much impressed by allies with bad reasons—they always leave when the fighting gets rough. Most of them, in this case, think that value-free science was the doctrine that scientists were or should be politically neutral. Although that was Weber's original doctrine, it soon acquired a massive logical rationale and transformation by connection with the fact-value distinction. This fortress is still held, and indeed is located nowhere near the fighting over the social content of science. Focusing on this issue, whether science can only legitimately generate descriptions rather than recommendations or evaluations, we find the usual failure of self-analysis; even the most cursory study of scientific reports shows them to be permeated with value judgments. Something very funny was going on in a subject which didn't notice that, or didn't understand its implications, or didn't care about inconsistency. The explanation had to be the desire of psychologists *not* to face the embarrassing consequences of their professional but suppressed commitment to evaluation. Speculation on that motivation is widespread, and you have heard much reference to it. I have examined the logical issues in some detail elsewhere; I will not repeat the discussion here. The position is totally devoid of logical merit.

You may feel that psychology has largely recovered from this charge of commitment to an untenable doctrine of value-free status. Not at all. The old guard still rules—it just talks less. The young Turks have their heart in the right place but their heads are still confused. That situation does not earn a passing grade on intellectual dimension. And the exceptions—the sturdy and brilliant few, like Don Campbell, who have turned to the evaluative tasks—have now run into a second methodological barrier, beyond the value-free taboo, the barrier presented by the irrelevance of classical psychological methodology, even when modified into "quasi-experimental" design to serious evaluation. (Not so incidentally, this problem is one that Dr. Miller warned us about in 1969.)

It would after all be a little surprising if a science built on the Newtonian model should turn out to be useful for social program evaluation. Of course, psychology makes valuable contributions to evaluation—most large-scale evaluations depend heavily on statistics and tests and measurement contributions from psychology—but those contributions cover only perhaps a sixth of the relevant skills. Yet most people appointed to the several thousand professional positions as evaluators in this country have only that training, because that was the only professional training that came near to being appropriate and/or because the people writing the job descriptions believed that to be so. As a result the dead hand of an irrelevant model still controls this area of application. For example, it has led to the fostering of the practice of evaluating the vast federal interventions by running hundreds of thousands of tests and feeding the results into computerized statistical programs. Out of the millions of dollars spent on this, the only thing that has emerged is that nothing significant has emerged. I am highly respectful of negative results—they do increase our knowledge—but I am convinced that it only takes one or two of these studies to show that little more is to be gained from them. We are now moving away from that approach, towards small experiments with better controls, but we are moving *very* slowly, *very* late, and with inadequate capabilities for handling the results. After all, amongst all the handbooks for doctoral theses or research article preparation in the social sciences, where do we find a serious (not a perfunctory) treatment of the ethics of experimentation, or of the analysis of sexist language or racist test bias, of affirmative action personnel practices, just to pick three issues. Not in the classical paradigms of psychological experimentation? The answer is "never." Yet these are key components of most applied social program evaluation. And equally important components, which are not covered at all, involve an analysis of the justice of the social program itself, the costs of delivery, the side effects of the process, the identification of unintentionally impacted populations, the location of the implicit decision structure, the assessment of needs, the distinction between statistical significance and social significance. One can hardly evaluate many programs without knowing intimately the arguments pro and con various types of affirmative action, the arguments about academic freedom, equality of opportunity, and so on—in short, applied ethics. Plus game theory. Plus cost-benefit analysis. And so on. As long as psychologists control the personnel input to evaluation as much as they do, and as long as their intellectualizing about evaluation is as limited as it still is, we must expect continued failure in this area. To bring in ethics is not to bring in something extraneous to psychology; only the mental block of the value-free doctrine leads us to see it this way. Ethics is—or at least has the latent function of being—a social strategy for meeting needs and maximizing expectations. Psychologists are no strangers to game theory and decision theory and group dynamics; yet they have almost universally stopped short of using these approaches to develop a systematic treatment of ethical problems as simply one type of social-psychological problem. Usually they mutter something about the difference between the normative and descriptive. One more example of the fact/value non-distinction; or to be more precise, a distinction that exists only in a particular context and has absolutely no intrinsic strength at all.

Exactly similar arguments apply to the cost dimension. The allergy of psychologists to cost analysis reflects itself in the curriculum—no social science department teaches it and few business schools teach it competently. But cost is just as much a constraint on the solution of human practical problems as is ethics, or for that matter physical strength. And it is just as absorbing an intellectual challenge. One might as well face the fact that training psychologists for practical contributions will mean quite a reform in the *curriculum* (and not just the orientation) of psychology departments.

Putting the ethics and costs aside for the moment, let's look in closing at an example that's much closer to "home," that is, to the classroom—an example that will illustrate some other deep problems for psychologists in moving to the practical realm. My theme here is of course that psychology is not just handicapped by value-allergy but by methodology-inadequacy. Not just a change of heart but a change of mind, a change in intellectual training, is required. Thus consideration of the value-failure leads quickly to problems in the intellectual domain.

Consider what at first sight appears to be a good example of psychology moving into the self-analytical and practical domain, the development of Keller plan teaching or the Personalized System of Instruction. This originated from a psychology professor, teaching a psychology class, and applying to it (so he believed) psychological principles. Most of you are familiar with the approach—replacing lectures as the main teaching vehicle with reading materials, using frequent tests and tutors to review them one-on-one, stressing occasional lectures as (optional) reinforcers, providing self-pacing and multi-tracking and so on. This movement is now very strong in higher education; it has its own journal, newsletter, association, workshops, annual meetings, and disciplines. I have recently collaborated with Barbara Davis on a review of the substantial literature of studies of the success of PSI. They often meet the standards of traditional psychological design validity; but they never approach adequacy as studies which speak to the practical decisions and questions about adoption or support that are obviously waiting in the wings, particularly questions about the dropout rate, verification of grades, the increase of work, the hidden costs, or exploitation of tutors. I'll add two other comments. The widespread view—shared by Keller—that PSI represents an application of behavioral psychology and hence is a practical contribution from that movement, is simply fallacious. It is considerably nearer the Oxford and Cambridge tutorial model with its five centuries of humanistic teaching than it is to Skinnerian shaping technology. The rhetoric of behaviorism here is a veneer which has no logical basis and incidentally serves to turn away many potential users. It is an exact parallel to the mistake of supposing that psychoanalysts can count to the credit of Freudian theory those patients (if any) who are in fact aided by their time in treatment.

My second comment is that the results—so far as we can work them out—from these studies are not very good. It is certain that they are not very good; it is possible that they are not even positive on balance. Yet a thousand or so psychologists and other scientists are sold on the approach to the extent of changing their courses to fit the model. In short, even within the discipline, the capacity to identify solutions to practical problems is extremely inadequate. The mythology of PSI says it's very successful: it isn't, on the evidence we have. The mythology of "Sesame Street" says *it* was successful. Again, the evaluation was done by psychologists (at ETS, as it happens); again, it used the wrong methodology, in particular concluding from a statistically significant difference to the existence of a practically important difference. In fact, it is nearly impossible to find in that report any discussion at all of the absolute magnitude and the educational significance of the differences between control and experimental groups. Yet you get only the absolute differences for your money.

The mythology of "Sesame Street" as a success is so strong that NSF is apparently about to fund its developers for a "Science Sesame Street" because they're so good. But their actual track record is: one multi-million dollar effort with negligible results ("Sesame Street"), a second with almost the same results ("Electric Company") and one which was so bad it had to be stopped in midstream. What a winner!

CONCLUSION

So the study of the value-free fallacy shows up a terrible intellectual failing of psychology and it leads us to see experimental design failings and hence practical and ethical failings. The net is tightly woven. In a sense, I think Miller's stress on hanging on to the science is right—but the theoretical must be reformed to serve the practical. In so doing it will not lose intellectual content but be revitalized, instead of increasingly losing in the competition for new majors and professionals.

And the same message we get from PSI must be applied to the popularization of psychology, the "sloppy stuff" of Esalen and Synanon. Those avenues *must* be explored. But the revolution of social and even psychological legitimacy that made it acceptable to consider them was not accompanied by a revolution in methodology to fit such studies, though it *was* accompanied by a revolution *against* the old methodology, in the sloppy sense of abandoning the standards of scientific investigation.

Psychology has flunked—and the failure runs deeper and goes wider than most critics have realized. Only if we realize this can we hope to build on the necessary revolution a new and more useful science.

General Discussion of Scriven's Paper

Miller: We have a few moments for discussion and since Professor Scriven will not be with us tomorrow—am I wrong?—this might be a good time for it.

78   An Evaluation of Psychology

I'm at a low ebb. Perhaps my blood sugar is low at this time of day, but I think that's not really it. It's my intellectual sugar that's down. Two men whom I admire enormously have just destroyed my life. Professor Koch told us that he didn't want to give psychology away, he wanted to take it back. He felt that we don't have any true scientific results worth giving away and probably, on principle, we can't have any, and there can't be an integrated coherent discipline in psychology or in any other science, and no paradigm can be preemptive, and what the hell are we doing? And then we had lunch and come back and get our "grades" from the man who I must regard as the Master Evaluator and . . . straight D's. I haven't had a D since I almost flunked out as a freshman.

Koch: It might have been good for you.
Miller: Well, it would have saved everyone here a lot of trouble. Just to get things started—since that's what moderators are supposed to do—I remember conversations with John Pierce, who used to be director of research at the Bell Telephone Laboratories. John liked to point out that in the history of science it was frequently the case that practical discoveries were made first in technology and industry. For maybe the first two or three hundred years of modern science, scientific progress was made by taking up things that had been found in the workshops by artisans and trying to figure out why they worked. I don't know the history of science well enough to provide examples, but certainly things like thermodynamics came out of noticing that steam engines were pretty useful devices and so on.

Well, I remember a conversation with John when he was trying to give some direction to a group of psychologists who were working at the Bell Telephone Laboratories in Murray Hill, New Jersey. He asked me, What are the practical things that a group of psychologists should work on? And. . . Never mind what I told him! I'm not . . . wouldn't be proud of it even if I remembered it, I'm sure. But his decision was that the teaching machine was a practical discovery, something that worked, and he tried to get his psychologists to work on it in the hope that some real science would come from that kind of a practical discovery. I didn't know about Dietrich, I don't know whether that would lead to anything beyond the practical way of increasing reliability and validity of evaluation of freshman compositions or not, but it conceivably could.

The point of view that Professor Scriven was advocating

is not a new one. It's a very powerful one. It wasn't until the twentieth century that certain branches of science became sufficiently well formulated that they could actually make predictions that went beyond what any practical person knew. And it may well be that psychologists are unlike chemists or physicists or molecular biologists or astronomers. We are still back in the nineteenth or maybe the eighteenth century with respect to the problems that we want to understand, so Scriven's is very good advice.

I'll shut up now because somebody else will surely say something. Do the members of the symposium . . . do you want to . . . [*pause*] Aw, come on, fellas! There must be somebody who can put in a good word for psychology.*

Question and Answer: Miller and Scriven**

Miller: I'm sorry tht Michael Scriven is not here, but I will proceed as if he were. I agree in principle that psychologists should apply evaluation techniques to themselves as he urged us to do. But I disagree on the grade he gave us on our self-evaluation. I believe we have applied those methods to ourselves. I've wandered through a number of scientific societies in my dilettantish career and I can assure you that psychology is the most self-concious profession that I have ever had any contact with. We're constantly examining our own entrails.

Now, the journals are full of reports of studies evaluating psychotherapy. There was recently in the *American Psychologist* a summary of some three or four hundred of these which

---

*The remainder of this discussion serves as the general discussion following Koch's paper, because of the obvious relevance of the ensuing comments for that presentation.
** Michael Scriven was able to be part of the symposium panel for only the first of the two days of meetings. Since Professor Miller's direct questions to each speaker were delivered at the end of the symposium, Scriven was later given an opportunity to respond by telephone with no more time to "plan" an answer than those participants who remained throughout.

you may have had a chance to see, coming out with the rather surprising result that psychotherapy did do some good, but different kinds of psychotherapy were indistinguishable in their effects. So, whatever kind is cheapest, take that. I can remember my revered Professor Edwin Garrigues Boring published a series of papers years ago on the role of women in psychology years before women's liberation became fashionable. Now, I suspect that Professor Scriven, having done most of his reading in philosophy, of course, is not as well informed as he might have been about the amount of self-examination that psychologists have done, in the extent to which we have turned our tools on ourselves.

My point would be that the problem is that we took so little action on the basis of what we discovered as a result of that self-examination. We knew perfectly well that there weren't any black graduate students, we knew perfectly well that women were discriminated against, we knew a lot of things, but in the old days it used to be the exclusion of Jews from psychology departments. So, the real scandal is not that we didn't evaluate, and the point is that evaluation is no panacea. You can evaluate until you're blue in the face, but if you don't do something with the result you've wasted your time. So my question to Dr. Scriven would be: What are your recommendations for forcing change as a consequence of the result of evaluation? How do we turn evaluation into action?

Scriven: Professor Miller thinks that psychologists have done more self-study than any of the numerous other professional groups with whom he has been affiliated. I support that judgment, yet they still have done very little. Studies of the outcome of psychotherapy, indeed, have been done, but only very recently have they been done with any technical sophistication. And studies of teaching are in the same situation—recently done to a considerable degree, but still not very sophisticated, in following on a very long period of habitual nonoccurrence. But there are many other areas where self-study is of the very greatest importance, where virtually nothing was done and where even today only a travesty of research occurs—for example, studies on the methods whereby research grants are awarded (i.e. peer review). Even though Gary Boring had done some writing about women in psychology, and some studies, this was not something which— if I recall correctly—he featured in any of his texts, and it's certainly not something which other psychologists featured in their texts. So there might have been an occasional individual doing some of this work, but it was not being treated with any kind of seriousness by the profession as a whole. Perhaps that falls under the heading of action rather than research, and I certainly agree with Professor Miller that the great gap here is between the evaluation and the action. But even in the case of psychology a very large gap still exists with respect to the research itself.

To give yet another example—studies of the extent to which psychologists have been influenced by the predilections of funding agencies for which they have worked are still rare and hardly the focus of attention that they surely should be, since we have in such an example a clear case of tension between commitment to scientific objectivity and interests in continuing to get financial support. So I won't clear the slate with respect to my original charge about the lack of self-study; and I'm certainly happy to add the extra charge of lack of effectuation of the results of self-study.

To turn to the question on which Professor Miller focuses—the question of how to improve change, how to effectuate change in a beneficial direction—I think that there are two parts of this that deserve considerable attention. One is improving the evaluations so that they speak directly to the actual alternatives of the decision makers. Evaluations are much too frequently still done on a scientific model instead of a decision-oriented model. For example, they will often simply investigate whether a program achieves its goals rather than the question of whether it is a more cost-effective way to achieve those goals than any other available program; which would, of course, involve cost analyses and all the dimensional effectiveness analyses which psychologists are chary about. So one part of the solution is to improve the revelance of the evaluation. A great deal of room still remains for improvement there.

The other part of the improvement is to improve the procedure for training psychologists—the moral and social education of the professional—so that these things are seen as more central, something about which professionals know more than they presently do, so that they in fact explicitly discuss questions of ethics. Not just narrow professional ethics—the clinical relationship, the use of tests—but the more general professional questions, such as the obligation of psychologists trained or funded on public money to return some kind of results or investigations that bear a social payoff. This kind of thing needs to be incorporated in the training programs much more seriously. Gary Boring—the man who appointed me to the editorial consultant role on *Contemporary*

Psychology in order to review works on scientific method and parapsychology—quite well exemplified the deficiencies in training that are typical. And in this case the deficiencies were with respect to learning about the ethics of handling controversial areas within psychology. Boring never did learn how to achieve some kind of balanced approach to parapsychology. He would simply switch from Monday-Wedesday-Friday thinking that it deserves a hearing to Tuesday-Thursday-Saturday thinking that it should be thrown out bag and baggage. He didn't ever acquire a sense of what you might call fair play in these things.

So I think that's fairly typical. You find that constantly in the journals and in the meetings. There's still a very poor sense of a large scheme of ethics as far as psychology is concerned. The most obvious example of that lies in the fact that the APA—which is made up of slightly more than half clinicians and slightly less than half researchers and academic teachers—has still never managed to take any kind of stand on the ethics of psychotherapy as a legitimate kind of treatment on the one hand, or on the ethics of teaching without a reliable system of teaching evaluation on the other hand.

I guess that's most of my comment directed toward Miller's point. It isn't that psychologists can plead ignorance. He's right . . . they don't even have that excuse.

Testing—The Limits of Social Responsibility

Miller's Introduction of Williams

Miller: For a change of pace, the next speaker is not a university professor. E. Belvin Williams comes to us from the Educational Testing Service in Princeton, New Jersey, where his title is Senior Vice President, Program Areas. I remember Bel from my days as president of the APA, when he was one of a group of black psychologists who undertook to educate the APA in general—and me in particular—about the social responsibilities of psychology. I remember looking at that group and being very frightened by them; I didn't know what violent, radical thing they were going to do. Then I looked down the list, I saw Belvin Williams' name, and I said, "Well, they can't be all bad. Look, this guy is running the computer at Columbia Teacher's College. They must be all right."
Jackson: And it didn't hurt Bel!
Miller: Anybody who can relate to a computer can relate to me is the implication, I guess. I assume he's presently performing similar, valuable educational services for the Educational Testing Service, and his title today does concern social responsibility. It is "Testing—The Limits of Social Responsibility." Bel . . .

Williams' Opening Statement

Thanks, George.

I'm not in the computer business any more, but I do some things that are related to it. I wanted to say that I'm not—as he did point out—I'm not in the university any more. I've changed my self-image from that of an academic to a practitioner. As I was listening both to Sig Koch and Michael Scriven some of it seemed a little bit unreal, since my world is quite different these days.

As a matter of fact, these matters of social responsibility and responsibilities of institutions and psychologists are major ones for us at ETS. I thought that just to show you some of the currency of the issue, on April 5—today's April 7—on April 4, April 5, and April 6 there was a series of articles run in the New York *Daily News*, the newspaper with the largest daily circulation in the United States, on testing. I can give you a brief look at how she started—Miss Kiki LaBais.

The first article is entitled, "The true measure of tests: Are they accurate? Are they fair?" And with a subtitle of: "Tests: The rating game." At the end of the article, which is a reasonable presentation of things, she points to the next installment with a question: "Who can be blamed?"

And in the next installment it has "Tests: The rating game" and "Testing: The gripes get louder." In a very early paragraph she mentions, "A lot of people write the giant Educational Testing Service in Princeton, New Jersey." Since most of the article is devoted to ETS, I suppose that the inference that one should draw—if one read the first article—is that you ought to blame ETS. We're not, by any means, the sole keepers and makers of tests. In fact, only a small portion of them. But, to the extent that it's convenient to draw the fire of the social critics, I suppose that's a worthy function that we might serve.

I wanted to sketch out my remarks, and this might be a little bit different from the previous speakers. Namely, I wanted to look at two central statements of George Miller's paper. One, "give psychology to the people," or "give it away." I want to agree with that statement. I think that's a pretty good idea, being a populist by heart. And I would also want to argue that there is much to be given, and probably the only fault is that we haven't given quite enough.

The second statement, however, that I'd like to look at in his paper is that "psychologists have no stated obligations to solve social problems," and if you did revisit the article you remember the particular quote, which I will read to you momentarily. I think that I want to take issue with that perhaps and to—depending on his present view—perhaps disagree very strongly with it.

Then I thought that I would organize some of my comments around the question that was asked of us in the paper sent by Dr. Kasschau, of reexamining the issue or notions of application, relevance, and policy-setting. I think I will agree with some of the comments made by both Professors Scriven and Koch regarding those terms. Then I'd like to focus a little more sharply on what I think are some issues before the American Psychological Association or the profession at large. I'll also focus on some issues before us as individuals and issues that necessarily confront testing organizations such as ETS.

Testing—The Limits of Social Responsibility

E. Belvin Williams
Educational Testing Service

> Because morality is so elusive a concept, the careful researcher may be inclined to exclude it from his considerations, arguing that it's largely a matter of personal or cultural style. But I believe we are living through an age when morality is becoming a stronger and stronger force in the whole world, and for us to ignore it in our decision theory research is for us to become largely irrelevant. (Churchman 1973, p. 4)

In his letter of invitation to me regarding participation in the first Houston symposium, Professor Richard A. Kasschau suggested that our purpose "is to revisit the notion of 'giving psychology away,' to analyze more carefully the rhetoric, and debate the issues and pseudo issues." I am grateful for this opportunity to share with you some of my ideas on the topic and, in particular, to set them forth against the background of concerns voiced by Miller (1969) almost a decade ago. Professor Miller has been a model for many of us who would pursue areas of inquiry within psychology. I am most pleased to participate in this discussion with him today.

For purposes of easy reference, permit me to cite two passages from Miller's presidential address; the first is one with which I heartily agree, and the second is one with which I strongly disagree. But both provide parameters of thought which shall limit my remarks in this session. Miller argued:

> The most urgent problems of our world today are the problems we have made ourselves. They have not been caused by some heedless or malicious inanimate Nature, nor have they been imposed on us as punishment by the will of God. They are human problems whose solutions will require us to change our behavior and our social institutions. (1969, p. 1063)

With this statement, I agree.

Miller goes on to say:

> Moreover, there is nothing in the definition of psychology that dedicates our science to the solution of social problems. Our inability to solve the pressing problems of the day cannot be interpreted as an indictment of the scientific validity of our psychological theories. As scientists we are obliged to communicate what we know, but we have no special obligation to solve social problems. (1969, p. 1063)

With this statement, I disagree. Have we no obligation to solve those problems that we have helped create? Surely, the moral principle supporting an affirmative reply to this query is the same as that which prompts the United States government desperately to seek a radiation-free, uncrowded, and life-supporting island for the Bikinians some thirty years after the atomic experimentation on that isolated and unimportant, to us, atoll.

Is it not both reasonable and morally proper for corporations which for decades have released tons of chemical waste into our streams, urban air space, and tillable land to seek strategic solutions for correcting these lethal hazards? Similarly, can physicists be indifferent to the problems of atomic waste? Perhaps they can, but at their own peril. It was this concern with the consequences of scientific invention that the late J. Robert Oppenheimer wrestled with, and he concluded that our country and our world would be the better were it to curtail rapid and thoughtless expansion of our atomic arsenal. Perhaps his solution was faulty, but the concern and sense of obligation remain. In sum, this concern with the conjunction of scientific inquiry and social consequences would qualify as a moral principle under Kant's maxim, i.e., *"I am never to act otherwise than so that I could also will that my maxim should become a universal law"* (Jones 1952, p. 853).

The attentive layman and psychologist are likely to agree with the above formulated relationships between scientific inquiry and the responsibility of the scientists to monitor and correct the social problems created by their scientific discoveries and inventions. But what has this to do with psychology? It has created no nuclear weapons, owns no chemical plants, threatens no world order, but tends to focus on the individual and aggregates of individuals. For psychology, Kant's second formulation of the imperative of duty would apply. *"So act as to treat humanity whether in thine own person or that of any other, in every case as an end withal, never as means only"* (Jones 1952, p. 855).

Let us look more closely at our country, our science of psychology, the ways in which we have given psychology away, and our unmet obligations. Churchman's observation provides a starting point:

> So I begin with the outrage that in our society we keep treating people as means—like inanimate instruments—instead of as individuals. We send 19-year-olds to a far land to fight and possibly die, because we

regard them as essential means for our defense. We number people, we train people, we make people work in incredibly dull jobs, all because this is thought to be the best means to our ends. (1973, p. 6)

Of the many parts of psychology, none has been more widely used than that described as mental measurement. Holtzman (1971) and Thorndike (1971) have described the historical progress of educational and psychological measurement and its success. Few Americans have gone untouched by some psychological measurement device. Selection and classification for the armed services began with World War I and continues. Evaluation of the educational progress of students within school systems has been in place well over a half decade and could very likely become more widespread. Note Joseph A. Califano's remarks at the most recent annual meeting of the College Board:

In short, basic competency tests, used skillfully, and sensitively, are useful and necessary—they are a limited, but very important tool for charting and improving the process of education. We need to do more testing and we need to do better testing. (Califano 1977)

Selection and placement of students entering college or graduate and professional schools have a history of almost three quarters of a century and continue. Likewise, selection of employees within local, state, and federal government, as well as in industry, is on an upward spiral. Indeed, we test, we label, we exclude, and we include, but not always with the individual as an end in mind.

The technology that has been created to support large testing activities is impressive. Among other things, the supporting technology enables us to gain reasonably precise estimates of the reliability and validity of information gained. These two attributes are fundamental considerations for any information regardless of how it is collected, e.g., through interviews, on-site observation, dreams, or physical measurement. With the present technology, it is possible to collect information from large numbers of people quickly and in a short span of time. Further, it is possible to score or in some sense evaluate the responses of persons in automated ways at levels of accuracy, reliability, and speed not possible a few decades ago when this phase of the process was done by human scorers. In addition, it is possible to design the information collection effort in such a way as to be able to support reasonably well generalizations to domains of knowledge, performance, and skills beyond the scope of the immediately observed. Finally, public repeatability and/or empirical confirmation of the entire process is easily done. This is the essential characteristic of objectivity.

There can be no doubt that a nuclear set of psychologists, psychometricians, and educational measurement theorists have been highly successful in creating instruments with high social utility. For the most part, the larger purposes served by these functional social artifacts have served institutional objectives and in some instances created problems—institutional problems, social problems, and problems for the individual, which, now more than ever before, are receiving intense social attention. What are some of the problems?

Thorndike (1971) points out that the social concern regarding testing has been, in general, of two sorts. First, there is the view that there is too much testing and too much weight is given to it. Second, there is the fear within the educational sector that testing will pervert the learning and pedagogical processes either because trivial outcomes or criteria are measured or because the test themselves are poorly constructed. Ten years earlier, Thorndike and Hagen had noted that social criticism seemed to be determined by "(a) the incompleteness and imperfection of the information yielded by our measurement procedures or (b) the unwise things that we do with that information" (1961, p. 13).

Part of the "unwise" use can be understood from the angry criticisms of various minority students who view normative tests, as Holtzman notes (1971), as instruments used to deprive them of access to better colleges, jobs, and social positions. When it is pointed out that the tests do not prevent access, but the decision makers using the tests and other relevant information do, the retort is simple and strong. Seligman articulates a particular response for legal education, and its characteristics are generalizable. He argues:

> By acting as gatekeepers to the legal profession, American law schools cease to be merely educational institutions. They now are also political institutions, helping determine who can afford to be represented by counsel and who cannot; whose rights will be defended in courts of law and legislatures and whose will not; inevitably, which citizens shall receive "equal protection under the laws" and which shall not. (1978, p. 46)

But the counter claim to the Seligman argument has been made, not only by test makers and educators, but also by members of the public press. Zonana of the *Wall Street Journal* poses the essential social dilemma:

> At the same time, society is being pushed toward greater reliance on testing, by increasing competition for a limited number of places in graduate and professional schools, and by the quantities of student applicants with uniformly high grade point averages. Professional certification and licensing boards are using more tests to be sure they comply with government antidiscrimination regulations. (1978, p. 1)

And as cited earlier, federal government spokesman Califano (1977) urged not less testing, but more and better testing.

There is a strong temptation on the parts of some to view the present controversy swirling around mental testing as transitory and perhaps fickle. But a more temperate view would entertain the thought that profound movements are underway in our society, and psychologists are indeed a part of it. Kant's second maxim, i.e., treating individuals as ends and never as means only, is worthy of careful consideration. It is one thing to argue during a time of war or national emergency that various members of the society are used primarily as means to ensure the survival of the society. Testing for the intermediate areas of diagnosing, selecting, and placing gains wide support.

But during periods absent national emergencies, a different sort of specter is raised when major institutions depend heavily upon testing. Although few can disagree with the observations of Zonana (1978), Holtzman (1971), and Thorndike (1971) regarding the need for rational and socially justifiable methods of allocating scarce resources, i.e., means, among a large number of consumers, i.e., alternate ends, the way in which this is done may have fundamental and pervasive implications. Consider yet another, and earlier, articulation of Seligman's (1978) remarks as set forth by Bell:

> Thus the university, which once merely reflected the status system of the society, has now become the arbiter of class position. As gatekeeper, it has gained a quasi-monopoly in determining the future stratification of the society.
>
> A post industrial society reshapes the class structure of society by creating new technical elites. The populist reaction, which has begun in the 1970's, raises the demand for greater "equality" as a defense against being excluded from that society. Thus the issue of meritocracy versus equality.
>
> In a meritocracy as it has traditionally been conceived, the assessment of individuals and the allocation of social rewards proceed on the assumption of a close relation between achievement and intelligence and between intelligence and its measurement on the Intelligence Quotient scale. (1972, p. 31)

It is not here claimed that the social problems noted above result primarily from the uncritical and overuse of psychological tests, but it is asserted that the mental measurements movement and the technologies created to facilitate it have indeed contributed to our current perplexities. And while it is true, as Miller cites, that "there is nothing in the definition of psychology that dedicates our science to the solution of social problems" (1969, p. 1063), I submit that at the very least we must dedicate ourselves to clearing up or finding solutions to the problem we have abetted.

Within professional psychology there has been a general acknowledgement of a responsibility to guard against over-reliance upon test data and a misuse of it. The professional interest in test construction, administration, and interpretation spans almost a half century. Recognized and widely accepted guidelines regarding the construction and publication of tests were developed almost a quarter of a century ago (American Psychological Association 1954) and have received periodic review and revision (American Psychological Association 1966, 1974). Despite the early effort, professional sensitivity to issues of test misuse was not as sharp twenty-five years ago as it is today. Witness the absence of indexed reference to "test use" in *Educational Measurement* (1951) when the '54 guidelines were already under discussion, relative to that of *Educational Measurement* (1971). Thus, for both the professional and the layman, there has been an increasing awareness of problems generated by casual or uncritical test use. Fundamental to the rise in popularity of both psychological and educational tests has been the heightened "decision demand." As expressed by Thorndike and Hagen,

> the educator or the practical psychologist is continually faced with the necessity of arriving at some decision as to a course of action. He must decide what to do about an individual or individuals, or he must help the person himself decide what to do.
>
> Our basic assumption is that *sound decisions arise out of relevant knowledge* of the individual or individuals.
>
> We assume basically that knowledge is good, that knowledge is power, that knowledge is the basis for effective control of the problems that confront us from day to day. This is a basic tenet of our faith. (1961, pp. 7–8)

If this tenet of faith is accepted, it can then be asked whether "test misuse" has only social and ethical meaning, or whether it has a technical definition as well, subordinated to the more encompassing universals of ethical behavior. In the first instance, one might ask whether in a world of perfect instrumentation, e.g., no error of measurement, there can be anything other than social or ethical "test misuse." In the second instance, one necessarily asks whether, in a world of imperfect instrumentation, e.g., acknowledged error of measurement, there are only the usual parameters defining errors of inference. Hence, there is not a technical meaning to the notion "test misuse," but only errors of inference which should be guarded against as effectively as possible.

Accepting the basic tenet of faith set forth by Thorndike and Hagen (1961), one must ask how it is ascertained that relevant knowledge has been gained. With respect to tests, it is usually said that the confirmation of relevance is gained through the validation of the test. Commenting on this phrase, Cronbach argues that

> one validates, not a test, but an *interpretation of data arising from a specified procedure*.
>
> Because every interpretation has its own degree of validity, one can never reach the simple conclusion that a particular test is valid. (1971, p. 447)

Given Cronbach's formulation, it is possible to conceive of situations in which judgments based on interpretations of data may be misapplied, should two or more specific validation procedures be confused. Consider the different procedures that pertain to criterion-referenced relative to norm-referenced testing. In the latter case, the interest is to gain reliable discrimination between any two individuals at arbitrary points on the scale; in the former, the overriding interest is to gain reliable discrimination only at a single point on the scale. Given the different objectives, the test construction and psychometric estimates are likely to be based on quite different procedures. Hence, to judge two persons as different when both are above or below the criterion point, but do not have the same score, might be said to be a misuse of technical information.

But even if judgments on validated interpretations were appropriately related to specific procedures, one can ask whether use of the test at all could constitute test misuse. The situation identified by Meehl and Rosen is frequently encountered by the potential user of some psychometric instruments:

> The efficiency of the great majority of psychometric devices reported in the clinical psychology literature is difficult or impossible to evaluate for the following reason:
> a. Base rates are virtually never reported. It is, therefore, difficult to determine whether or not a given device results in a greater number of correct decisions than would be possible solely on the basis of the rates from previous experience. When, however, the base rates can be estimated, the reported claims of efficiency of psychometric instruments are often seen to be without foundation. (1955, p. 194)

Meehl and Rosen demonstrated the disutility of test use in that situation in which the occurrence of the phenomenon, e.g., poor adjustment, good adjustment, or college success in the real world, differs markedly from the test's ability to detect or reflect the phenomenon faithfully. Indeed, fewer correct classification decisions could be made with the test than without it.

In more instances than one would care to list, test data are too heavily weighted. Thorndike (1963) calls attention to certain misuses frequently noted in educational settings. Clearly the concept of overachievement may in fact be undergirded by the uncritical acceptance of errors in prediction. The same is true for the concept of underachievement. Psychometric limits and realities have in numerous instances become significant bases for social and educational decision making.

Emphasis of the limitation of tests such as those used in college admission decisions does not guarantee correct use. It is well known that test scores or the combination of test scores and grade point averages from high school are insufficient to account for all of the determinants of college success (Angoff 1970). Yet, evidence is scarce to support the view that decision makers either collect or evaluate in a systematic way the contributions of other data sets in reaching admissions decisions.

Even if the tests were used with proper caution, the problem of fair test use as identified by Thorndike (1971) and Darlington (1971) would still remain. As pointed out by both of these authors and further articulated by Gross and Su (1975) and Petersen and Novick (1976), integral to the technical problem is a value decision that must be made by someone on someone's behalf and probably imperfectly, regardless of the amount of data or information available.

The problem of test misuse is inextricably intertwined with specific technical limitations of tests, and the general limits of all empirical inquiries. For this reason the corrective steps indicated for curtailing test misuse are varied. Clearly, test publishers have a major responsibility in such efforts. They must set forth clearly and precisely the limitations of their instruments. At the very minimum, the burden of providing relevant information about testing objectives, validation strategies, and interpretive constraints lies with test publishers for their particular instruments. Conjointly, there must be almost unilateral effort on the part of test publishers to investigate possible sources of error that are both controllable and uncontrollable. Professional groups—be they psychologists, educators, lawyers, or others—certainly must critically question in constructive and knowledgeable ways the uses and possible misuses of test instruments.

To this point it has been argued that we face profound social problems, that psychology as it has been given to the people has contributed to the development of certain of these problems, and to some extent has taken steps to correct the imbalance and troublesome circumstances. But the well-intentioned social steps have been insufficient to quiet the larger social concern. Somewhere in our effort to join the movement of social efficiency, the well-being of the individual has been subordinated. Even now in the historic debates before the nation's highest court the issue of discrimination based on group attribution is being considered. Earlier Supreme Court decisions had affirmed the view that decisions to exclude individuals on the basis of group membership were unconstitutional. Now, through debate of a variant of that claim—namely, the inclusion of persons because of group attribution and the exclusion of other persons because of a different group attribution—has the constitutional principle been subverted. In all of the debate, the person has been lost. And one is strongly inclined to say that, in psychology's haste to become a science, and to respond to the institutional requests of education, government, and industry, the individual has been lost.

It is ironic that a strong historical interest of early workers in educational measurement focused on individual differences. For some educators, the search for and identification of dimensions along which individuals could be ordered was justified by the promise that more efficient planning or placement could be achieved for each person. But rarely does one encounter in the psychological literature claims to the effect that test results could be and should be used by the test taker for the enhancement of self-understanding and self-respect. More typically, test data were, and still are, turned over to institutional decision makers for the purpose of achieving institutional objectives. In this sense, psychology has not been given to the people but to sets of institutions whose interests are not one and the same with those of the individuals tested.

The reverberating echoes of public concern reflect, in part, the impotence of individuals before the information armamentaria of institutions and the test publishers that serve them. But such a relationship is not a necessary one, albeit historically a convenient one. The opportunity for fundamental public service and problem solution remains.

Florence Nightingale is reported to have said upon entering a hospital in the last century that "whatever else hospitals ought to do, they ought not spread disease." This sentiment was echoed years later by an eminent philosopher and teacher, Morris Cohen, when he stated that "whatever else systems of logic should do, they ought not enable errors of inference." In brief, there are limits and there ought to be limits which permit us to talk about the integrity of the system and the responsibility of those working in it, for it, or through it. For psychology, whatever it may be in its manifold forms, ought not undermine the foundations of the individual.

What is fundamental about our lives and our living? Surely self-respect must be counted as a foremost consideration. Rawls has argued that self-respect is a primary good. A definition of self-respect not alien to psychologists has been formulated by Rawls:

> First of all, as we noted earlier . . . it includes a person's sense of his own value, his secure conviction that his conception of his good, his plan of life, is worth carrying out. And second, self-respect implies a confidence in one's ability, so far as it is within one's power, to fulfill one's intentions. When we feel that our plans are of little value, we cannot pursue them with pleasure or take delight in their execution. Nor plagued by failure and self-doubt can we continue in our endeavors. (1971, p. 440)

If we in the educational measurement community were to ask ourselves what is it that we do to enhance a sense of self-respect for each individual who takes our tests, a ready answer would not be easy. It is clear that we assist institutions in maintaining their institutional respect since many of them point with pride to the test scores of their applicants and their admitted cohorts. But, about what can the individual feel proud or good, even for a moment, for having taken one of our tests? More often than not, self-doubts are raised by incremental failures to answer successive items satisfactorily. We need to give more to the individual, to treat him or her as ends and not solely as means to institutional "gratification."

To do so is to act in accord with a long and strongly held moral principle embraced by lay and scientific communities. At the very least, we should not destroy the sense of individuality in aggregating individuals.

Regardless of whether we choose to approach the minimum boundary (i.e., avoid harming the individual) or the maximum boundary (i.e., enhancing the primary good of individual self-respect) we begin to approach the limits of our social responsibility.

References

American Psychological Association. *Standards for educational and psychological tests.* Washington, D.C.: APA, 1974.

American Psychological Association. *Standards for educational and psychological tests and manuals.* Washington, D.C.: APA, 1966.

American Psychological Association, American Educational Research Association, and National Council on Measurements Used in Education. Technical recommendations for psychological tests and diagnostics techniques. *Psychological Bulletin*, 1954, 51. (Supplement)

Angoff, W. H. (Ed.) *The College Board technical manual: A description of research and development for the College Board Scholastic Aptitude Test.* Princeton, N.J.: Educational Testing Service, 1970.

Bell, D. On meritocracy and equality. *The Public Interest*, Fall 1972, 29, 29–68.

Califano, J.A., Jr. *Excellence and equity in the search for standards.* Speech delivered at the annual meeting of the College Entrance Examination Board, San Francisco, October 24, 1977.

Churchman, C.W. Morality as a value criterion. In J. R. Cochran & M. Zeleny (Eds.), *Multiple criteria decision making.* Columbia, S.C.: University of South Carolina Press, 1973.

Cronbach, L.J. Test validation. In R. L. Thorndike (Ed.), *Educational measurement.* Washington, D.C.: American Council on Education, 1971, 443–507.

Darlington, R.B. Another look at "cultural fairness." *Journal of Educational Measurement*, 1971, 8, 71–82.

Gross, A. L. & Su, W. Defining a "fair" or "unbiased" selection model: A question of utilities. *Journal of Applied Psychology*, 1975, 60, 345–351.

Holtzman, W.A. The changing world of mental measurement and its social significance. *American Psychologist*, 1971, 26, 546–553.

Jones, W.T. *A history of western philosophy* (Vol. II). New York: Harcourt, Brace, 1952.

Lindquist, E. F. (Ed.) *Educational measurement.* Washington, D.C.: American Council on Education, 1951.

Meehl, R. E. & Rosen, A. Antecedent probability and the efficiency of psychometric signs, patterns, or cutting scores. *Psychological Bulletin*, 1955, 52, 194–216.

Miller, G. A. Psychology as a means of promoting human welfare. *American Psychologist*, 1969, 24, 1063–1075.

Petersen, N.S. & Novick, M. R. An evaluation of some models for culture-fair selection. *Journal of Educational Measurement*, 1976, 13, 3–29.

Rawls, J.A. *A theory of justice.* Cambridge, Mass.: Harvard University Press, 1971.

Seligman, J. Selecting the chosen few at Harvard Law, it's points that count. *Student Lawyer*, 1978, 6, 43–50.

Thorndike, R.L. *The concepts of over- and underachievement.* New York: Teachers College, Columbia University, 1963.

Thorndike, R.L. (Ed.) *Educational measurement.* Washington, D.C.:American Council on Education, 1971, 3–14.

Thorndike, R. L. & Hagen E. *Measurement and evaluation in psychology and education.* New York: Wiley, 1961.

Zonana, V. F. Who gets ahead? *Wall Street Journal,* February 28, 1978, pp. 1, 21.

General Discussion of Williams' Paper

Miller: Thank you.

Williams: I thought you needed a friend.

Miller: I . . . There's a silence, so I suppose I'm supposed to say something. What would you like me to say, Rick?

Kasschau: We might want to leave it up to the audience. We've heard a lot of information and opinions today. Perhaps we should interpret ten seconds of silence as a cue to go call it quits for the day.

Miller: I felt that the problems with tests have more to do with their use than with their structure, and I think that was in my mind even as early as 1969. I felt that more public knowledge about what they really are and what they mean and what they don't mean would be in the public interest, and also in the interest of the profession. Those issues have become more and more exacerbated in the meanwhile, and we've gotten into legislative situations that I think probably—as you say—could've been avoided if we'd taken appropriate action at the appropriate time.

Frank, you opened us up this morning. Would you like to close us down this evening?

Kessel: The meeting is adjourned.

Question and Answer: Miller and Williams*

Miller: Dr. Williams, I was most impressed by the difficulty of defining particularly in any legally satisfactory way what is meant by the misuse of a mental test. That is clearly a very difficult problem. But there are some cases, I think, where anyone looking objectively at what has happened would agree that the tests have been misused, regardless of whose fault it is.

So I would say, suppose we shift from the question of admission to universities, where each university might want to set its own cutoff level for various reasons, to questions like employment. And then I'd like to know what are your recommendations for achieving a better match between the measurement of an applicant's qualifications and the level of ability that's required to perform the task for which he's applying? I think rather than worry about marginal cases of misuse, let's take one that's blatant, like requiring police officers to pass a test at a level that would ensure admission to an Ivy League college before you hire them as police officers. Something of this sort. A situation that I'm sure you're perfectly familiar with.

Williams: George, I think you gave me an easy question that I'll try to answer fairly quickly. I did want to sneak in a response. I don't know what Michael Scriven would have said, but it seems to me that after you do an evaluation study, what really then counts are effective administrators and leaders to get things done.

But you asked the question about employment tests. How you match up things that are required on a job with what you are . . . with your measures? And you use for example selecting candidates for the police force or training firemen, and so on.

What I'd like to do is just briefly sketch out this response. Your question sort of goes to the heart of a criterion problem

---

*Composed from exchanges occurring at the end of the second day as Miller analyzed each paper and re-directed a question to each member of the Symposium.

that psychologists have done by and large less work on, but within the domain of industrial psychology there are some steps that are usually outlined for that task. First, one would start with some general notion called a job analysis and that means that you either go in and look directly at what people, the incumbents, are doing or get some indirect set of evaluations of what they are doing, that is from supervisors or whatever. Or you might get some comment or assessment from the incumbents themselves as to what they think they are doing. So you have both that set of direct and indirect observations.

After completing the job analysis, one then has to construct some kind of criterion measure, and upon doing that one has to evaluate two things of the criterion. One is relevance to the job analysis. And secondly, its reliability. But in examining its relevance one tries to use some kind of validation strategy called—as Gulliksen would have called it—intrinsic content validity where one first, after identifying the variables to be used in the criterion by the investigating team, by whatever rating procedures or scanning procedures they use, one then identifies a panel of experts to assess them and make differential predictions with respect to them. Meaning if one of these variables is absent, what would you expect to find in the behaviors of those individuals without it, those with it, and so on. After doing that, one subjects it to an empirical test of some kind to confirm or infirm the predictions of the experts.

Having completed the assessment of the reliability of the measure, one takes a third step of raising the question, What will be the modality of the predictor? Namely, should one use simulation, interview, paper and pencil, or some kind of brief work exposure, work sample where you put the individual on the job, let him or her stay there for awhile and you observe it, him or her. Or you could have, obviously, a variety of simulation procedures and interview procedures and, of course, paper and pencil tests.

After you have made the choice of the predictor, one then has to evalute it with respect to its reliability and, of course, its validity, which would then be defined as its relationship to the criterion measure which started back up at the top of the list.

Now, my third part of this is that there is a pretty good example of that procedure that we did in a Philadelphia study which was for the purpose of hiring policemen for the city of Philadelphia in which those steps were gone through, and you'd be interested to know that the test was the sort that you would not give to a candidate trying to gain admissions to Harvard or Boston or Michigan. In fact, the candidates were given the tests materials to take home, study, look at, and then come back and take the examination.

Miller: May I? . . .

Williams: Yes.

Miller: The misuse of the testing material to exclude certain segments of the population from such jobs as policemen, firemen, whatever . . . uh . . . I'm not saying this well. Let me grant you, yes, that we do know how to do that. You know how to do it. ETS knows . . . There are people in our profession who can do that. The other side of the problem is how do we get the opportunity to do that? Do we sit in Princeton and wait for them to come to us or . . . I mean . . . Where are the customers for this? How do we suffer?

Williams: Well, that's a difficult answer for an ETSer to answer. If I were a non-ETSer I'd give you another answer. I'll tell you why . . .

Miller: Take your hat off and answer . . .

Williams: I'll tell you why it's a difficult answer for an ETSer. That is, we pride ourselves in not selling anything. That is, in fact, we sit in Princeton and wait.

Miller: On a salary!?!

Williams: However, I think that much of this is shared through the professional mechanisms of meetings and so on. It has been an interesting thing because ETS has followed a so-called academic model of not putting . . . we don't have salesmen, and we don't go peddle our wares and so on. That's been a part of a tradition, the academic tradition, that it was a little bit demeaning and dirty to do those kinds of things. But we would offer our expertise—research and others—to anyone who would like to come and ask about it. But that's a problem.

Now, in other instances, I think, other organizations—Psych Corp, for example, through Harcourt Brace does have a sales mechanism and they do take their wares out. But to clients like municipalities and governments and so on, most of that has been their coming to us. What we do do, in all candor, however, we do have nine regional offices around the country, such that they interface with government agencies and with professional groups and make known various things that we have and can do.

But that's not a very well articulated procedure for ETS.

	We've avoided by and large. That's not to mean I'll be satisfied, but I'm just describing the state of affairs.
Jackson(?):	Can I make a comment? I think psychology has avoided trying to monitor situations of that sort. And the result has been massive government regulation, as Dr. Bevan points out, in that area.
Miller:	Well, that's one way to do it. Pass a law that you have to match the test with the job, but we've got enough laws . . . blowing them out like bubbles, more or less . . .

Psychology in All Sorts of Places

Miller's Introduction of White

Our first speaker of the morning is Professor Sheldon White from Harvard University, where, since 1965, he's pursued his longtime interest in the study of how children learn. His early work was on conditioning and generalization in children, but since going to Harvard I'm glad to say that he's become interested in interesting things, pursuing a wide range of child learning problems, and has been an active consultant to many organizations concerned with the health and education of children, a career that's admirably prepared him to talk about "Psychology in All Sorts of Places." Shep . . .

White's Opening Statement

I'm going to give you a somewhat abstract talk today. When I was first approached about coming here to talk on the theme "Psychology and Society: Giving Psychology Away," my first thought was to maybe prepare a talk which was full of war stories in which I tried to describe the somewhat obscure and intriguing processes of trying to have conversations with people who make policy, trying to take what you know and relate it to them. It's much more complicated to give psychology away than most people think it is. But instead I went off a distance from that.

I'm not going to talk directly about social programs for children, social policy. Most of my experiences were piled up during the time of the poverty programs, during the Great Society era that started in about 1963 and went on for about ten years. What I know best are the complex of federal programs—Headstart, Follow Through, Title I, some of the health programs, OEO. There is a kind of official record of that time which says that the poverty programs failed, and which says also that psychology in some way failed. But that's not quite clear. All accounts of why psychology failed do not agree.

Some people believe that Headstart was an experiment designed to test a theory by psychologists about IQ modification. Since Headstart didn't raise IQs, this wonderful, practical suggestion that psychology had was disconfirmed by the evidence.

Some others take a different position. They argue that Headstart was not an experiment in child development but a component of a larger experiment in community action. Nevertheless, these people too say that psychology failed. Psychologists among other social scientists tried to use their data to project the directions of social policy and they couldn't do it. Not only that, but when they came to evaluate these social programs it's their fault that (a) they evaluated the programs and they found out they weren't working or (b) they weren't able to evaluate them and find out they were really working. It depends on who you talk to whether it's a or b.

I think Frank Kessel in his opening talk has eloquently traced a lot of the threads that run in and through the relationship, the difficult relationship between psychology and the federal government. The problem is that I believe some different things about that period. I believe that the poverty programs succeeded to a remarkable extent. I'm not going to take the time, but I believe that one can easily count about a dozen major, positive features, things that are now in the government that were not there at the beginning of the 1960s that don't seem likely to go away. Some of them are very large residues of the poverty program; all of them generally intended to further the purposes of the poverty programs.

And furthermore, I believe that during the course of my interactions with Washington and other sites I've seen a lot of psychology given away. I've felt it given away and received. To make a very long story short, I've come to have the opinion that whenever a psychologist talks to a non-psychologist, deals with him by working on a common problem, some psychology gets given away. And I think we don't readily detect this giving. I think it's hard to see this giving because we have a somewhat vague image of what it means to give psychology away. And I think we have a poor picture of psychology, of what it is and what the practice of psychology is and what the relationship is between knowledge and practice.

And so I've been writing a series of papers about the history of psychology—the organization of the field and so on—trying to work through some of these issues about how knowledge gets made by groups of psychologists and how their knowledge is related to that of others. The paper that I'm going to present today really deals with that theme. It deals not so much with what exactly is happening on the interface between the psychologist and programs for children, programs and education, but will take a broad view of psychology and its relevance.

I have an opening quote, an epigraph by Ernst Cassirer. It's from *The Philosophy of Symbolic Forms* . . .

Psychology in All Sorts of Places

Sheldon H. White
Harvard University

> Thus for Plato, too, myth harbors a certain conceptual content: it is the conceptual language in which alone the world of becoming can be expressed. What never is but always becomes, what does not,like the structures of logical and mathematical knowledge, remain identically determinate but from moment to moment manifests itself as something different, can be given only a mythical representation.
> Ernst Cassirer, *The Philosophy of Symbolic Forms.*

For purposes of discussion, let us distinguish three zones of organized human activity with regard to psychology; an inside, a middle, and an outside. The inside is a body of organized inquiry variously known as academic psychology, research, the ivory tower, scientific psychology, basic research, the knowledge base, etc. Most people agree, roughly, that there is such a zone of psychology and, if one does not push things too far, they agree on what is in it and not in it. This zone holds individuals who follow characteristic, highly organized practices. Following convention, however, we will call this a zone of "knowledge." The middle zone holds a group of individuals practicing activities that are understood as bridging between the inner zone and the outer zone—clinical psychologists, educational psychologists, industrial psychologists, military psychologists, etc. The outer zone holds the activities of society in general, practice.

There is something not quite right about the way this system is working. Otherwise we would not be confronted with a contemporary argument. We have to find ways to give psychology away (Miller 1969). We have an organized bureaucratic system—men, money, buildings—all supposedly designed to give psychology away perpetually. Within the American Psychological Association a dwindling minority of academic and research types fight to keep psychology as they see it from *all* being given away. And yet some psychologists worry about the problem of giving psychology away. The worries are not entirely unreal. Outside the discipline of psychology, significant others—congressman, administrators of research-funding agencies—keep asking, "What are you giving us?" "When have you ever given us anything?" "When will you help?" "Why should we give money to irrelevant and slightly snooty basic researchers when we can instead give our money to contractors who have a nice quality of humility and eagerness to please and who will work on whatever we think we want?"

If, in fact, our system designed to give psychology away seems not to be doing so, then there would seem to be two possibilities. Maybe the system isn't working. Or maybe the system is working but we don't know how. We don't know what "working" looks like.

The fact is that the middle zone of psychology seems to be growing. Each year we find in it more men, more money, more career lines, etc. What's feeding it? Some hard-nosed economists would argue that the many career lines characteristic of the middle zone of psychology are really part of a welfare program for a middle class increasingly being displaced by automation, make-work. The middle-class intelligentsia, always slightly dangerous to the political system if idle and disgruntled, is kept busy and reasonably happy by the social distribution of slots like "clinical psychologist," "educational psychologist," "remedial reading teacher" . . . for that matter, quite conceivably by slots like "professor of psychology," or "professor of economics." The social welfare argument may be one truth about the matter, but I doubt that one argument, one cause, one why, can express the whole truth about any phenomenon of human behavior.

I suspect that our definition of "working" is wrong, a limiting stereotype, which hinders us from seeing many of the things that cross back and forth among psychologists and people. Let us now try to come to closer grips with that stereotype.

HISTORICAL MYTHS OF ORIGIN IN PSYCHOLOGY

At the beginning I set forth the three-zone image of psychology's relation to the world in complete confidence that all psychologists were familiar with the conception. I know that psychologists all have this idea because it is expressed in the bureaucratic structure in which psychologists live and because it is latent in hundreds of things that one hears or reads every year. Together with thousands of people whom I have never met, I form an "it," the discipline of psychology. We are working together. Our itness was formed by our training, and it is rehearsed in thousands of everyday activities with colleagues. Where did this shared itness come from? Was there a Big Bang? . . . somebody sitting somewhere and writing out a constitution which we all now follow? We have no record of that.

It looks as though the itness arose out of a historical process. We may be able to understand the itness a little better if we try to see its formation. There is a second reason for looking at the history. There are some reasons for believing that narrative histories, by their very existence, are an important device for creating and sustaining the itness of a social group.

Some anthropologists have argued that narrative histories serve as a kind of binding force for tribal cultures, bringing disparate acts and facts of everyday life into a perceived unity. In discussing the roles of mythic stories, Bronislaw Malinowski says:

> The cultural fact is a monument in which the myth is embodied; while the myth is believed to be the real cause which has brought about the moral rule, the social groping, the rite, or the custom. Thus these stories form an integral part of culture. Their existence and influence not merely transcend the act of telling the narrative, not only do they draw their substance from life and its interests—they govern and control many cultural features, they form the dogmatic backbone of primitive civilization. (1948, p. 12)

Mythic stories help people to see the way in which they are composed together into one group. Using anthropological materials, Mircea Eliade, the historian of religion, has offered some detail about how this group composition process takes place. According to Eliade, it is common for myths to take people away from present time to a past time, a special time, a dream time. This time is a point of organization for the present; in it, special beings perform acts that create linkages of meaning among the things of the present.

> The man of the societies in which myth is a living thing lives in a World that, though "in cipher" and mysterious, is "open." The World "speaks" to man, and to understand its language he needs only to know the myths and decipher the symbols. Through the myths and symbols of the Moon man grasps the mysterious solidarity among temporality, birth, death and resurrection, sexuality, fertility, rain, vegetation, and so on. The World is no longer an opaque mass of objects arbitrarily thrown together, it is a living Cosmos, articulated and meaningful. In the last analysis, The World reveals itself as language. (Beane and Doty 1975, p. 8)

In a time outside the present time, special things have happened to make many things of the present speak in one tongue. The narratives of the myths transmit, in imagery, a semantics of existence. To bring novitiates into the group, one brings them towards the special time and imagery, which serves to map the world and the place of the individual in it.

> Through the initiation rites the neophyte is gradually introduced to the tribal traditions; he discovers all that happened *ab origine*. This "knowledge" is total—that is to say, mythical, ritual, and geographic. In learning what took place in the Dream Time, the initiate also learns what must be done in order to maintain the living and productive world. Moreover, a mythical—or mystical—geography is revealed to him: he is introduced to the unnumerable sites where the Supernatural Beings performed rituals or did significant things. The world in which the initiate henceforth moves is a meaningful and "sacred" world, because Supernatural Beings have inhabited and transformed it. Thus it is always possible to be "oriented" in a world that has a sacred history, a world in which every prominent feature is associated with a mythical event. (Beane and Doty 1975, p. 53)

The language of the present created out of the dream time tells people what the prominent things are, why they are prominent, and how they are oriented or related to one another.

You will have seen where I am going by now. I am about to argue that narrative histories of psychology set forth a dream time, in which special beings and events create meaningful relationships among things and acts and places of the present. The leap is huge, but there are some considerations in its favor.

- It might be argued that there is a vast difference between tribal myths and documented and verifiable accounts of the past created by scientists and historians. To this it might be said that a story is a story, and perhaps stories with footnotes may create much the same effect on listeners as stories without footnotes. We can verify our stories by evidence, of course, but the anthropologists say that tribal people regard their myths as continuously confirmed by everyday evidence. The fact that our myths are linked to much documentary or physical evidence does introduce an important feature—the possibility of a myth that may be explored or elaborated by empiricism, and the possibility of debatable and corrigible myth systems.

- It might be argued that we need some evidence that modern groups of individuals use stories and images for organization of their experience. Such evidence seems to be available in abundance. Research on small groups (Bales 1970; Dunphy 1974) has repeatedly turned up observations that stories and images may serve as organizers for the groups. Bales says:

> In group interaction, symbols (words, metaphors, images), which have the power to stimulate fantasies, are presented by persons to each other in their communication and action. . . .
>
> Once such a process is set in motion, others tend to get drawn in because of their own unconscious associations to the things being said and done. . . . A confusion sets in between the images talked about and the persons talking about them. The chain reaction of associations is *enacted* by the persons. The chain of fantasy begins to develop a certain

coercive power over the participants. People are forced into the roles portrayed by the fantasy, by projection, seduction, or manipulation. (1970, p. 138)

For working groups, images or ideas put forth by members may be supercharged by group feelings to form a contemporaneous "dream time," shaping and organizing the work of the group. As working groups go through stages of development, it appears that a succession of images are called forth to give coherence to the special issues and organization characteristic of each stage (Bennis and Shepard 1956; Dunphy 1974).

• It might be argued that the cognitive properties of myths are unexplored and obscure. To this it can be said that there is a rapidly rising literature of story analysis which may now locate such properties. Schank and Abelson (1977) have recently described a computer program that generates stories, using as a central basis "scripts," generic representations of that-which-is-to-be-expected in human settings like picnics, wars, etc. The conception of scripts as a basis for ordering experience seems similar, on the one hand, to Minsky's conception of frames (Minsky 1975) and, on the other, to the idea that cognitive mapping in humans may order human experience in both spatial and nonspatial frameworks (Siegel and White 1975; White 1977a; White and Pillemer, in press). It is quite possible that one function of stories may be to transmit scripts, or frames, or cognitive maps from the teller to the listener. It is exactly this which Eliade claims as the function of tribal myth, and something like this may hold for narrative histories of psychology.

• A fourth, final, and most telling argument against the claim that psychological history sets forth mythic frameworks for the field is a pragmatic one. The fact is that most psychologists do not use their history in the way tribal groups use their myths of origin. They do not rehearse their cosmogonic myths very much; indeed, a good many psychologists have only a cursory understanding of the history of the field. If our analogy was really good, then we might expect to find initiation rites in which our young—our graduate students—were taken out of real time into sacred time and there, hearing and reliving the supernatural history, become one with the special beings of the dream time. One can identify some cultish subgroups of the field where something like this may take place but, in general, our graduate training takes place without anything like this—and indeed, with some special effort and emphasis given to demythification. We train our students to challenge the past. But we train them to do so within a framework, within an understanding of legitimate procedure, methodology, and ideas of a proper and improper way to offer and meet challenges. It is this framework which, I believe, has a special and sensitive relationship to the history of psychology.

I believe this simply on the basis of some years' experience teaching the history of psychology. Most students who become familiar with the conventional history of the field—generally, students who become familiar with Boring's (1950) or Murphy and Kovach's (1972) histories—express a kind of feeling of relaxation, of understanding, of organization. "*Now* I see how the pieces fit together . . ." "*Now* it all makes a little sense . . ." That sort of thing. And, in my experience, students who venture a little further into history, who examine sources and writings not woven into conventional writings often emerge with expressions of disturbance, questioning, real doubts about the conventions of the field. So I have come to believe that, even though one can find no explicit rituals of transmission, the history of the field carries in a very charged way an image of what the field is supposed to be about; and the deeper explorations of that history, one advantage of having a corrigible mythic system, may facilitate attempts to revise or review that charter.

The idea of three zones of psychological activity, a zone of central scientific inquiry, a zone of professional work based on applications of that science, and a zone of practical activities to which the knowledge refers, seems deeply embedded in the history of psychology.

REVISITING THE DREAM TIME

We view psychology as a kind of continuation of traditional philosophical inquiry, armchair philosophy become scientific. Our histories give a clear story that pictures things that way. If we view the past through a slit pointed in just the right direction, then we see clearly a well-documented history that seems to say just that. Our dream time begins, roughly, at about the time of Sir Francis Bacon, the *Novum Organum,* and the rise of the spirit of science. A rising tide of scientific inquiry begat, on the one side, Hobbes and Locke, patriarch of the house of Skinner and, on the other, Descartes, patriarch of the house of Piaget. A moving body of philosophical inquiry into epistemology comes from that time towards the present, with distinguished figures on both the empiricist side—Berkeley, Hume, Hartley, the Mills, Lewes, Bain, Spencer—and on the rationalist side—Leibnitz, Kant, Hegel.

In 1879 there begins, in Wundt's laboratory, the scientific and experimental pursuit of psychology, philosophy being pursued by other means. The laboratory psychology grows, at first expressed in introspectionism, then in functionalism and behaviorism, finally emerging at present in information-processing and genetic epistemology.

Modern research traditions in cognitive psychology, in particular, seem to represent a rather satisfying culmination of the process of scientific development. Questions of thought, of the construction of knowledge, of a priori ideas versus a posteriori ideas, of the relation of perception to conception, now fill the journals. They are being debated on evidence. In the real time of today, we relive the questions and the issues of the dream time; we apply the methods of Wundt to the issues of Locke and Hobbes and Descartes and we realize the special value of our house, which is progress, scientific movement.

I mean no disrespect to Boring when I here argue that this view of the history of the field is limited. Boring knew, and said, that history can be rewritten, that history writing is a contrivance of the present for the purposes of the present. This is neither the time nor the place to undertake a revision of psychology's history, but I would like to argue that most of us today share some restrictions of view about the history of the field, and these restrictions seem related to restrictions involved in our framing of the question of relating knowledge to practice. Suppose we widen the slit through which we view our history. We see a slightly different pattern.

1. *We view the past as epistemological philosophy becoming epistemological psychology. Everywhere we look in that past, we find that these epistemological movements are part of a larger picture, a broad effort to reconstruct knowledge in the interest of creating reformed government.*

Sir Francis Bacon is typically addressed as an early philosopher of science. He fought to separate knowledge based on the words of man from knowledge based on observations of things:

> Words are but the images of matter . . . to fall in love with them is all one as to fall in love with a picture.

Bacon established what we now regard as the basic principles of scientific induction. But it is important to recognize that his major effort *The Novum Organum*, was part of a larger, five-part effort, *The Great Instauration*, which he projected but never completed. First the reconstruction of methods and of terminology. Then, upon that the reconstruction of the biological and social sciences, and then, finally, the reconstruction of government so as to give it a firm foundation on truth and rationality. Bacon never completed his great program of reconstruction because, of course, he held high posts in the British government and led the active, chance, up-and-down existence of a courtier of his time. But he saw his scientific work as directed towards practice; he had little use for work that began and ended in ideas (Robinson 1976, pp. 200–207).

This program of comprehensive reconstruction caught the imagination of Thomas Hobbes and René Descartes; the epistemological writings by which we know them are but fragments of a series of works which they projected for themselves, again not completed. If we look along the lineage of philosophical writings that come forward from them towards us we find that those writings were, in the minds and lives of the writers, usually subordinated under broader political pursuits—on the empiricist side, generally Benthamism, utilitarianism; on the rationalist side, generally, early precursors of socialism. Something like a fulfillment of Bacon's project of a Great Instauration—philosophical, scientific, and governmental truths all inter-rationalized to offer a social directive—emerges in the middle part of the nineteenth century. Towards the right, the ten volumes of Herbert Spencer's *Synthetic Philosophy* serve as the nucleus of an ideology of laissez-faire free enterprise justified as naturally right under the rubrics of Social Darwinism (Hofstadter 1955). Towards the left, the series of writings of Karl Marx and Friedrich Engels serve as the nucleus of an ideology of Communism. Marxists, no less than free-enterprisers, felt that nineteenth century science, and Darwin's theory of evolution in particular, provided a triumphant scientific vindication of their political arguments (Hofstadter 1955, pp. 115–118; Engels 1940). So our precursor lineage of philosophical psychology comes to us deeply immersed in a broader lineage of political thinking.

When, in 1879, a psychological laboratory is created and a discipline of psychology begins to form, this, too, is part of a broader picture. (1) Not only psychology, but the full range of the physical and social sciences were being established as disciplines. The American Psychological Association was founded in 1892, the American Historical Association in 1884, the American Physical Society in 1889, the American Mathematical Society in 1888, the National Statistical Association in 1888, the American Economic Association in 1885, and the American Political Science Association in 1902. Bledstein (1976, p. 18) states that in the 1870s and 1880s at least two hundred learned societies were formed. (2) What was a series of American colleges begins to become transformed into the modern research-and-teaching university. Many Americans, not just psychologists, make the pilgrimage to Germany, to use the German university as a model. (3) The romance of "scientific management" of men and human affairs fills the air. Men are to be measured, their capacities and activities scientifically assessed, their institutions—factories, schools, governmental agencies, homes—bettered by rational analysis and calculated planning. (4) Human service to other humans, once under the governance of religious or private charitable auspices, or not undertaken at all, begins to be covered under law and begins to be professionalized. There begins a series of governmental movements establishing programs for the young, the old, the handicapped, the unemployed, the poor, that climaxes a first time in the New Deal of the 1930s, a second time in the War on Poverty of the 1960s. The psychology that emerges in American universities is tied to, and formed by, contemporary concerns to build a rational basis for education, social work, psychiatry, the courts. Applied psychology does not emerge after the creation of basic psychology. It emerges with it, in it.

So we have to see the emergence of psychology historically as part and parcel of a broad movement towards rationalized social practice. The giving away of psychology is arranged for at the instant psychology is arranged for.

2. *We view the development of psychology as the creation of one discipline. In actual fact, what seems to have emerged is a multiparadigmatic, pluralistic set of inquiries.*

In 1979, one year from now, we celebrate the centennial of the founding of Wundt's psychology laboratory at Leipzig. Some ceremonies are being planned, celebrating the establishment of scientific psychology. I hope that sometime during that year we will discuss some of Wundt's reservations about the scope of an experimental psychology. Wundt never meant to create a fully experimental psychology. He said, in 1918, that a fully experimental psychology would be "trivial." Wundt did believe that psychology could be partially pursued by experimental means—thus expressing a mild deviation from some formidable and highly respected dicta of Immanuel Kant before him—but part of it, he believed would have to be pursued by "folk psychology," the analysis of humans in their natural milieu, in society, pursued through the study of human products. Wundt wrote a ten-volume series on folk psychology to stand beside his physiological psychology (Haeberlin 1916). Wundt's folk psychology is conscientiously mentioned by the major histories of psychology, but not really discussed. Despite Wundt's high place in the mythology of American psychology, his belief that laboratory psychology must be supplemented by folk psychology was not carried forth in the mythology of the discipline.

The basic problem was Kant's (1790) analysis, in his *Critique of Judgment*, which precipitated a century of writing about the fundamental differences between the *Naturwissenschaft* versus the *Geisteswissenschaft*, the natural sciences versus the human sciences. The kind of science you can have depends upon the kinds of things you have to deal with. Consider one of the things the physical sciences deal with, say a rock. A rock is there. You can turn your back on it, look again, and it is still there. You can measure it, wait a while, and repeat the measurement. Put another rock beside it and you have two rocks. Rocks have a nice quality of permanence, stability, and independence of normal variations in environmental conditions. They are subject to cause-effect relations. Now let us take a thing of psychology, say a smile, representative of what we usually call a behavior. Smiles don't just stand there; they come and go. Suppose you watch a human being for a while and watch smiles. The human smiles twice. Have you seen the same thing twice? Have you seen two different things? Have you seen a thing at all? If you say that you have seen the same thing twice, as psychologists usually do, then exact measurements of this presumptively same thing—say, the smile-width as measured in centimeters—do not always give the same value. So the thingness of smiles, like the thingness of most of the interesting terms in the human sciences, remains distinctly problematic.

The basic problem is that a smile is a temporal, teleonomic system. Its "itness" arises out of an orderly series of muscular transformations over time, and since this "itness" recurs we can infer that this orderliness is by design, is programmed. Kant argued that teleonomic and temporal entities were of such a vastly different character from the static things of the physical world that one could not use the methods of the natural sciences to deal with such entities—since they contain cause and effect within them. If we want to get very sticky about things, of course, a rock seen twice is not exactly the same rock, and rocks have some features that might suggest that they are in reality temporal systems with some limited teleonomy of design. But I do not want to open the door to a long dark corridor. I am here trying to present an issue of psychology's susceptibility to the methods of the natural sciences, an issue which was of some concern to Wundt and which is still with us today.

The early psychologists tried to build upon Wundt's foundation one laboratory and one discourse for the field, and they very rapidly failed. Adherence to Wundt's exact kind of laboratory and Wundt's broadly psychophysical program, as brought to the United States and expressed by Munsterberg and Titchener, hardly lasted past the turn of the century. The heart of Wundt's program was the idea that a limited kind of psychological thing could be defined, a sensation, which could be observed and measured and which could be meaningfully related to the things of physics. Americans rather rapidly set that program aside. They had trouble making precise observations of the Wundtian things. More importantly, perhaps they were dispersing into multiple arenas of inquiry—animal study, child study, abnormal psychology, mental testing, industrial psychology, social psychology—in part drawn by scientific curiosity, in part drawn by the multiple demands of emerging social practices around them. They proclaimed themselves as "functionalists" together.

Titchener shrewdly protested that you can't have a science of functions. You can't see or measure a function. He took to calling his kind of psychology "existential psychology." He studied things that existed and could be seen; the functionalists didn't. The problem of Kant emerging. Nevertheless, the separating body of American psychologists proceeded forward. By the 1920s, American psychologists were forced to recognize that they had become a pluralistic discipline, and so a series of books appeared that tried to list the pluralism: Murchison's *Psychologies of 1925*, Murchison's *Psychologies of 1930*, Woodworth's *Contemporary Schools of Psychology* published in 1931, and Heidbreder's *Seven Psychologies* published in 1933. These books differ on their exact count of extant psychologies. They underestimate the pluralism of their time; there are bodies of work in physiological psychology, industrial psychology, clinical psychology, educational psychology, social psychology, and developmental psychology which do not fall into their lists. But the restricted lists show a multiplicity, and that multiplicity is to continue to the present.

One more attempt was to appear to form a central laboratory of psychology and a potential unification of discourse. The learning theory movement appeared in the 1930s and waned in the late 1950s. One could not hope in the 1930s that psychological inquiry could be contained in one laboratory, but one could hope that one grounding laboratory, the laboratory of conditioning and learning, could form a discourse and a basic theory that would ultimately encompass the theoretical work of all laboratories. We have the program of stimulus-response psychology at Yale, the attempt to form a mathematical theory of conditioning and learning accompanied by a shower of papers attempting to demonstrate that ultimately everything—social psychology, human thinking and problem solving, psychoanalytic psychology (White 1976, 1977a)—can be encompassed in a network of S-R lawfulness.

If one looks carefully at the "behaviors" that were examined in the learning theory laboratories, one sees that they were functions being treated as things. That is, in fact, exactly what you do when you count a series of smiles, bar-presses, codings of "acts aggressively," "runs down the runway," etc., as successive instances of the same thing. It turns out you can go a limited distance by doing so. By virtue of the fact that they are organized systems of transformations over time, functions have a degree of what Donald Campbell (1968) would call "entatitivity." So meaningful statements about behaviors in relation to events have emerged from this tradition. But, inevitably, problems of time and teleonomy emerged and so we find that the newer psychologies—information-processing, Piagetian genetic epistemology, Bowlby's translation of the ethological approach—express time and control systems analysis in their approach.

Most important for our discussion, the learning theory tradition did not resolve the pluralism of inquiry. That pluralism continues today, and psychology appears as a multiparadigmatic body of inquiry: disparate data bases, discourses, and frames of reference. What, then, is the form of psychological knowledge that we bring towards practice?

THE STRUCTURE OF PRACTICE

In a rather discomforting little essay on practical psychology, Lloyd Etheredge (1976) sets forth what appear to be some unfortunate consequences of a pluralistic knowledge base. He poses a hypothetical case, "The Case of the Unreturned Cafeteria Trays": the manager of a high school cafeteria is distressed because students using the cafeteria are not returning their trays to the front and he seeks advice from a psychologist about why this is happening and what he ought to do about it. Etheredge shrewdly directs his manager to a series of theorists about human behavior and he is able to generate no less than thirty(!) explanations of why the students are doing this, accompanied by no less than fifteen or twenty different policies for behavior change. Etheredge is a political scientist interested in the application of knowledge to practice. His use of the psychological literature seems sophisticated and fair; I don't imagine that all the rival theorists would bet much money on their suggested explanation or cure but one can easily imagine each of them running his or her idea "up the flagpole," offering it tentatively and speculatively. As uncomfortable as this little story may be, most psychologists will instantly recognize the validity of the argument. There are a lot of fragmentary conceptions in the field, and a lot of ambitious and imaginative proponents. Something like this could happen. If our knowledge base allows us to explain the same issue in thirty different ways, offer one or two dozen approaches to resolution, can it reasonably be said that we have a usable form of knowledge? I am not absolutely sure, but I think there is a reasonable possibility that we do. We have talked so far about the structure of our knowledge. Let us talk for a few moments about the structure of practice.

An emergent problem in the history of psychology, suppressed in the beginning but now irresistibly upwelling, is the differentiation of the study of physical things from psychological things. If we try to study psychological things in exactly the same way we study physical things we fall short or we run into trouble. Our notions are really grounded on experience with physical things. When we run into trouble with the psychological things we have difficulty seeing where the trouble is. Pretty much the same kinds of problems emerge in the practical management of psychological things. We are used to managing physical things; we export ideas formed by that usage towards the management of psychological things; we regularly run into difficult problems because, in fact, psychological things do not happen in the same way and cannot be controlled in the same way.

Let us consider two problems in the management of human activities, the problem of what causes what, and the linked problem of division of labor.

I owe to Robert Savoy a rather nice way of expressing the problem of causation in psychology. He provided, in a paper in a graduate seminar, an analysis of the question, "Why did Gary Gilmore die?" I propose here to discuss "Why has Johnny learned to read?" leaving it to the listener's imagination to construct the parallel analysis for Gary Gilmore.

Why has Johnny learned to read?

>1. He has learned to read because a successive series of translations from light-dark configurations in the visual field, translated into patterned retinal firings, have progressively established a set of presumptively biochemical transformations in his nervous system.
>
>2. He has learned to read because a series of oculomotor activities have been formed into organized sensorimotor routines and because parallel routines, much harder to localize or specify, have been established to form a basis for cognitive comprehension.
>
>3. Johnny has learned to read because he is motivated to learn to

read. He wants to grow up and so he puts in effort and intensity and attention in the classroom, and this has brought him to reading.

4. Johnny has learned to read because his teacher, trained and experienced and willing to exercise suitable routines of classroom organization and management, has put before him a set of experiences that have led him to read.

5. Johnny has learned to read because his parents have from the preschool years on led him to have faith in what reading can do, and in the school years have allowed and encouraged, and even forced, him to regularly attend school.

6. Johnny has learned to read because the laws of his state require that all children attend school after age 6 and be taught reading.

7. Johnny has learned to read because the emergence of high technology and a high degree of development in his country has required that schools be created to give literacy to all children of the population.

8. Johnny has learned to read because the school committee and taxpayers of his city have appropriated the funds with which to support the buildings and personnel of a school equipped to offer reading training.

I have rather rapidly generated eight different answers to the question of why Johnny has learned to read. I would claim that they are all valid answers in the sense that they all approach the "Why?" question with an acceptable form of a "Because . . ." answer, if not a fully substantive reply. One could generate more answers. For each "because" one can imaginatively generate a context in which the particular form of "because" is the cogent form. Biochemists, historians, psychologists, teachers, politicians, physicians all have quite different interests in the whyness of Johnny's reading.

This pattern of multiple control and multiple causation seems to exist for all aspects of human activity, particularly in a complex and bureaucratically controlled society. Different disciplines and, within psychology, different paradigms of inquiry seat themselves at different lines of the web of causation, seeking to understand what causes *this* system of whyness to function as it does. So, too, are the practitioners distributed. An immense apparatus of social control stretches out over Johnny's head, as it were. There is a local school system and school committee; a state department of education; a federal bureaucracy of HEW. Within these groups we find people managing all the whynesses: the whyness of teacher presence and teacher willingness and teacher competence, the whyness of money, the whyness of parental willingness, the whyness of the law, the whyness of medical remediation of learning problems, etc. If, in fact, it takes many different people managing very different things to bring Johnny into reading, then perhaps we need a pluralistic knowledge base. Maybe the discourse that would help the school principal may not be the discourse that would help the school treasurer or the parent or the federal commissioner of education.

In short, I believe that the emergent pluralism of psychological inquiry in this century may have something to do with the pluralism of social control and management that tends to be directed towards human activities in a complex society.

We think of the many people who are occupationally concerned about Johnny's reading as distributed according to division of labor, their different activities converging on one end, and this is in a sense true. The common goal of all their efforts is to get Johnny to read, but there is a peculiar incalculability of their synergy which is worth some discussion. We are used to division of labor as applied to physical things. That kind of division of labor is easily calculable, and so we regularly ask children to calculate it in school. "If a carpenter can build a wall in two days, how long will it take two carpenters?" Children can perform such simple calculations on humans dealing with physical things, and managers can perform much more complex calculations. Someone building a house involving wood, wiring, brick, and plumbing can easily estimate that he is going to need a carpenter, an electrician, a mason, and a plumber, and with a little effort he can calculate when and for how long he will need each and how much each is going to cost him. Enormously complex synergies of human effort can be calculated in this way; I am told that it took twenty thousand workers together to get the first rocket to the moon.

Let us see if we can make some similar calculations about Johnny's reading:

> If one teacher can give Johnny decoding skills in one year, how long will it take two teachers?
>
> If Johnny has a reading problem and an emotional problem and a vision problem, can we get Johnny to read by using a remedial reading teacher plus a psychiatrist plus an opthalmologist? How much time from each will we need?
>
> If Johnny has learned to read with an overall school budget set at $860 per year per child, how much will we increase Johnny's reading if we augment the budget by $300 a year?

It would be easy to proliferate calculational problems that are fundamentally nonsensical. The fact is that we have this vast social network hovering over Johnny's head and all the people are in one sense necessary to get him to learn to read and they are in another sense not necessary at all. Johnny might just himself learn to read, just pick up a book and acquire reading without them. Many children do. Try getting a rocket to the moon without the twenty thousand men working at it. Johnny is an active, temporal, teleonomic system. So, too, are all those people in the bureaucratic network about him. They form a vast system of interactive social purposes. There is not one goalfulness in the system, the goal of building and flying the rocket, towards which other goal-setting may be subordinated with some clear understanding of the part to the whole. Someone with the task of designing and ordering control-panel knobs for the rocket can understand that if he is late the knobs will arrive late. If he does not do his job the rocket will not have knobs on the control panel. Suppose Johnny's superintendent is very late in his work, or he suspends activity because of illness for six months. There may be many calculable consequences, but it might be quite difficult to relate his or her performance in any way to Johnny's reading.

Let us consider a set of individuals located at various points in the bureaucratic niche system that we imagine rising above Johnny in the process of learning to read. Let us consider, say, the teacher in his classroom, the chief of the learning disability unit in his local hospital, the principal of his school, the Title I coordinator for his state, the head of the National Education Association, and the United States commissioner of education. There are literally hundreds of such individuals, people who consider Johnny's reading somewhere within their legitimate purview. These people, this heterogeneity, is Practice. We wish to benefit this practice system with Knowledge, to give psychology away to it. How shall we do so?

What is each person doing?

1. All the people on our short list are interested in Johnny's learning to read, among other things. No one above the level of the teacher can see Johnny or speak to him. Except under special circumstances, no one above the level of the teacher will know that Johnny, specifically, exists. Most of the people on our list do not deal with children in the flesh; they deal with paper and with other people in the bureaucratic web. Johnny appears before them in the form of symbolic indices that reflect some limited aspect of Johnny-and-others-like-him.

2. Each person on our list deals with Johnny in the midst of a certain kind and level of aggregation. The teacher does not deal directly with Johnny. He or she deals with a classroom that includes Johnny, and that is something quite different. The chief of the local learning disability unit has only a statistical chance of ever seeing Johnny; he does think about Johnny regularly, Johnny in the midst of statistics used to estimate service personnel and facilities necessary for various outreach areas of the city. The Title I coordinator of the state is concerned about a transfer of federal funds, by formula, to cities in proportion to the number of poor children they have. He considers Johnny in the midst of statistics portraying the proportion of poor children in his city; he deals with money and with paper-and-pencil reports describing Title I programs for poor children in Johnny's city. Each person glimpses some very limited aspect of Johnny in a unique way, relevant to unique options for decision characteristic of his role.

3. When each person acts, he acts on symbols—generally, symbols representing people or money. The higher you go above Johnny, the more people act on symbols representing money.

4. The efficacy of any action at the higher levels is always argumentative. People and money are very generalized agents of action. Sending labeled people towards Johnny—e.g., teachers, pediatricians—specifies

their agency to some extent, but, as noted above, their output is not very calculable. Sending labeled money is twice argumentative. The effect of the money is not very calculable, and, beyond that, in the governmental system we have, labeled money tends to wander as it goes down the pipeline. It changes its label or it turns into just planning money. Some have argued that because of the very restricted vision of people in the upper bureaucratic cubicles—the very limited vision of Johnny I am here trying to portray—money has to be labile as it comes down the pipeline. Only the people who are very near to Johnny can really see what he needs, and only they can decide how to bring money to bear on his needs.

5. Herbert Simon has defined all problem-solving as, essentially, a process of translation. This is a good way to look at the actions of people in the bureaucratic niche system we have been examining. Each person in the system uses symbolic representations of the state of the world and, using judgment and experience, translates those representations into decisions about symbolized people, resources, and regulatory permissions and constraints. Every single person has a unique translation function—he or she faces a unique set of inputs and options for output. That is one way to define a job or a role in a bureaucratic hierarchy. There is, practically speaking, no way for any social scientist to tell this web-as-a-whole exactly what to do. The social scientist may, however, be essential in constituting the symbolic world these individuals live in and in forming or influencing the translation functions they perform.

HOW PSYCHOLOGY IS GIVEN AWAY

The social structure we have pictured as rising above Johnny's head, all concerned about his reading and almost all trying to deal with him through symbols, is a comparatively new phenomenon. It took a lot of social change to bring it about, and the establishment of psychology as a discipline was part of that social change.

Chandler (1977) has traced the rise of the modern corporation and modern management structures in business. Before 1840, American businesses were run by people who dealt directly with the work and the workers, at most standing one step removed behind an overseer. The coming of communications facilities, the railroad and the telegraph, and associated needs for heavy concentrations of capital began an elaborating change. More and more people appeared whose function was executed in a management hierarchy, with work away from direct contact with the physical execution of the business. These people lived in a paper-and-pencil world. The elaboration of the hierarchies was accompanied by a constant pressure for new systems of accountability—new ways of representing the functioning of aspects of the business in symbolic indices. Eventually, after about 1900, the modern vertically integrated corporation appears, production integrated with distribution.

Chandler argues (1977, pp. 130–131) that national associations of industrial professionals—the American Society of Railroad Superintendents, the American Railway Master Mechanics Association, the Railroad Travelling Auditors Association, the Association of Railroad Telegraph Superintendents, etc.—proliferated before the professional academicians began to set up similar societies. Chandler's "managerial revolution" was initiated by technological inventions, but in his history he repeatedly takes the position that it was the demands created by managerial innovations that stimulated and precipitated many of the industrial inventions of the nineteenth century. Businesses were becoming all at once capital-intensive, technology-intensive, and management-intensive.

Science and engineering enter into American higher education in the 1850s and 1860s, competing with the classics curriculum in the established colleges and standing alone in newly created institutes of technology. The physical sciences got established earlier, the social sciences later. The modern graduate arts and sciences faculty was established in the colleges in the late 1800s. Harvard created its Graduate School of Arts and Sciences in 1890. In the 1880s and 1890s, Johns Hopkins, Clark, and Chicago vied with one another for first position among American graduate, research-producing universities. These changes in education are reviewed by Bledstein (1976, Chapter 8) who argues that between 1870 and 1900 a "culture of professionalism" emerges in American society. The center of that culture was the American institution of higher education, transformed from a set of small finishing schools for ministers and classicists into the comprehensive American university of today.

It seems reasonable to believe that the emergence of Chandler's managerial revolution had something to do with the emergence of Bledstein's culture of professionalism, and that both together had something to do with the creation of that hierarchy that now rises over Johnny's head. In the first place, it was during this time that there began to be enhanced pressure to make sure that Johnny could read. The states, one by one, passed and enforced compulsory attendance laws between 1880 and 1917; twenty-eight had done so by 1900. In the second place, it was at this time that strenuous social efforts began to create national, centralized, scientific standards and management practices in American education. Tyack (1974) reviews the efforts of administrative progressives to bring about a "one best system" for American education. He pictures it to some extent as a conspiracy of an elite group together with academics trying to regain control over urban school systems that had fallen into the hands of local ethnics. But movements like these are never single-minded. One might well believe that the administrative progressives meant some of what they said. They said they wanted to bring to schools some of the benefits of that professionalization and management they now saw rising about them in American industry.

What the movement brought about was professionalization, bureaucratization, the schools of education within the universities. The vast majority of the bureaucratic niche system that exists around Johnny, virtually the entire system outside his local community, was created by that movement—regional and state and national educational coordination.

The new psychology of the twentieth century may have had particular relevance to the new superstructure. Suppose we divide the educational occupations around Johnny into two groups. One group—the teacher, the principal, the local school committee member—is relatively proximal, either deals directly with Johnny or with people close to him, and can examine the teaching of Johnny directly if it wants to. The occupations of this group are quite old and exist far back behind the turn of the century. Another group—the Title I coordinator for the state, the head of the National Education Association, the U.S. commissioner of education—is relatively distal, dealing with Johnny only through symbols or through negotiations with people who are at a far remove from him. These occupations are new, they were either created or given enhanced prominence after the turn of the century.

The identification of the proximal occupations with older management of education is, of course, imperfect. The chief of the learning disability unit of the local hospital holds a proximal occupation, and yet the role is new in the twentieth century. Johnny's teacher, most proximal and oldest of the occupations, in one sense, is not the same person he or she was in the nineteenth century. In the twentieth century, Johnny's teacher has most likely been credentialed at the college level, operates under constraints imposed by national achievement testing, uses complex national curricula of a kind that did not exist in the nineteenth century, was selected for the job under hiring policies imposed by affirmative action, draws upon auxiliary professionals who deal with counseling, speech pathology, and reading disability, teaches deinstitutionalized handicapped children whose presence in the classroom is mandated by P.L. 94-142 coming down from the federal level. One might say that what is new in the twentieth century is the distal superstructure together with modifications of the proximal superstructure, in some ways quite considerable modifications, that coordinate it with the distal structure and transmit its purposes. Psychology and, more generally, the new social sciences were particularly relevant to this distal superstructure and its proximal ramifications.

The possibility of this special relevance was seen by the turn-of-the-century reformers who tried to lay down a knowledge-building system in parallel with their new management system. Psychologists—G. Stanley Hall, Edward B. Thorndike, James McKeen Cattell—were among those who stumped for scientific administration of the schools. Nicholas Murray Butler made psychologists like Thorndike, Cattell, and Dewey a prominent part of his Teachers College at Columbia, in its day a model for schools of education and a national leader in the campaign for administrative progressivism. And schools of education provided for psychologists their first substantial home outside of the philosophy departments. In 1910, Walter S. Hunter contemplated becoming a psychologist and had to deal with the fact that the only teaching positions available for psychologists involved a combination of either philosophy and psychology or education and psychology (Hunter 1952, p. 165).

The three-zone conception with which we began our discussion took form near the turn of the century. There would be a basic science of psychology, creating knowledge about things like learning, motivation, emotion, individual differences. There would be bridging disciplines like educational psychology, translating that basic knowledge into scientific teaching methods and creating tests and measurements for the schools. And there would be teaching, now professionalized and sitting on a knowledge base.

While there was something generally right about the three-zone conception, there were some things that were specifically wrong.

First, there was the assumption that the most traditional and proximal educational function, classroom teaching, could be transformed by the provision of scientific methods. William James (1900) among others, protested, saying that teaching was an art and not a system of rational management. But from that day to this, teachers have taken their obligatory educational psychology course and methods courses, have gone to their classrooms and closed the doors and practiced the ancient art of human communication with children. As recent counter-certification movements would suggest, teachers are still not persuaded that science has brought much to everyday teaching. One thing the reformers had to consider was that their new disciplines might have their most direct relationship to the newer and more distal educational functions.

Second, the three-zone conception rested on an analogy with science, engineering, and the revolutionizing of industry through technology. From that day to this, psychology has been haunted by an acute case of physics-envy and has lived nervously with the notion that the "immaturity" of the discipline would give way to the "maturity" of the physical disciplines. And psychology has sat waiting, with increasing impatience on all sides, for that little demonstration of practical power—that transistor, that penicillin, that pill—something that you can hold in your hand that would invincibly demonstrate the technological fruits of psychological basic research for society. What the early psychologists might have considered were contemporary arguments that psychology could not be, in whole or in large part, an experimental science. But such arguments were set aside.

Suppose we consider the possibility that the new psychology, and associated new disciplines, had particular cogency for the distal superstructure and its proximal ramifications. Suppose we consider also that this superstructure manages human beings in the process of becoming, not the movement or assembly of physical things. What psychologists might be giving away might be the following:

1. *They create symbols representing characteristic functions of people.* Distal bureaucrats make decisions involving large numbers of people. They live in windowless rooms, importing and exporting symbols. There are only a limited number of ways of creating symbolic representations of the functions of aggregates of people. One way is to use stereotypes, ideas in the culture about what groups of people are typically like. Another way is to draw upon statistical estimations of the generality. During the 1920s and 1930s, child psychologists spent much time in efforts to portray norms and averages—the average child's height at age 4, size of vocabulary at age 6, knowledge about families at age 10, etc. The "average child" is, of course, a legendary creature to a teacher or a parent, who always find themselves confronted with particular children. But the legend has a peculiar solidity to a distal bureaucrat. That individual is in fact often in the process of trying to visualize something about an "average child," towards which he will try to direct an "average action."

2. *They create symbols representing characteristic functions of social action.* Having acted, distal bureaucrats have problems sensing the consequences of their action. They need feedback. School achievement tests are widely taken today as indices of the school performance of a child. They have some serious deficiencies in that regard. But there is good reason to believe that in their inception they were regarded as useful indices of the performance of a *school*. Near the turn of the century, American schools were very uneven in facilities, personnel, and quality. School achievement tests make much more sense as instruments if one envisions them as aggregated over a school or a school system, to be used as *rough* indices of comparability of educational standards—to be used, say, to estimate whether the teaching offered in a turn-of-the-century small town was roughly comparable to what was being offered elsewhere in the country. During the 1960s, with the creation of the poverty programs, the federal government set up manifold legislative requirements for program evaluations. Psychologists are still involved in the fulfillment of much of those requirements. The requirements demand that credible symbolic representations of the output and efficacy of preschools, Title I programs, mental health centers, etc., be created. Without such symbols the federal government is, in a real sense, blind to the consequences of its actions.

3. *They offer myths to organize perception, value, and action.* Psychology and the new social sciences gave distal bureaucrats important elements of a statistical sensory system, creating the symbolic equivalents of vision, audition, and kinesthesis. But something more is needed. In order to exercise his translation function, a bureaucrat needs some kind of a theory that tells him how actions in the face of perceptions lead to consequences that are of more or less value. Many bureaucratic activities are prescribed by formula, by regulation, or by rational manipulations of fixed and calculable commodities such as money, personnel slots, etc. But, particularly as one goes towards the higher levels of the bureaucracy, where policymaking and decision making go on, a distressing kind of openness often appears. Administrators may need help in deciding which signals are more crucial and less crucial, what questions they should ask, how inchoate signs of stress may be interpreted to form a pattern. If one looks

closely at points where psychological findings are brought into practice today, one often finds that the findings are offered as components of mythic stories. They are not brought in as isolated facts but as parts of consistent systems of facts and arguments that, all together, say something about where the social system has been, where it is going, where favorable or unfavorable consequences lie. One finds this in the social use of IQ tests (White 1977b). One finds this going on, conflictedly, in the contemporary social use of policy research (Rein & White 1977).

I argued earlier that historical myths of origin may play an important organizing role for psychology as a discipline, helping to make it an itness, making disparate acts and phenomena into a language that speaks meaningfully, organizing and dimensionalizing experience. Now the argument is that psychologists contribute to the statement of myths that organize social and political practice in our society. They contribute to a modern form of empirical, corrigible, debatable mythmaking.

The argument, so far, is that the new psychology and the new social sciences had direct relevance for the emergence of a distal bureaucracy in education, and that they have helped in constituting the symbolic world in which the individuals in that part of the web must necessarily operate. But, even with that help, the distal bureaucracy in education is not very knowing or powerful. What the distal bureaucracy sends down towards Johnny today is mostly money subdivided according to very crude categories—income, special minority status, handicap, etc. The distal bureaucracy does not know enough or feel enough to do anything more complicated. I think this is because of very basic problems in locating causation and dividing labor with regard to human beings in the process of becoming. Chandler (1977, pp. 372–375) points out that despite serious efforts and a variety of apparently favorable circumstances, industries that were more labor-intensive and less energy-intensive (less technological) never attained great size and never attained vertical integration in the late nineteenth century. He points to a variety of business factors that might account for this. One factor, conceivably, might be the fact that complex human functioning is very hard to manage at a distance.

The labor-intensive core of education is, of course, the teacher teaching. What do psychologists do for the proximal superstructure near Johnny?

4. *They categorize children. They assist in moving children from less-favored to more-favored categories.* In rural America in the last century, Americans placed a high value on schooling, but people went to primary school when they could and as much as they could. The penalties for not having much schooling were not great. Communities arranged for whatever level of schooling they felt they could afford. Now, with compulsory education and universal schooling, with national achievement tests, with a great felt sense that schooling is crucial for social survival, with a middle class that pushes for optimal child development and poor families that push for educational equity, the factors that control or condition a teacher's performance are much greater. The poor performance or the slow performance of a child calls for explanation and, if possible, correction. So IQ testing has come in, in some part to rationalize children's educational

standings, in large part to justify difficult decisions to place children in special classes. A number of special designations have been developed for children who have trouble in schooling: "reading disability," "familial retardation," "learning block," "underachievement," "learning disability," "educational handicap," "hyperactivity." Most of the time, these are not absolute and clear problems of children, identifiable in all contexts. They are problems in the ability of the child to keep pace with what the school demands.

Where psychologists have become heavily involved with local school processes is in the effort to create unbiased methods to assign children to such categories, and in efforts to assist children out of them. A disease-model terminology is sometimes applied, so that this kind of agency may be discussed as "diagnosis," "therapy," or "treatment." That terminology may more appropriately be applied to children who are "emotionally disturbed," "acting out," or with "behavior problems" (where the child's difficulty may arise out of something other than its imperfect relationship to the school). But the disease model is today quite argumentative for much of classical psychiatric practice. What seems most salient about the work of psychologists in schools is that they play a role in mitigating among the interests of the child, the parents, the schools, and the laws, to place the child in a special status with regard to schooling. At times, the "diagnosis" of a child in these terms is empty and looks exactly like a social settlement; at times a "cure" returns the child to a normative, optimal social status. The work of the psychologist here is with the administration of a category system.

5. *They teach psychology.* If the art of teaching is not much different today than it was a hundred years ago, the role of the teacher is immensely different. The teacher is in the midst of bureaucrats and constituencies, all of whom in one way or another want coordination, justification, and explanation. Teachers must be able to explain all this to themselves. They need to know what the myths of the distal bureaucrats are, whether or not they agree with them. They need to be able to articulate their teaching, say what they are doing and why they are doing it, to questioners with various interests and levels of sophistication. So there comes about a rising need to be able to discuss child development, the process of learning, the goals of education, the meaning and the justification of educational practices, the art of teaching. Psychologists study many of these things. They have ideas about them, special ways of looking at children, frameworks of interpretation, facts about children that fit into the frameworks. In courses on psychology, in encounters with writings by psychologists and about psychology, the teacher absorbs some of the perceptions, ideas, discourse, frameworks. Some things about the children and the schools, about the teacher are made coherent, given order and dimension. Events are made into a language.

It is not completely clear that a teacher who has developed a kind of broader consciousness and a broader ability to articulate teaching is any better at the traditional functions of teaching than was the teacher of one hundred years ago. Accepting William James' characterization of teaching as an art, one might ask whether a painter or a playwright or a novelist immersed in the educational and cultural milieu of today is better than his counterpart of one hundred years ago. One would have to say in some ways yes and in some ways no. Some of the evocative ability of great art is timeless and, by implication, context-free. Some classical art, once significant for its day, has gone stale; some modern art speaks with a peculiar cogency to the special human concerns of today. But the analogy of the teacher to the artist is not fully satisfactory: Teachers live in a political and bureaucratic world in a way that artists do not. Psychology seems to have become a part of teacher's lives as that world has grown more complex around them.

ON GIVING

I have tried to argue that psychology is today being given away in a considerable amount, but that we do not fully recognize or credit the giving. We have a view of psychology that does not recognize or legitimate it. We can stick with the traditional view that psychology is a quasi-physics in the process of maturing; there are some things about the field that will fit with this view. But if we stick with this view, we will have to keep on repressing the fact that the field is pluralistic and growing more so, that there are a lot of components of the field that do not *look* like they are moving towards mathematical modeling, and that there is an enormous amount of "applied psychology" out there that does not seem to connect well with "basic" psychology, and that people out there seem to have an enormous appetite for popular psychology, the holy and the unholy.

In order to make the argument that much of psychology is made and given away by means other than those of the natural sciences, I have told a story with footnotes. The medium is the message. Not being able to offer proof for such a large argument I have tried to appeal to consistency (White 1977a), the argument that the story makes a pattern of the facts. I have dwelt on psychology in relation to education, in part because education has been one of the earliest and most obvious practical targets for psychology, in part because education writ large (becoming) is a good deal of what psychology is all about, in part because much of my own experience has been with attempts to relate psychology to education. But I believe that psychology's relation to education is prototypic for its relations to psychiatry, social work, industry, the courts, etc., and that with minor modifications one could trace out parallel histories and a parallel structure of contemporary interaction in these areas as well.

To some extent I have been following publicly available facts, to some extent private experience. Having been on a faculty of education for some years, having consulted with a variety of educational programs and agencies, I have repeatedly faced the problem of being (a) a psychologist and (b) useful. It is pretty hard to use psychological knowledge to make up conclusive, forcing recipes for action for a teacher or a policymaker. A number of psychologists seem to cherish the vague belief that this is possible and that, off in the distance, it is the incompetence of educational psychologists together with the fuzzy-mindedness and willful romanticism of the public that blocks the public use of scientific findings from psychology. To such psychologists, I would recommend that they try making their suggestions to an articulate, critical teacher or policymaker.

And yet, although this legendary path does not really seem to be there, one does find that both teachers and policymakers can get quite absorbed and intrigued by psychology. The teachers who are most intelligently responsive seem to be experienced teachers who have taught for a few years and who return to the university struggling to come to terms with issues that seem to be at the same time incoherent and important. They seem to be trying to know what they know. As novitiates in psychology courses they can be at times surprisingly decisive and judgmental. They will offer summary negative judgments about bodies of work that seem to psychologists to be scientifically sound and important—"No, not *that*"; they can become quite intrigued by a paper, or part of a paper, that to the instructor seems like a piece of obsessive obscurantism; they will hold high a piece of "soft" work—with some taste and discrimination, knowing that it is soft—because they feel it goes directly towards something crucial in their experience. This paper is, in part, an effort to explain what psychology is giving to those teachers.

I have been in dozens of meetings with federal agency people, the distal bureaucrats, and have watched them again and again struggling to find indices that will tell them what is happening "down there," what their programs are doing, what the problem is. And, of course, I have watched them culling through stories; I have watched social scientists and agency people offering stories; I have read stories in congressional testimony. There is an incessant governmental traffic in stories. Martin Rein and I wrote an analysis of this (Rein & White 1977). This paper is, in part, an effort to explain what psychology is giving to those distal bureaucrats.

To some extent I have been following theory in this paper. When Wundt partitioned his psychology into a physiological psychology and a folk psychology he was responding to Kant's classic distinction between the *Naturwissenschaft and the Geisteswissenschaft*. The folk psychology was an attempt to set forth an empiricism appropriate for the *Geisteswissenschaft*. There was a "philosopher of science" for the human sciences, Wilhelm Dilthey, whose work received minor attention from psychologists in the years when the dominant hope was that the field would be physicalized. Successive editions of Woodworth's *Contemporary Schools of Psychology* (Woodworth 1931, 1948; Woodworth & Sheehan 1964) show, nonetheless, that the field was partitioning into two masses—one experimental, building on behaviorism, oriented towards explanation; the other built on clinical and conversational encounter and projective testing, building hormic and motivational themes, oriented towards understanding. Dilthey appears in the second group as proponent of an "understanding psychology" (White 1977a, Table 1). This is rather consistent with what most of the things were that were called "systems" in the books of the 1930s, or "learning theories" or "personality theories" in the 1950s. They were in only minor ways theoretical structures for a psychology-in-existence; they were for the most part prospectuses and agendas for a possible-psychology-to-come.

Dilthey (Dilthey 1961; Hodges 1944; Makkreel 1975) was concerned to set forth a methodology for the social sciences. He held that psychology was the key to that methodology. Part of psychology, he felt, was approachable by the methods of the natural sciences; he held this view in common with Wundt but not with all turn-of-the-century philosophers. Part of it, he felt, would have to be approached by the hermeneutic method. Human behavior, or the products of human activity, are approached as a text. The text is interpreted through one's "lived experience." One "reads" the text for meaning, to use a psychoanalytic term, through a kind of identification with the author. What would the author have to have been like to have delivered these signs? (This may sound a little farfetched, but then one can regularly watch an animal psychologist trying to "think like a rat" in an effort to interpret his data. Maybe Piagetian Animism is not an intellectual aberration of early childhood; maybe it is a powerful intellectual tool.) The text so construed is offered as a myth by the social scientist, a story with footnotes. A quasi-text is turned into a literal text. The process is essentially a process of translation.

Could a psychology that creates mythic forms be regarded as legitimate for those ideals that psychologists espoused when they sought to be "scientific"? Conceivably, it might. Instead of regarding psychological research as a means towards the construction of so-far-rare mathematical models, one might regard it as a means towards the construction of stories with footnotes, of a kind that psychologists now manufacture in abundance. Popper has incisively argued that the sine qua non of a science is *falsification*. He had in mind the sudden, sharp challenge to a scientific idea that is posed by the classical *experimentum crucis*. But I have here in some sense been trying to falsify the conventional story-with-footnotes of psychology's history and of its relevance. It is possible that a psychology composed of debatable, corrigible myths might be empirical and progressive through gradual, evolutionary processes of trading in conjectures and refutations. Dilthey felt that it could. But, of course, this scientific process and its relationship to everyday activities would be badly misunderstood if one looked at it through a lens made by the mythic form of the natural science.

References

Bales, R.F. *Personality and interpersonal behavior.* New York: Holt, Rinehart and Winston, 1970.

Beane, W.C., and Doty, W.G. *Myths, rites, symbols: A Mircea Eliade reader.* Vol. 1. New York: Harper Colophon, 1975.

Bennis, W.G., & Shepard, H.A. A theory of group development. *Human Relations,* 1956, *9,* 415–437.

Bledstein, B.J. *The culture of professionalism: The middle class and the development of higher education in America.* New York: Norton, 1976.

Boring, E.G. *A history of experimental psychology,* 2nd ed. New York: Appleton-Century-Crofts, 1950.

Cassirer, E. *The philosophy of symbolic forms: Vol. 2. Mythical thought.* New Haven: Yale University Press, 1955, 2–3.

Chandler, A.D., Jr. *The visible hand: The managerial revolution in American business.* Cambridge, Mass.: Belknap Press, 1977.

Dilthey, W. *Pattern and meaning in history: Thoughts on history and society.* New York: Harper Torchbooks, 1961.

Dunphy, D.C. Phases, roles, and myths in self-analytic groups. In G.S. Gibbard, J.J. Hartman, & R.D. Mann (Eds.), *Analysis of groups: Contributions to theory, research, and practice.* San Francisco: Jossey-Bass, 1974.

Engels, F. *Dialectics of nature.* New York: International Publishers, 1940.

Etheredge, L.S. *The case of the unreturned cafeteria trays: An investigation based upon theories of motivation and human behavior.* Washington, D.C.: American Political Science Association, 1976.

Cobb, C.M. Group metaphor: Its function, form, theme and evolution. Unpublished doctoral dissertation, Harvard Graduate School of Education, 1973.

Heidbreder, E. *Seven psychologies.* New York: Appleton-Century-Crofts, 1933.

Hodges, M.A. *Wilhelm Dilthey: An introduction.* New York: Oxford University Press, 1944.

Hofstadter, R. *Social Darwinism in American thought.* Boston: Beacon Press, 1955.

Hunter, W.S. Autobiography. In E.G. Boring et al. (Eds.), *A history of psychology in autobiography,* Vol. 5. Worcester, Mass.: Clark University Press, 1952.

James, W. *Talks to teachers on psychology.* London: Longmans, Green, 1939 (orig. 1900).

Kant, I. *Critique of judgment.* New York: Hafner Press, 1951 (orig. 1790).

Makkreel, R.A. *Dilthey: Philosopher of the human studies.* Princeton: Princeton University Press, 1975.

Malinowski, B. *Magic, science and religion and other essays.* Glencoe, Ill.: Free Press, 1948.

Miller, G.A. Psychology as a means of promoting human welfare. *American Psychologist,* 1969, *24,* 1063–1075.

Minsky, M. A framework for representing knowledge. In P. Winston (Ed.), *The psychology of computer vision.* New York: McGraw-Hill, 1975.

Murchison, C. (Ed.) *Psychologies of 1925: Powell lectures in psychological theory.* Worcester, Mass.: Clark University Press, 1926.

Murchison, C. (Ed.) *Psychologies of 1930*. Worcester, Mass.: Clark University Press, 1930.
Murphy, G., & Kovach, J.K. *Historical introduction to modern psychology*, 3rd ed. New York: Harcourt Brace Jovanovich, 1972.
Popper, K. *The logic of scientific discovery*. New York: Harper Torchbooks, 1965.
Rein, M., & White, S.H. Policy research: Belief and doubt. *Policy Analysis*, 1977, *3*, 239–271.
Robinson, D.N. *An intellectual history of psychology*. New York: Macmillan, 1976.
Schank, R.C., & Abelson, R.P. *Scripts, plans, goals and understanding: An inquiry into human knowledge structures*. Hillsdale, N.J.: Erlbaum, 1977.
Siegel, A.W., & White, S.H. The development of spatial representations in children. In H. Reese (Ed.), *Advances in child development and behavior*, 1975, *10*, 9–55.
Tyack, D.B. *The one best system: A history of American urban education*. Cambridge, Mass.: Harvard University Press, 1974.
White, S.H. The active organism in theoretical behaviorism. *Human Development*, 1976, *19*, 99–107.
White, S.H. Social proof structures: The dialectic of method and theory in the work of psychology. In N. Datan & H. Reese (Eds.), *Life-span developmental psychology: Dialectical perspectives on experimental research*. New York: Academic Press, 1977 (a).
White, S.H. Social implications of IQ. In P.L. Houts (Ed.), *The myth of measurability*. New York: Hart, 1977 (b).
White, S.H., and Pillemer, D. Childhood amnesia and the development of a socially accessible memory system. In J. F. Kihlstrom & F.J. Evans (Eds.), *Functional disorders of memory*. Hillsdale, N.J.: Erlbaum, in press.
Woodworth, R.S. *Contemporary schools of psychology*. New York: Ronald, 1931; 2nd ed., 1948, 3rd ed. (with M.R. Sheehan), 1964.

General Discussion of White's Paper

Miller: Thank you, Dr. White. As they say, "Hope springs eternal" doesn't it?
White: Well, you wanted hope, George!
Miller: I know. I've been listening for it. This is the first I've heard.
Williams: I gave you hope.
Miller: Yes. I apologize to Dr. Williams.

All right, now we come to that embarrassing silence when the moderator is supposed to say something. What should I say? I think I'd like to save my comments until this afternoon, but I do appreciate the attempt to put the whole enterprise into some kind of historical perspective, and—as a student of Gary Boring myself—I agree that *he* knew that he was creating a myth, and that's why he called it *A History of Experimental Psychology*, refusing to call it *The History of Experimental Psychology*. And it's about time, I think, that we rewrote that history.

I don't know whether anybody out there in psychology—perhaps that's what you're doing, Shep—is writing a myth for our time that will make sense to students who want to go on within a tradition. The process of socialization when transferred to the graduate student level is usually called the process of professionalization, but I think it's a very similar process of picking up your local myth, and in psychology we do have a lot of myths. You pay your money and you take your choice, and what happens to truth along the way is a little hard to think about.

Dr. White and I—yesterday afternoon—had a discussion about the difference between a correspondence theory of truth and a coherence theory of truth. I think what he was saying is that most of what passes for knowledge in psychology does so by virtue of its internal coherence, rather than by its correspondence to reality. That's a dangerous way to go, as you can have a coherent system that is totally unrelated to anything you might want to do with it. What we really need is a way to satisfy both a correspondence and a coherence theory.

Please, somebody rescue me. We have a comment? Good!

Audience: If we lose "physics envy" in terms of our methodologies, what's out there? What's post–physics-envy methodology?

White: Maybe we ought to do what Michael Scriven said yesterday. Maybe we ought to look at ourselves and figure out what we're doing. There's an argument—George would know more about this than I would—in a book by Laird called *The Miracle of Language* that I read years ago and I enjoyed. Laird says that the grammar that we learned—most of us in the public schools—was all wrong. I don't know whether you ever parsed sentences and made sentence diagrams . . . Well, Laird says that most of that grammar is wrong. It was put on America, and it's an inflectional grammar. It was put on the

English language by medieval historians who just assumed that Latin grammar would work for English. And in recent years we've discovered that English is a distributional language as opposed to an inflective language, and the grammar is very different. Now we've been going on for many years assuming that the grammar of psychology is in effect a physical grammar. And one consequence is that we don't identify any effectiveness of the field. That's not the only consequence: There are others. For example, we use our theory of knowledge and practice in psychology to manage things like research grants. Now I personally believe that the government each year spends hundreds of millions of dollars, in effect, acting on the premise that they're driving research towards relevance, while in fact such funds are driving research off the cliff into entropy. That is, there is no meaning to the research at all; it's neither relevant nor is it basic. And I believe the government regularly spends tens of millions of dollars in forcing an image of scientific propriety—what it takes to make a grant look good—that doesn't fit many of the people in the field.

I don't know how many of you saw a joke letter from Ivan Pavlov in the *American Psychologist* about fifteen years ago. "Help! I am a young investigator. I am doing a very expensive kind of research. I have to use one dog at a time. I can't get many dogs, so I can't pile up a lot of data. Nobody believes my data. They won't publish it because I only use one dog at a time and because they won't publish it I can't get grants. Will sombody figure out something for me to do? Signed Ivan Pavlov."

Now, that's . . . Piaget would have a hard time getting some of his stuff through editorial journal processes. We need, I think . . .

Miller: Is that bad?
White: Yeah, I think that's bad. At this point I would say . . . I wish somebody would edit him. Don't take me wrong.
Miller: That's what I meant.
White: Yeah.
Miller: I wish he would read what he wrote.
White: I think if he were to randomly throw away about two-thirds of each of the books we'd all be better off. And he could, by the way, for many of them. But at any rate, I'm saying that the fact that we have an image of science based on physics envy is very crippling for the field. Because evey one of us knows of work that seems valid but is outside the canonical forms.

So I propose that we venture in, into the unknown. If Chomsky can flail away trying to figure out what English grammar is, maybe we can flail away trying to figure out what it is we're doing. I don't have any answers. I don't have, in effect, laws of methodology for the field. All I have is a certain conviction that they're different than those which we've been using. And I'm proposing that it's now almost become necessary that we go out into the void and figure out what they are.

Williams: I have one more question on this whole issue of the physical grammar that we use. You were suggesting therein a transformational study, after one has observed . . . if one were to do the sort of thing that Kohlberg has done where you free the observations from the age scales that have been used. You mentioned in passing that one investigator might be concerned with certain invariant relationships as well as variant relationships, and what struck me about that is whether that term "invariant relationship" is the preferred one in the system that you are suggesting; as opposed to a covariant or covarying relation or set of observations, where I always get stuck in my own connotation of the word. [For you] something's stable back here while something else is moving, whereas I'm quite comfortable with the notion that everything's moving, some things more or less rapidly, in some space or spaces.

White: O.K. No, that's true.

Williams: I'm curious about that.

White: Yeah, I guess what I would call that would be higher order invariance, and I'm quite sure that simple invariances—things remaining the same—are few and far between in most psychological analyses. So most invariances are really covariances of a higher order sort.

There are forms of modeling which are coming forward now—mostly A.I. types of modeling—which seem complex enough to be able to handle this sort of thing. And the fact is we're moving towards them. All I'm trying to do is to raise to consciousness what it is we're doing. We're really trying to revise the canonical forms of the field. And in the past, in the not very recent past, I've been in Washington and people have come and said, What have you done for us? Why are we giving you this money? What difference does it make?

Take a committee just last year. We were doing this under the august auspices of the National Academy of Sciences. Mathematicians and physicists and chemists who were—of course—our betters, looked in on us and told us whether we were right or wrong. I found it immensely restrictive. It has nothing to do with status envy among professionals. I just felt that they were asking the wrong questions about the issues and that we ought to have guts enough, if you want to call it that, to say, "O.K. maybe we can create our own trough, feed from our own trough, and maybe we can construct our own arguments about what we do and why it is we do it."

Miller: Years ago when a man named Kennedy was President, I occasionally went to Washington and talked to people. I remember talking to a man in the Bureau of the Budget, which is what the Office of Management and Budget was then called, about funding a program in psychology that was very important to a group of us. He put the question in a very straightforward way. He said, "Well, all right, we could give you this money, but how much is it worth in terms of the children's supplemental milk program?" That's the level at which those people have to think. Do you take milk away from children to give it to somebody who wants to do a particular program of research? At that time it blew my mind. I didn't want to take milk away from little children.

Jackson: Sure you did!

Miller: I tried to get him to look at some of the waste in the Department of Defense and channel that our way.

Audience: I'd be interested to know how Shep would respond to the question, How would you try to move this milk man to a different level of conciousness?

White: Well, that man in OMB is a classic type—I've never met George's friend, but I've met his uncle and his cousin. They always ask the same question. Because in actual fact he's living in that windowless room; he's supposed to translate all kinds of things into money, and the only arguments he feels are compelling are arguments that measure different goods against the same goal. What he'd like to do is, in effect, monetize preschool programs, foster parents, and rockets, and then do a cost-benefit calculation which would allow him to make a value judgment. But he can't do it. I think that fundamentally what he does in the end is to use a political process. Political processes are designed to adjudicate values. And what he really does is to put the money where he thinks all of the values that converge on him come to rest. I doubt very much that we can offer him an algorithm. However, I'm quite sure that the fantasies of P.E.R.T. and P.P.B.S. are fail-

Koch: ing now. That is, they don't dream as much as they used to about getting to it [an algorithm].

Koch: Well, they've failed all along. Now it's being recognized.

White: Yeah, yeah.

Miller: Yes, but even I predicted that they would fail.

Koch: We agree on something!

Williams: Yeah, but there's still a very strong theme to try to quantify and make the decisions on those sorts of bases. It would seem to me that one alternative for psychology would be to strengthen its political bases. That might mean either in APA or AAP or whatever else that has a voice here.

Bevan: I think that would make the difference and tells you what Shep is talking about, because there is one criterion that the government uses to justify all expenditures and that's an investment good. What is the payoff in one way or another? And unless you can find a criterion—a different base for a policy for supporting research—you're not going to sell that guy in the OMB.

White: I think that maybe the first thing would be to take a different image of where the research may be landing and look for the consequences of it. Greg Anrig, who is state commissioner for education in Massachusetts, once said what I thought was the right thing. He said, "I don't need people who can bring me answers. I can use people who can bring me questions." Maybe we ought to look at the flow of questions. Maybe we ought to look at the flow of formats, of myths, of metaphoric forms. Maybe we ought to trace the influence of psychology in a very different way. Then when we know a little bit about where we're going and how we're getting there, then maybe we ought to address the question of turning it into money. But, since we keep defending ourselves against the "transistor" saying, "Look at this. You don't think that's a transistor, but we invented it, and it really is a transistor," we're going to fail every time, because we really have never made many things that look like transistors.

Audience: One of my philosophy teachers said, and I imagine he quoted and I don't know from where, "A more beautiful answer to him who asks a more beautiful question."

White: Isn't that nice. Yeah.

Miller: One of the tasks of the moderator is to protect the time of the next speaker, isn't it? That was a beautiful note on which to end. Let's take a break and start again in fifteen minutes.

Question and Answer: Miller and White*

Miller: Dr. White, I enjoyed the trip into the past. It's always more comfortable in the past than in the future somehow, because of its mythic character. I assume that's why you took us there. And I agree that much of what passes for knowledge in psychology is accepted as true largely because it forms a relatively coherent mythology, and that in this respect it resembles the knowledge of everyday commonplaces that children in any society acquire as part of their process of socialization. And I also agree that different groups of psychologists are sustained by different and sometimes incompatible myths. But I'm concerned about how we determine what's worth doing. One way to do that, I suppose, is in terms of carrying the myth—we want to memorize nonsense syllables because we live in the myth of Ebbinghaus. Or another possible way of deciding it is to say it's socially important. A lot of people are suffering from problem x and therefore we should choose that as our problem to work on.

But neither of those approaches seems to me to ensure that the problems to which we devote our research and our deepest thought will really be intellectually interesting. Or perhaps my question is, What are your criteria for something being intellectually interesting?

To say that an organism adapts itself to its environment is an old idea, a true idea, an important idea. I just don't think it's interesting scientifically, intellectually. The problem is how are we going to discover something about the adaptive process that will be new and unexpected, not an extension of common sense, or mythology, or notions of social importance? Something that will stand to adaptation as the double helix stands to the theory of evolution, let's say. Something that you didn't expect. Something that is what scientists are really expected to do.

White: I wasn't really sure that I understood the question that Dr. Miller addressed to me. That is, I didn't understand how I

---
*Composed from exchanges occurring at the end of the second day as Miller analyzed each paper and redirected a question to each member of the symposium.

had, in effect, evoked the question. One question was, How do people who do science decide what to do? How do they decide that anything's important? How do they . . . that's it. I didn't understand it, so I'm paraphrasing it. And maybe it was . . .

Miller: That's a good question, too. [*general laughter*]

White: Well, I think that during the course of my talk, I appealed to the notion of myths several different ways and several different times. And I did that, I must admit, in part as a kind of rhetorical device and in part as a kind of historical device, because the way I got into consideration of these issues myself was by becoming, in fact, interested in myths as something apart from maps—myths as doing something for social groups that maps don't do. I got into attempts to analyze them, in part because I felt that in analyzing aspects of social policy there was a strong presence of something that looked like myths; and in part because I'd become aware—in a happy coincidence over the years—of a kind of historical tradition, this hermeneutic tradition, in which in fact something like myth is seriously analyzed. But someone said to me over coffee that myth was a bad word to use, and I can see it carries unfortunate overtones; because whenever I use the term "myth" I leave the impression of a world lost in dreams. And I would assume that an unperturbed coherence theorist would be smoking pot on a campus at Berkeley or some . . .

Miller: Or Harvard! . . .

White: . . . I really was trying to sketch a more complex picture of a very complicated communications system which, in my mind, stretches between a very differentiated group of scholars—and scientists whom we call all psychologists—and a very differentiated group of people in practice. And I was trying to sort of build the network in midair, so to speak, and try to line up what passes between them.

There's a great deal that goes on in the development of knowledge in the scientific group that is not easily conveyed by the image of a myth, and there's a great deal that goes in the management of social policy that represents something more than the carrying forth of myths. But for a group of people distributed across space, myths, I think, serve a very important function of allowing these people to recognize the possibility of their relationship to one another.

Are these people (in working with these myths) trying to adapt? Is that all that I've said? I didn't think that I was really arguing for the concept of adaptation, which covers anything. I will admit I didn't talk about the motives that animate people in a system like this. That was one of the things that I just didn't build in the talk, but I think is worth talking about. In any bureaucratic system stretching high in the air above Johnny's head, one of the things you have to take into account is the intense frustration of most bureaucrats because, in fact, there's a great deal of idealism loose in the government. I think you meet more idealism in Washington than you do most other places. A lot of the people in that system really want to help Johnny to read. And what's frustrating them is that they're in those little cubicles, they're getting information they can't trust, and they're making actions the efficacy of which are not very clear. They all know what the problems of action are in a bureaucratic system. And they have a strong motive somehow to get things a little clearer, to get a clearer idea of what's coming in and what's going out so that they can enforce their basic motives which, among other things, have to do with good will toward kids and freedom.

The interesting thing is, How does the person who lives in a situation of constant ambiguity express his motives, whether they are holy or unholy? One motive I think that they have is to try to get a clearer picture of what it is they're doing. And one thing that psychologists do is provide them with different registers of what's going on in the world, with certain images of how the system is working, and, in so doing, give them a clearer picture of what their competency might be, what their agency might be. But is the motive of people simply to adapt to their bureaucratic niche? No, I don't think so. I think the motives of someone who's working in government is generally, though not always, a motive that I'd call idealistic.

Now, why does a scientist or a scholar—someone pursuing the variety of things in psychology—why does he ever find out anything new? What perturbs the system? I really feel that there I probably just talked too quickly. I've written—just prior to this talk—a rather complicated paper on "Social Proof Structures: The Dialectic between Method and Theory in the Work of Psychology." In it I tried to picture a group of psychologists working in a laboratory or at large, and their attempt to confront disturbing reality, perturbations in what they see, and then to wrestle with. I tried to picture what kinds of messages get sent back and forth, what kinds of compromises occur in people's behavior; what are the systems by which a group of people act together to build common knowledge of the world. And I tried to picture a set of schools of psychology, if you like. In the modern day, schools of psychology are grouped around action programs. They're grouped around what we call research programs. And it's very interesting to contemplate a group of people who, in effect, belong to a club; and they all own Skinner boxes and they write back and forth to one another about what they see in the Skinner boxes. And then compare and contrast them with another group of people who own couches, and yet another group of people who all own short, fat glasses and tall, thin glasses. Imagine a set of clubs like that writing back and forth to each other trying to agree about what they can all see by acting in common and trying to erect, from what they can all agree that they see, some kind of picture of reality.

Now I guess that was not expressed in my talk. But such an image of the scientific process or the processes of psychology is what I was trying to telegraph in the first part. What are the motives or why does this group seek to enlarge its vision? I suppose the idealism that's expressed in any scientific or scholarly group would be something like the pursuit of truth or the pursuit of competence, perhaps, if truth is an aspect of competence. Since some of us are coherence theorists (as George and I agreed over drinks provisionally) then I would say perhaps they're pursuing something that may be a little higher than truth . . . which is beauty: But that for another day. Thank you.

Miller: Let me try again. Okay?

I hope you won't give up your use of the term myth, because to me it evokes a much richer notion of social integration over time than would, say, a Kuhnian paradigm of normal science. But I assume that, like the Kuhnian paradigm, a myth has a very conservative function to play in any social group. Now, I think that's the point you made early on in your talk, that that is the function that it serves. It's strange that a man as conservative as Tom Kuhn should have been cast in the role of the advocate of revolution. (It's won him as strange an advocacy as I won when I said let's "give psychology away.") Tom [Kuhn] did say there have to be revolutions, that you work out to the end of a paradigm and then something intellectually interesting happens; you invent a new paradigm, you grow a new myth, you get a community of people working around another idea. I didn't expect you to tell me that you eat ice cream and pickles the night before and you wake up with this nightmare which is the great new idea of the future. I don't know where those new ideas come from, but I missed in your talk an appreciation of the absolutely crucial nature and crucial importance of that flash of genius that keeps us in business, whether it is eyeballing crotches or the parity principle in physics. It must come from somewhere, you know, whatever it is. And that was what I wanted to draw you out on. Not how we talked to each other about what we agree on.

White: Let me just . . . the right answer is, I wish I knew. But let me just say a few words about that.

I think that inevitably myths break down. That is, myths will not hold things. There's a very lovely paper by Ernst Mayr called "Two Hundred and Fifty Years of Evolution." It appeared in the . . . in *Science*, I think, about three or four years ago, and he talks about the coming of evolution not as something that happened on the day that Darwin published *Origin of the Species*, but as something that was accumulating a hundred and fifty years before Darwin. Moreover, Mayr argues—as do a number of biologists—that it hasn't completely "happened" yet. But the question is, How does the climactic event occur? How does one . . . how does a new myth emerge?

Well, I don't exactly know. I do think, however, that there is a growing period of incoherence. There is a period during which the old image, the old form stands while anomalies accumulate. Having been raised in the learning theory tradition, I can tell you that there was a lot of drum-rolling among the S-R psychologists. They looked like an impervious group. But as a matter of fact accumulating for many, many years in the S-R literature were "set effects," "expectancy effects," etc. There were all these damn things that didn't work right in the experiments, and they were always accumulating in the discussion sections of journal articles. You couldn't deal with them in the results section because you didn't know how to talk about them, but there they were in the discussion section. And so people kept inventing terms . . . they kept seeing things that they couldn't deal with, so they kept naming them "sets." These anomalies accumulated in the articles for years, and then someone wrote a paper, saying, "Let's throw the word 'set' out of psychology because it's become a wastebasket word." Of course what they were discovering was mind, attention, and so on; but nevertheless there was a long period during which the system held and anomalies accumulated.

What causes the system to erupt and revolutionize? I'm not completely sure, but Kuhn has made an interesting comment: "When things get very bad, then people who hold a

	paradigm suddenly start brooding. They start reading philosophy." That's him, not me.
Koch:	That's what happened to Kuhn.
White:	Since we live in a time of corrigible myths I think what scientists do is they go back to the dream time, and they say, "Gee, maybe we came out the wrong way." And maybe they try exactly the kind of exercise that I was trying here today. They try to go back into the historical origin of their myths, and try to reconsider whether their definition of the game is exactly the right one. Now, that's just a guess based on something Kuhn said, and I don't honestly know.
Koch:	Well, that's the Pollyanna reading of framework change, and at times and places it may have a certain truth. But there is also a phenomenon known as boredom, and it seems to me that many framework changes in psychology are simply a result of two factors. First, that people—even those who espouse a theoretical framework of a gappy and overpretentious sort very religiously—are secretly divided people because they have to have insight into the gaps. And people of this sort who entertain that kind of framework over a sufficient time span—during which you have an enormous amount of cognitive time-marking because there's no real forward movement, and you're closing your eyes more and more to negative evidence, counter-arguments, and so on—ultimately get bored somehow.
White:	That's a good point.
Koch:	Yes.
White:	I agree.
Koch:	Right.
White:	I think that happens.
Koch:	Yeah.
Williams:	Well, but that's . . .
Jackson:	Then they start reading philosophy.
White:	They've got to have an alternative.
Williams:	Well, sometimes . . .
Koch:	Yes, I think that point of view has been rather overdone, initially by people like Conant. You don't abandon a theory until you have a better one, etc., etc. You can point to historical junctures in the psychology of the past forty or fifty years when people have just been appalled at the cognitive thinness of what is in the public domain. Some have looked for an alternative, and have been willing to buy virtually any alternative that is as different as possible from this very thin-thing that bores and appalls them.

White: Touché.
Koch: Okay?
White: Okay.
Williams: Well, it does seem to me that the term "boredom" ought not to be passed over too quickly. At least when I took courses in psychology that was always used as a surrogate for some kind of conflict.
Audience: May I try one comment based on what Shep was saying? Certainly one looks at the data, and it doesn't fit, and then you go read the philosophy. Another . . .
Koch: That's what Kuhn says.
Audience: Okay, for another reason of where that comes from is that somebody who has already read the philosophy, programmed a computer, talked with linguists, comes to look at the data, and looks at it in a different perspective.
White: I am Pollyannaish. I was accused of it, and I am. I have a sort of view that all's for the best in this world. Panglossian, I think it's called. But I do feel that you can find what I've suggested in history. I guess the group that I know best is the learning theory group. Though it's happening in Piaget right now, the anomalies are accumulating. The system is holding, but anyone who knows the system can give you an enormously long list of all the things that shouldn't be happening that are now happening. And people are waiting to jump on something better as soon as somebody suggests either a new idea or a new set of procedures or something. So there is a kind of integrity. The process does correct itself to some extent.

Promoting Human Welfare Through Legislative Advocacy

Miller's Introduction of Jackson

Our next speaker is Dr. James Jackson of the University of Michigan. I met Dr. Jackson when he was still a graduate student ten years ago. At that time he was actively campaigning to increase the admission of black students into graduate programs in psychology. I'd lost contact with him in the intervening years, and therefore one of the benefits of this symposium to me has been to meet him again and to find that he has fulfilled his promise to become a social psychologist and to learn that he's still active in his advocacy of the rights of minority groups. Dr. Jackson's topic is "Promoting Human Welfare through Legislative Advocacy." Dr. Jackson . . .

Jackson's Opening Statement

Actually George didn't tell the whole story. I actually met him during his speech. I really mean that "during." It was in 1969; I had come to Washington—being the only black graduate student at that point at Wayne State University (from which I got my degree)—and I ran into a number of other black graduate students from other universities who were in similar sorts of straits. It was interesting to meet all these black graduate students. I was very happy to see them. It was hard to believe because I had thought I was the only one in the United States. So it was kind of nice to see that there were others. And during our conversations while we were there we decided that perhaps we should try to do something about this particular situation. So we had a discussion, and we met several evenings. Days merged into evenings. We write manifestos, and we got very involved.

As you can see I was a very, very activist type then, and I'm going to come back to that in a little bit. My whole history has been that way.

One decision we made was that we needed to get APA to do something about black graduate students. We needed to increase the number of black graduate students, other minority students, and so on. We thought we'd try to do something dramatic, so we planned this thing that during the presidential speech—I didn't know who the president was . . . [*laughter*] . . . I mean, what I'm trying to say is that it was nothing personal . . . it was all accidental. We planned that we would get up, and that we would make a statement to the whole APA about trying to do something about black graduate students.

So there were about twelve of us, I think, and we were sitting out in the audience waiting. We had planned this whole thing. Just before they were going to give the microphone to George we all got up, marched up in front of the podium, took the microphone, and said that we were going to hold this microphone until the APA listened to our demands, until our demands were met.

George . . . I looked at him, and it was really funny. He had the most bemused kind of expression on his face. He didn't know what was going on, what this was all about, and what was happening. So we made our demands and they agreed that they [the Council of Representatives] would meet with us the next day and we said fine. We all got up, we marched out, out the door, and I never did get a chance to hear the speech! [*laughter*] It was incredible. So I am particularly happy to be here today because it gave me an opportunity to read the speech! [*laughter*] I know it now, know what he had to say, and basically I agree with a lot of it, as you'll see as we go along.

I guess I want to talk a little bit more kind of at a practical level, because I'm going to be talking about advocacy—legislative advocacy, psychology, and society. The title of my talk was "Promoting Human Welfare through Legislative Advocacy" when I submitted the title. I've changed that title somewhat. See, I'm messin' with George again! I have added a subtitle now: "A Proper Role for the Proper Science of Psychology?" In an attempt to talk about how can we devise roles for psychologists' being involved with social policy that seems to be appropriate for the science and the profession, I'd like to read just two quotes to start my talk. I think they demonstrate what some of the problems have been historically regarding the involvement of psychology in the whole social policy process.

Promoting Human Welfare Through Legislative Advocacy

A Proper Role for the Proper Science of Psychology?

James S. Jackson
The University of Michigan

As a science concerned about the social consequence of its applications, psychology must also fulfill a broader obligation to society by bringing influence to bear on public policies to ensure that its findings are used in the service of human betterment. (Bandura 1974, p. 859)

The psychologist's job as a scientist is to search for data, principles and laws that enlarge our understanding of psychological phenomena. . . . There is no reason why psychologists should not advocate political viewpoints, but they should advocate them only as individual citizens. The psychologist's role as a scientist is to set forth the facts, and to set forth these facts in as value free a fashion as possible. (Atkinson 1977, p. 207)

These two statements illustrate a continuing controversy regarding the role of social science and the social scientist in the formulation and implementation of social policy. It has become increasingly evident in recent years that science has assumed a more activist stance in relationship to social policies which affect the integrity and operation of science and, perhaps more importantly, the welfare of the general population (Price 1974, 1978).

In the beginning of the current decade Irving Horowitz (1971) proposed that the dominant organizing principle of the seventies, as far as the history of the social sciences is concerned, might well be policymaking. The subsequent years have supported this observation as discussion and debate have escalated regarding the proper role of social science, if any, in the policymaking processes of government (Price 1974; Roberts 1974; Goodwin & Tu 1975; Smith 1973; Rie 1977). Given my own personal history as a social scientist, I had never seriously questioned the appropriateness of an active role for psychology.

There exists, however, a lack of consensus regarding the proper role of science, particularly social science, in the various aspects of government policy decisionmaking. In the nearly ten years since George Miller (1969) suggested one possible orientation of psychology (with a little p) to societal problems, giving psychology away, no agreed-upon stance has evolved regarding the relationship between the science of psychology and the process of social policy development. If anything, it has been the strong difference of opinions concerning the role of the field in this arena that has provided one major wedge between academic and non-academic segments of the discipline (Dörken 1977) and resulted in the lack of agreed-upon roles guiding psychology in an admittedly important area that directly affects human welfare.

I would like to propose that psychology should take an activist/collaborative role in the development of policies which affect the welfare or well-being of individuals in this society. Although I would agree that these policies are not always created in federal or state legislative bodies, I do contend that it is the policies developed by these latter entities which have the most significant and pervasive effects. I include here, of course, the various regulatory activities of the bureaucracy which are an integral aspect of the legislative process. This is a somewhat bold proposition, but one, however, that has a demonstrable reality in the lobbying arm of American psychology, the Association for the Advancement of Psychology (AAP). The activities of this organization provide the model of legislative intervention on behalf of psychology, and hopefully in the service of the public welfare, as well as the source of my observations.

LEGISLATION AND SOCIETAL NEEDS

The discussion at this symposium occurs within a context of societal problems that have become more complex and seemingly more intractable over the last ten years. Unemployment, particularly among groups such as young black urban males, approximates rates only observed during depressions. The scarcity of energy sources and related environmental problems are reaching critical proportions. Acceptable housing is becoming more and more unavailable, with private homes soon to be possible only for upper income groups. Similar observations could be made about race relations, education, food production, and the high incidence of crime. It could be argued that these are not new problems but problems which have confronted this society for decades. We as citizens, however, have maintained hope that the promises of more sophisticated technology would result in new energy sources, provide new jobs, lower the cost of housing, remove at least the physical bases of racial tension, improve our educational system, and lower an intolerable crime rate.

As we prepare to enter a new decade (with an appropriate social science dominant theme to be coined), the solutions to these extant problems seem no closer than they were at the end of the previous decade. One may question, Haven't we made some progress? And the answer would be, of course. But have we been equal to the task of keeping pace in providing approaches to problems which seem to multiply at an almost geometric rate? I believe that the answer is an unequivocal no!

But this is not the issue that I would like to specifically address. I have no doubts that we could muster very strong agreement that our nation is experiencing severe and perhaps chronic social problems. In fact, I am certain that many of you have heard this theme too often in the past, its mere repetitiveness soon falling on sated ears. What I would like to suggest, however, is that the major government response to these issues is the introduction of legislation (or new regulations) purportedly designed to redress some imbalance, oversight, history of neglect in some social group or, for those of you more cynical listeners, as a response to some vested interest. Although this is true at almost all levels of government, I would like to restrict my comments primarily to the federal legislative process.

Although we can all point to the failures of the Great Society programs as an example of social policymaking gone amok, perhaps other more acceptable examples of large-scale social programs—e.g., Social Security, various housing acts, and old-age assistance packages—are also the products of federal legislation. While we may debate the relative merits of any given congressional act and its implementation, it is clear that federal legislation has been used as a major method of both directly and indirectly confronting human societal problems (Gross 1966; Kramer 1970). This is not to ignore the role of private concerns and local governments in the welfare of the general population. The sheer size and scope of the social programs initiated by federal congressional action, however, generally assumes potentially broader impact upon individual well-being and thus provides the justification for examining the proper role of psychology in social policymaking at this level.

As I proceed I would like to comment briefly upon some of the major factors that seem to provide impediments to the full participation of psychology (and science more generally) in the development and implementation of social policy. I do not in any manner, however, wish to imply that consensus exists regarding the role for the discipline. On the contrary, it is the existence of several major unresolved issues which has hindered agreement regarding whether *any* active role is appropriate. In the following discussion I will touch briefly on the problems of psychology as a unique scientific/applied social science, scientific and human values, psychology's more recent flirtation with direct legislative advocacy, and my observations regarding the positive aspects of the activist/collaborative model of involvement in social policymaking.

PSYCHOLOGY AND SOCIETAL PROBLEMS

Defining Social Problems and Human Welfare

We could undoubtedly achieve considerable agreement among most psychologists, no matter what their orientation, that as *citizens* psychologists should play an active role in the process through which policy is developed and implemented (Atkinson 1977; Miller 1969; Smith 1973). On the other hand, some social scientists assert that this involvement is not enough and that psychology as an applied science (Varela 1977) and perhaps as a basic science (Bandura 1974) has some unique contributions to make to the solution of problems which confront society and thus to the general welfare of the population (Freeman & Sherwood 1970). Although the arguments regarding the applicability of psychology to social problems have generally involved the field as a basic science, it is clear that we may also question whether even the more applied and technological aspects of the profession have any relevance to the solution of these problems (Beit-Hallahmi 1974; Campbell 1975; Rappoport & Kren 1975; Rie 1977). A specific example of the latter issue in clinical psychology involves the ongoing debate regarding the effectiveness and value of psychotherapy, particularly in the treatment of non-white, non–middle class, and non-verbally skilled individuals (Albee 1977; Cummings 1977).

One major factor contributing to our inability as a science/profession to achieve any unanimity regarding a stance toward social problems is the difficulty in clearly identifying the phenomenon which is the object of our science, particularly in natural settings. Unlike the physical scientist or engineer, social scientists, particularly psychologists, find it to be no simple task to determine meaningful rules of inclusion and exclusion. Given our definition of the science as one that studies behavior and mental processes (McKeachie 1976), we are often hard-pressed to discover issues or societal problems that could *not* be conceptualized as having some relevance for psychology (Miller 1969; Rappoport & Kren 1975). The potentially all-encompassing definition of the nature of a relevant social issue or social problem has resulted in some psychologists deeming the concept essentially a useless one for psychology: "We need to develop generic criteria suggesting the kinds of social problems that can be approached intelligently from the standpoint of psychology. Psychology is not cogent to everything" (Rappoport & Kren 1975, p. 840).

Similarly, since behavior occurs within a social and historical context, some psychologists have suggested that our theories are no more than reflections of contemporary history, non-enduring, emphemeral, and affected most strongly by historical/cultural changes (Gergen 1973). Within this same vein others have gone so far as to propose that there are social problems, involving behaviors and social interactions, that cannot be solved in the traditional enduring meaning of scientific explanation; and are, in a sense, intractable as far as scientific psychology is concerned (Sarason 1978).

Regardless of this strong pessimism, however, there appears to be rather broad agreement that the social relationships, processes, and behaviors involved in what are generally labeled social problems are legitimate areas of study for psychology (Miller 1969; Smith 1973; Varela 1977; Zuniga 1975). This is particularly true if we focus our attention more narrowly on mental health and health issues involving the provision for and delivery of psychological services.

Related to this issue is the work on what is generally called social indicators and the closely related focus on quality of life (Andrews & Withey 1976; H.E.W. 1969). Social indicators are statistics, similar to economic indicators, that hopefully provide barometers on the well-being of individuals in a number of important social domains (Andrews & Withey 1976; Land 1971). In the early formulation of the concept (Gross 1966), social indicators were viewed as an approach for clearly assessing the incidence and degree of social problems. More recent work has focused on basic underlying structure (Andrews & Withey 1976) and more applied concerns as to how these estimates of social problems can be used by policymakers (Rodgers & Marans 1975). Although other examples could be presented, the work on social indicators stands as a possible approach both for defining and assessing the incidence and extent of social problems and as a procedure for discussing and formalizing what is meant by human welfare (Andrews & Withey 1976; Campbell, Converse, & Rodgers 1976; H.E.W. 1969).

Contributions of Scientific Psychology to the Amelioration of Social Problems

Some consensual agreement exists regarding the importance of social problems and even the fact that psychology as a science might have some potential relevance to their solution (Zuniga 1975). Similarly, we are beginning to develop procedures, such as social indicators, that may provide a method for unequivocally defining social problems and other elusive concepts as well-being or human welfare (Andrews & Withey 1976; Gross 1966). With regard, however, to the level and intensity of involvement of the social sciences, as science, in the solution of social problems there seems to be a lack of agreement and clear guidelines (Atkinson 1977; Freeman & Sherwood 1970):

> The social scientist should direct his work toward the solution of contemporary social problems and . . . the amelioration of the ills of our society should be a guiding force in the work of social researchers. (Freeman & Sherwood 1970, p. 1)

This viewpoint considers the total role of the social scientist as direct involvement in research explicitly addressed to social problems. Equally strong statements have been made by psychologists opposed to any involvement of the science in social problems. This latter perspective is probably best summarized in the following by Tyler:

> It became almost naive to assume that what was discovered through research could have much effect on man's nature or institutions. . . . Psychology was to be thought of as a pure science, and the implicit slogan was "science" for science's sake. (1973, p. 1021)

This view of the basic social scientist is of course extreme and unlikely to be found in any pure form. On the other hand, there has been the often unspoken (and perhaps overly stressed to funding agencies) assumption that because of the unique nature of the phenomena in psychology (behavior and mental processes) that anything studied is relevant and potentially of benefit to society (Varela 1977).

There exists a strong belief on the part of basic social scientists that within a free and open society relevant discoveries lead without fail to appropriate technologies for use in solving human problems (Atkinson 1977; Price 1974).

> The question for the future of science is whether, in the public forum, the justification for support of basic science will continue to be the argument that basic research leads inexorably, through application, to technological innovation. (McElroy 1971, p. 296)

There is a belief, whether articulated or tacitly assumed, that our scientific pursuit of the intricate nature of human behavior and mental processes will result in theories that can be applied in much the same manner that engineering stands in relationship to physics (Atkinson 1977; Miller 1969; Roberts 1974). Within the context of this view of science and social problems, then, much of the concern of psychology has historically focused on the fostering of appropriate scientific values (Vallance 1972) and promoting strict neutrality in the implications of basic scientific findings (Roberts 1974). The maintenance of scientific objectivity was viewed as a goal almost as important as the scientific discoveries themselves (Vallance 1972).

During the present decade, however, we have seen several myths regarding the supposed objectivity of the social sciences questioned (Roberts 1974; Vallance 1972). The touted value-free nature of the enterprise seems no longer defensible, if it ever was, and individual and societal values have been demonstrated to impinge upon problems chosen for study, approaches, and interpretations of findings (Bevan 1976; Caplan & Nelson 1973; Zuniga 1975).

> For when you recognize science as a human activity, you recognize that it is perfectly capable of good and bad outcomes and that scientists like all other human beings, as agents of social activity, are thus necessarily involved in value judgments and are accountable not only to their peers but ultimately to society at large. (Bevan 1976, p. 481)

Similar variations on this theme can be found in almost every corner of the discipline (Garner 1972; Roberts 1974; Segall 1976; Vallance 1972). Although new models are being proposed, what the final implications are for psychology is unknown at the present time (Buss 1975; Garner 1972).

The value-free, scientific-objectivity argument has also been continually used in the debate over psychology's role in the legislative process and through this process in the solution of social problems (Atkinson 1977; Miller 1969; Smith 1973). Given the belief that "good ideas" and relevant psychological theory somehow find their way into public use, psychology has historically defined its role, as a basic social science, in social policy-making as objective expert (Atkinson 1977). Thus, the implementation of social policy was (is?) viewed as an essentially political process which exists outside of the scientific purview (Bevan 1976; Dörken 1977; Miller 1969; Smith 1973).

> Concern with legislation, negotiations with insurance firms and governmental agencies, and workshops for the aspiring practitioner have seemed to them much too undignified, much too public, possibly irrelevant, and not at all scholarly. (Rie 1977, p. 1)

It is clear that the political process has been viewed, particularly by academic psychologists, as a procedure diametrically opposed to the scientific process; one which would taint the respectability of any psychologist who became involved.

> Psychologists and social scientists more so than other scientists, need to carefully distinguish between providing scientific data and making policy. If a psychologist is fascinated by political power and the ability to shape public policy, he or she should run for elective office and not try to disguise political efforts by cloaking them in the framework of psychological research. (Atkinson 1977, pp. 207–208)

Obviously, this perspective on the political process clashes with scientific values of objectivity, nonpartisanship, and openness of mind in the pursuit of scientific knowledge. Any institutionalized set of social behaviors that conveys vested interest, compromise, or is self-serving would be viewed as anti-ethical to the disciplinary canons.[1]

ACADEMIC AND PROFESSIONAL PSYCHOLOGY

As I alluded to previously, the perceived schism between psychology as a basic science and psychology as an applied profession has also contributed to the confusion regarding the discipline's role in the legislative process. Unlike other social sciences, psychology trains individuals both for basic science careers and professional service. Although one may question the success of this dual-training model (Meehl 1972), the objectives of the bulk of our clinical and other more applied areas is to produce scientist/professionals. Recent statements and changes in the "harder" areas of the discipline (e.g., experimental) also demonstrate a move toward more applied areas, e.g., developmental, human factors, and clinical. It is of course the dual training which makes psychology such an important mental health discipline. In comparison to other social science professions, it is the nature of the training which justifies our relatively expensive costs in the delivery of service (excluding psychiatry) and our increasingly important and prestigeful position in the mental health arena. Instead of capitalizing on this extraordinary strength, however, psychologists have found themselves in an unending controversy over the value of one orientation or the other (Garner 1972; Raush 1974; Tyler 1973), even in light of supposed adherence to the Boulder and Vail models. This continuing debate has resulted in a proliferation of what can only be called specialized scientific or professional psychology associations. The fact that formal discussions regarding this issue are now necessary attests to its seriousness and, if not resolved, the potentially negative impact on, among other things, the political unity of American psychology.

It is not my intention, however, to relate all the reasons, both rational and irrational, for this apparent science-applied schism in psychology. That this difference is probably a pseudo one has been explicitly argued on many prior occasions (Bevan 1976; McElroy 1971).

> The quality of the basic research is improved by communication between the basic research scientists and the people who have problems to solve. Thus, for scientists to engage in goal oriented research, research aimed

---

[1] I have always wondered how this set of attitudes jibes with departmental and professional association policies that often involve important scientific issues.

at solving problems already known to exist, is both to perform a service to society and to improve the quality of the basic research itself. (Garner 1972, p. 945)

My reason for bringing this issue to your attention is to indicate how this applied versus basic science debate has affected the involvement of psychology in social policymaking.

Perhaps because of their day-to-day contact with individuals who have social problems, psychologists in non-academic settings have been more concerned with the legislative process and the formulation of social policies which facilitate or impede the delivery of human services. Unfortunately, I believe that often the political activities engaged in by applied psychologists are viewed as self-serving by the remainder of the discipline and evoke fears of bias, loss of government and societal respect, as well as an attenuation of effectiveness in gaining public support for basic scientific research (Atkinson 1977; Rie 1977; Smith 1973). In many ways this particular view, in light of an already tenuous relationship within psychology, provides additional impediments to a clearly defined role for psychology in social policymaking.

There is a common propensity to view our science as consisting of two separable components; academic/scientific and professional. Notwithstanding the growth of freestanding professional schools, the bulk of psychologists who work in non-academic applied settings are trained in Boulder-model programs emphazing both research and service. Many psychologists in academia combine elements of both in their work.

The general belief, however, is that non-academic psychologists have a greater stake in the legislative process (Rie 1977) in that it somehow serves their interest to the exclusion of academic psychologists and perhaps the public. I believe that these attitudes stem from a general misunderstanding and at times ignorance of the political process and particulars of legislation. For example, the National Research Services Award Act (NRSA) of 1974 is clearly a bill which has an important impact on the training of all psychologists. Including the unfortunate ADAMHA regulations attendant to the act, psychology is literally threatened with losing its capability of training mental health professionals with both clinical and research skills. Furthermore, the regulations themselves pose undue restrictions on our capability to effectively train purely research psychologists. Similar arguments can be made regarding the change in federal support from predoctoral to postdoctoral training. If academic psychologists have difficulties in recognizing the effects of such legislation and regulations on their training programs, it is not surprising that they fail to comprehend the potential impact of the National Health Planning and Resource Development (NHPRD) Act of 1974 which potentially lays one cornerstone for National Health Insurance. Although the regional planning boards at all levels are of importance to psychology, the bill possibly would require local and regional approval of grant proposals from academic psychologists. Of broader importance are the employment opportunities and consumer advocacy functions available to research-oriented psychologists under the evaluation requirements of the act.

Even further removed, apparently, from academic psychology are the current Colorado Medicare Study which assesses the advisability of including psychologists as independent providers under Medicare and increasing the ceiling on mental health benefits; and the Federal Trade Commission investigation of the Joint Commission on Accreditation of Hospitals (JCAH) to determine whether JCAH arbitrarily and unfairly excludes licensed clinical psychologists from the staff of JCAH-accredited private and public hospitals. On the surface, psychology's involvement in these bills and regulatory activities seems to be solely in the self-interest of clinical psychologists. But is this so? First, there is a major concern with the current and potential impact on the consumer of mental health services. While one may argue that benefits will also accrue to individual psychologists, shouldn't we be willing to fight for the inclusion of the science/profession in legislation designed to affect the well-being of the American public?

Second, it should be clear that the unequivocal recognition of psychology as an independent profession is in the best interest of our scientific advances. If there is a symbiotic relationship between basic and scientific research and more applied endeavors (not just clinical), then the expansion and further refinement of these applied activities are of direct benefit to scientific progress (Garner 1972).

Finally, though I believe that it is a relatively minor point, provisions under all these seemingly "clinical" bills and regulatory activities provide expanded job possibilities for non-clinically trained research psychologists, just as the community mental health center bills have done.

I do not mean to imply in these comments that academic/scientist psychologists have nothing to offer more applied-oriented psychologists. As I indicate later, the emerging recognition of the symbiotic relationship between applied interventions and basic research activities provides the possibilities of true advances in our knowledge, and through translation processes, new applications by psychologists traditionally not located in academic settings.

In general, while we may achieve some consensus regarding the identification of social problems (Andrews & Withey 1976; H.E.W. 1969; Land 1971), we do have great difficulty in determining whether psychology as a social science has any fruitful contribution to make to their solution (Campbell 1975; Rappoport & Kren 1975; Vallance 1972). This is true both because of disagreement about the relevance of our discipline to available solutions (Miller 1969; Price 1974) as well as traditional scientific attitudes that "science for science's sake" is the only legitimate objective of psychology (Tyler 1973). It is becoming increasingly difficult for a social science, dedicated to the scientific study of behavior and mental processes, to justify a traditional insulated existence or to deny the importance of social technology, represented by applied psychology, in both the solution of societal ills and as a guideline for basic research (Bevan 1976; Garner 1972; McElroy 1971; Vallance 1972; Varela 1977). Whether we accept Bevan's (1976) proposition that morally we can no longer afford the "valley of specialized intellectual interest" or Freeman and Sherwood's (1970) contention that the very nature of the social scientific research enterprise, whether intentional or not, is "intertwined with efforts to identify, understand and temper the social ills of our communities," it is clear that psychology is being forced to take more activist positions in relationship to societal ills and consequently social policymaking.

PSYCHOLOGY AND THE LEGISLATIVE PROCESS

Models of Possible Involvement

Although there are undoubtedly many psychologists who would *not* concur, changes in more traditional orientations toward social problems and social policy are evident, and even the most conservative of social scientists would undoubtedly suggest some role for science in confronting social problems (McElroy 1971).

In examining the available literature, three consistent themes or models emerge regarding the role of psychology in public policy (Segall 1976). The first model is that of expert witness and is the most common, receiving the broadest support (Carter 1970; Fraser 1970; Miller 1969).

> In this, the simplest model, the psychologist merely offers what he knows to those who could apply it. If it is acknowledged merely that psychological facts ought to be brought to bear on policy dilemmas, then policy makers, either elected officials or their appointed administrative agents could be encouraged to seek interpretations of existing psychological facts from psychologists. (Segall 1976, pp. 18–19).

The process of merely providing expert testimony or information on particular topics, generally initiated by policymakers, has been the least threatening to traditional scientific values. The psychologist need not concern himself or herself with value issues of whether a particular social policy is the "correct" one or not. Even decisions as to whether to use the expert testimony or not are left completely to the discretion of the policymaker.

The second model or role for psychology is the evaluator, most notably espoused by Campbell (1969) in his vision of the experimenting society.

Similar to the role of the psychologist under the first model, there is little possibility of value conflict or loss of scientific "objectivity." The psychologist brings to the social policy arena methodological skills with which various alternative policies can be evaluated. Once the evaluation is completed, the decision to implement or not is based upon the political process with little or no input from the psychologist. Although one would hope that social policies would be developed under this model consistent with the findings, the psychologist would not be able to affect the decision.

The third model suggested by Segall (1976) is more Orwellian in content and views the psychologist as social engineer. Although this possibility seems the most farfetched, it is this role which is most often offered as to why psychology should *avoid* active social policymaking involvement (Miller 1969; Price 1974; Smith 1973). One is tempted to quickly dismiss this particular model because of its lack of feasibility at present and the lack of responsiveness to political realities of decisionmaking. When reading about fears of psychological control of an unsuspecting public one is immediately struck by the arrogance of these statements in the absence of demonstrable technology for implementation. On the other hand, such statements can represent a sort of naiveté regarding political power. However, as Vallance (1972) suggests, while we do not yet have the technology, one day we might, and now is the time to develop the appropriate values and ethical guidelines for its use. As Segall (1976) indicates, the type of large, widespread environmental controls dictated by this view of psychologist as policymaker and social engineer is undoubtedly not feasible. Although one cannot always be certain what a democratic society will bring, I have a somewhat difficult time imagining psychologists possessing and utilizing the type of political power bestowed upon them through scientific techniques of behavioral control. Far more likely in a society and science in which scientists "give away" their knowledge to the public (Miller 1969; Roberts 1974; Smith 1973; Vallance 1972), this technology of widespread behavioral control would most likely be usurped by those with existing power.[2]

Both the expert witness and social program evaluator roles essentially leave the policymaking decision process unchanged. There is no attempt to influence the process outside of objectively reporting on existing knowledge on the one hand and providing new evaluative data of relative merit on the other (Segall 1976). While these are the least threatening roles for social policy intervention, I would like to argue that psychology must take a much more activist stance with regard to social policymaking and thus intervention in the legislative process.

[2] A good example of this, on a limited basis, is the recent exposure of the C.I.A. and the LSD experiments.

Activist/Collaborator Model

> As psychologists, we have perhaps been overidealistic in depending for legislative success on the consumer advantage of our services, on social pertinence, and on the public interest—and above all, on our integrity as a profession and science, on the prevailing facts, the accuracy with which we address the issues, and logic. This parsimonious approach, while sound, is in the long run naive. Legislative success requires more than just being "good"; we have to learn the system and work with it. (Dörken 1977, p. 738)

If we as psychologists believe that the science has something to offer in terms of redressing societal ills and thus contributing to the positive mental health of the nation, then we should be willing to advocate solutions which are appropriate. Since, as I have argued, much of what passes for social policy is made in legislative decisions, we should then be willing to utilize legal methods and procedures for influencing legislation affecting psychology and human welfare. It is this active, interactive engagement in the political process which I suggest as an alternative role for psychology in the policymaking process. For want of a better term we can call this the activist/collaborator model. I believe that it is the activities of the Association for the Advancement of Psychology which provide a test of this model in the "natural" setting of Washington, D.C.

The structure that has evolved over the four years of the organization's existence is one which includes professional lobbyists, staff, and a policy board composed of psychologists representing professional, academic, and public-interest segments of the field. Day-to-day activities include the identification of relevant legislation; coordination of testimony and other influence attempts; the development of potential legislation; contact with the federal bureaucracy, including regulatory agencies; and other activities of a similar nature directed toward the interest of psychology and the interface with societal needs. I believe that this model has been demonstrated to work while upholding the ethical concerns of the profession and providing rudimentary procedures for achieving goals consistent with the public welfare.

CONCLUSION

Just as science generally is beginning to enter the public policy arena in advocate roles (Price 1978), psychologists, including academicians, must begin to assess their actual and potential contributions to the public welfare. If psychology truly believes that it can be of benefit, then why should it not advocate legislation that is in the public welfare as well as psychology's interest? The activist/collaborator role in the development of relevant social policy is seen as consistent with the view of psychology as a socially sensitive science/profession. The model maintains the ethical standards of conduct adhered to by all psychological scientists in the profession. No claims are made for psychology which cannot be shown to have scientific support and forms of "overpoliticalization" are avoided where possible (Price 1974). Problems with implementing this role of psychology can be traced to problems in the field more generally, many that have been discussed earlier. Among these are the science-profession schism, lack of clearly defined societal problem areas where psychology is relevant, and a lack of translation rules between the basic findings in the field and applied social technology (Miller 1970; Varela 1977).

Both changes in and the increased urgency of societal problems (Zuniga 1975), as well as the gradual melding of the scientific and applied aspects of psychology (Garner 1972), are contributing to the greater willingness to accept a more activist orientation for psychology. Such an orientation as represented in the activist/collaborator model demands that psychology assume public positions in areas involved either directly or indirectly as objects of scientific study. It implies that psychologists must take greater responsibility and be more in the public view. Not only am I advocating that we give psychology away, but that we also give psychologists away as well.

References

Albee, G. W. Does including psychotherapy in health insurance represent a subsidy to the rich from the poor? *American Psychologist*, 1977, *32*, 719–721.

Andrews, F.M. & Withey, S. B. *Social indicators of well-being in America: Americans' perceptions of life quality*. New York: Plenum Press, 1976.

Atkinson, R.C. Reflections on psychology's past and concerns about its future. *American Psychologist*, 1977, *32*, 205–210.

Bandura, A. Behavior theory and the models of man. *American Psychologist*, 1974, *29*, 859–869.

Beit-Hallahmi, B. Salvation and its vicissitudes: Clinical psychology and political values. *American Psychologist*, 1974, *29*, 124–129.

Bevan, W. The sound of the wind that's blowing. *American Psychologist*, 1976, *31*, 481–491.

Buss, A.R. The emerging field of the sociology of psychological knowledge. *American Psychologist*, 1975, *30*, 988–1002.

Campbell, D.T. Reform as experiments. *American Psychologist*, 1969, *24*, 409–428.

Campbell, D.T. On the conflicts between biological and social evolution and between psychology and moral tradition. *American Psychologist*, 1975, *30*, 1103–1126.

Campbell, A., Converse, P.E., & Rodgers, W.L. *The quality of American life: Perceptions, evaluations and satisfactions*. New York: Russell Sage, 1976.

Caplan, N. & Nelson, S.D. On being useful: The nature and consequences of psychological research on social problems. *American Psychologist*, 1973, *28*, 199–211.

Carter, L.F. Psychologists and federal legislation. In F.F. Korten, S.W. Cook, & J.I. Lacey (Eds.), *Psychology and the problems of society*. Washington, D. C.: American Psychological Association, 1970.

Cronbach, L. J. The two disciplines of scientific psychology. *American Psychologist*, 1957, *12*, 671–684.

Cummings, N.A. The anatomy of psychotherapy under national health insurance. *American Psychologist*, 1977, *32*, 711–718.

Dörken, H. Avenues to legislative success. *American Psychologist*, 1977, *32*, 738–745.

Fraser, D.M. Congress and the psychologist. In F.F. Korten, S.W. Cook, & J.I. Lacey (Eds.), *Psychology and the problems of society*. Washington, D. C.: American Psychological Association, 1970.

Freeman, H.E. & Sherwood, C.C. *Social research and social policy*. Englewood Cliffs, N.J.: Prentice-Hall, 1970.

Garner, W.R. The acquisition and application of knowledge: A symbiotic relation. *American Psychologist*, 1972, *27*, 941–946.

Gergen, K. J. Social psychology as history. *Journal of Personality and Social Psychology*, 1973, *26*, 309–320.

Goodwin, L. & Tu, J. The social psychological basis for public acceptance of the social security system: The role for social research in public policy formation. *American Psychologist*, 1975, *30*, 875–883.

Gross, B.M. *A great society*. New York: Basic Books, 1966.

Health, Education & Welfare. *Toward a social report.* Washington D.C.: H.E.W., 1969.

Horowitz, I.L. (Ed). *The use and abuse of social science.* New Brunswick, N.J.: Transaction Books, 1971.

Kramer, J.R. The social relevance of the psychologist. In F. F. Korten, S. W. Cook, & J.I. Lacey (Eds.), *Psychology and the problems of society.* Washington, D.C.: American Psychological Association, 1970.

Land, K.C. On the definition of social indicators. *American Sociologist,* 1971, *6,* 322–325.

Lasswell, H.D. Must science serve political power? *American Psychologist,* 1970, *25,* 117–123.

McElroy, W.D. The role of fundamental research in an advanced society. *American Scientist,* 1971, *59,* 294–297.

McKeachie, W.J. Psychology in America's bicentennial year. *American Psychologist,* 1976, *31,* 819–833.

Meehl, P.E. Second order relevance. *American Psychologist,* 1972, 932–940.

Miller, G.A. Psychology as a means of promoting human welfare. *American Psychologist,* 1969, *24,* 1063–1075.

Miller, G.A. Assessment of psychotechnology. *American Psychologist,* 1970, *25,* 991–1001.

Price, D.K. Money and influence: The links of science to public policy. *Daedalus,* 1974, *103,* 97–114.

Price, D.K. Endless frontier or bureaucratic morass? *Daedalus,* 1978, *107,* 75–92.

Rappoport, L. & Kren, G. What is a social issue? *American Psychologist,* 1975, *30,* 838–841.

Raush, H.L. Research, practice and accountability. *American Psychologist,* 1974, *29,* 678–681.

Rie, H.E. Psychology, mental health, and the public interest. *American Psychologist,* 1977, *32,* 1–4.

Roberts, M.J. On the nature and condition of social science. *Daedalus,* 1974, *103,* 47–64.

Rogers, W.L. & Marans, R. Toward an understanding of community satisfaction. In A.H. Hawley & V.P. Rock (Eds.), *Metropolitan America in contemporary perspective.* New York: Halsted Press, 1975.

Sarason, S.B. The nature of problem solving in social action. *American Psychologist,* 1978, *33,* 370–380.

Segall, M.H. *Human behavior and public policy: A political psychology.* New York: Pergamon Press, 1976.

Smith, B.M. Is psychology relevant to new priorities? *American Psychologist,* 1973, *28,* 463–471.

Tyler, L.A. Design for a hopeful psychology. *American Psychologist,* 1973, *28,* 1021–1029.

Vallance, T.R. Social science and social policy: Amoral methodology in a matrix of values. *American Psychologist,* 1972, *27,* 107–113.

Varela, J.A. Giving psychology away? *Contemporary Psychology,* 1977, *19,* 468–469.

Zuniga, B. The experimenting society and radical social reform: The role of the social scientist in Chile's unidad popular experiences. *American Psychologist,* 1975, *30,* 99–115.

General Discussion of Jackson's Paper

Miller: Thank you, James. That leaves us some time for discussion.
Williams: I have just one comment. I don't know whether Dick Atkinson really believes that, Jim. He might. But it would seem to me as the director of NSF that sure is what he ought to say. I think it would be very difficult for him to voice a different view and keep his job, just because of the nature of NSF, the way in which the Congress and certain senators look at it, etc. And it seems to me that if he does believe that, then I suppose he does have a certain amount of cognitive dissonance. But if he doesn't believe that, then it seems to me it might be a model for what psychologists might have to become more comfortable with, and that is a public posture, a private posture, and a professional posture . . .
Jackson: Let me respond . . .
Williams: . . . A little bit like deception.
Jackson: No, no. I have some problems with that. I really do believe that in some ways politics can be a more open process than the way in which we perceive it. I think psychologists for the most part—and I meant to say this, and let me say it a little stronger—have some very, very naive views about what the political process is all about. Either we tend to take the view that there's not much to it, or we tend to take the other view that there is more to it than there really is; that somehow some very, very involved kinds of machinations go on. And I think probably the truth is not in between any of those two points. It's something else altogether again.

But Atkinson, being in his position—I'm responding after you brought it up—probably should say nothing, whenever making the kinds of statements which are reported in a forum like the *American Psychologist* in 1977. Certainly people can point to that; they can point to the fact that you have an advocacy organization involved in doing exactly the kinds of things that are argued against by a noted psychologist who is involved in the National Science Foundation, and that's been known as *the* distributor of funds for basic science.
Bevan: You think that brought abuse against the AAP?

Jackson: No. I'm not saying that at all.
Bevan: Or could?
Jackson: Yes, it could. Everything is "could" here.
Bevan: I see.
Jackson: I'm just bringing out a point. But again, you know, if he didn't believe that, then I think it's best not to say anything at all.
Bevan: Let me add something to that. I don't know what Dick believes, but if we take the statement at face value and not necessarily in the context of a larger article—I can't remember those details—there are two things, at least two things, that suggest that he's not following his own rules. When he prepares a budget proposal to go to the White House each year he's in effect proposing certain policies with regard to science for the next year in this country. Secondly, he's forgotten that there's an apparatus now created by law that provides for the scientific community to advise the government on matters of policy, and to advise the executive branch on matters of policy. This is the science advisor, which is now an official post created by the Congress, not any longer one which depends upon our stance with relation to the President. There's a science advisory group—that is, there is a science advisory committee—and there is a whole office—admittedly now a small one—that prepares for the science advisor recommendations on matters of science policy. And the science advisor isn't speaking as an individual, and when Atkinson presents his budget he's not speaking as an individual either. So . . .
Williams: I have no quarrel with that, but I guess I was raising another kind of question for professional psychologists, and that is: It seems to me there are many different worlds and/or universes in which we live and, for want of a better word, you can think about these—the political world, professional world—as sets with fuzzy boundaries. You never quite know where they end and begin, so we'll just call them fuzzy sets. But given that, in the center of them somewhere there might be things that one has to do, or things that one has to say, that are not completely compatible with the other sets . . .
Bevan: That's practical politics . . .
Williams: . . . And I think that sometimes we are a little bit harsh on our colleagues when we hear or see one of them doing that, when the necessities of that particular set are such that he or she has to behave that way . . .
Jackson: No, no. I don't . . .

Williams: Like Ralph Nader and his friend on the whole business of transportation.

Jackson: Now, I wasn't going to imply that. Obviously, in terms of practical politics, there are stances one has to take arising from one's position. This happens all the time in simpler politics, at departmental levels, state levels, other levels at which we do things . . . We say things in a public way, which is not representative of the kinds of behaviors which we have to be involved in.

But, I think though, in terms of our now initial thrust to get involved in advocacy, and many times I've said it before with regard to public welfare, this means getting involved in the legislative process. We have to be kind of careful in terms of what we say.

White: I'm in favor of psychology being relevant, but I think that we have to understand that as psychologists we pay a price for being relevant. I think it would be naive to assume that if psychologists used their weapons in the political arena—that is, put in facts which either are biased or seem in effect to weight an argument—that politicians won't strike back with their weapons. Now, in actual fact, if a group of people at the University of California make politically relevant statements, then Reagan almost by instinct would strike back at the University of California. What the scientists control at the University of California is the ability to manufacture facts that weight political arguments. What Reagan controlled was the budget of the University of California. So, in actual fact, you're going to get a system in which by natural reflexes politicians strike back at things that are hurting them.

Now, if a group of developmental psychologists regularly produced data saying that the family is declining, that the children are in effect deprived, and they need certain kinds of goods to have cognitive development—that is, generally speaking, data favoring something like a day-care bill—then right-wingers are not going to say these are a group of scientists pursuing their truth and it's too bad for us. They are going to say these are enemies, o.k., and let's go after them. And they are going to attack their credibility. They will, as a matter of fact, create institutes in which guys manufacture facts on their side, but they will also strike back at these people.

I think you cross into another world in which the weapons are different. It's naive to assume that you can sort of keep your above-the-fray position while being in that world. My guess is that Dick Atkinson has to spar with that all the time. He has to spar with the fact that relevant psychologists create enemies while doing perfectly valid things because that's the nature of the being . . .

Bevan: That's the nature of the process.

White: Yeah!

Bevan: At bedrock it's an adversary process. It's a matter of balancing, if you will, special interests—whether the scientist's special interest or not. And so it's not so much a question of how or what you advocate, but what your style is, what your strategy is, it would seem to me. And I think there are two very important roles that we've got to keep separate. One is the job of public education with regard to the roles of science, and the other is the advocacy role. I think it's extremely important that those two roles and the mechanisms for them be kept completely separated.

Jackson: That's one reason why . . .

Bevan: So, anyway, your credibility can be protected.

Jackson: Well, that's one reason why we've created an organization like AAP, which stands as an independent organization, separate from the American Psychological Association. Obviously it has ties to the American Psychological Association and it's an organization which is involved in advocacy. All right, it makes much less of a pretense with regard to taking some objective stance on a particular proposition. But as Professor Bevan says, this is the advocacy position we take. We believe that x, y, and z should be done, and if so, they have certain sorts of effects.

I guess I get a little concerned, and I guess because we're talking about society here. In the paper I was talking about the fact that we are now undergoing a severe crisis with regard to certain social problems, and these are not trivial problems we're talking about. When we start talking about unemployment rates of 30 and 40 percent in certain segments of our population, we're talking about the potential of having individuals who'll grow up never knowing and never having a job. The implications of this for society are absolutely incredible.

We find ourselves in a very, very difficult situation if we stand back talking about scientific objectivity, talking about how we have to be concerned about being perceived and being nonobjective in the face of certain sorts of potential problems. And I think that we have to start taking some chances. I think we have to start taking some chances about how we're going to be perceived. Now the problem we have, of course, is that we are so damn naive and so damn inexperienced that we get out there and are perceived as being a bunch of do-gooders, and cause a lot more damage than we would by perhaps staying out of it and staying back. There's one thing about this kind of detached, aloof sort of scientific orientation which we've found in the past that's of value—you certainly *can't* do any harm. You might not do any good, but people have a belief that they can't do any harm.

I've talked to a lot of colleagues who take this position, who do basic research, who say that their research may have something to do with social problems, but they could care less. And at the heart of what they have to say is this feeling that if I did try to get involved in social problems I might make things worse than what they are. I mean [they have] a sincere belief about that, not just with regard to what scientific values are, but a sincere belief that maybe they really don't have anything to say about some particular social problem. And you have to respect that to a certain extent.

Audience: James, it may well be true that if they got involved, they'd do more harm than good.

Jackson: That's exactly what I'm saying. I'm saying you have to respect that particular attitude. What I'm saying though, is that psychology as a field . . . that if we do think that we have anything at all to say about the solution to particular societal problems, particular societal ills, then we also have a duty, duties of a higher value, a higher moral stance, to say something about it. You know, to step back to say well, . . . you could do x, y, and z if you want to . . . See, I think that is a worse particular position than the other one in terms of being value free and objective.

Bevan: I don't think that James is saying that every psychologist or every scientist needs to be involved in the public process, but the other side of the coin is that not all of us should stay out of it. That is, there are some of us who are temperamentally or otherwise inclined in that direction and we should exercise those roles.

Koch: May I get a word in edgewise this time?

Jackson: This is the first time I've seen you ask for it.

Koch: I've asked constantly. My hackles begin to rise a little bit and, as an old and superannuated character, I begin to get very concerned when we make such large statements as psychology being a field which has to be involved. Now, I like the statement on which you ended better than almost every pre-

Jackson: ceding statement which is . . .
You don't like my preceding statements?
Koch: Which is that you feel that not only are we giving psychology away—and I feel, as you know, that we're giving psychology away all the time, though in a counterproductive way—but you feel we should give psycholo*gists* away. Now *that* distinction is very important. I've been much more happy about relevantly sensitive and specialized owners of insight into socially important problems making themselves available. I'm terribly afraid of the fact that psychology has been for decades issuing enormous promissory notes with respect to which even in principle, it *must* fall on its face, and of the growing tendency of our professional institutions to exacerbate this humorous state of affairs.

And I'd like to supplement that by saying that three of the speakers thus far have reveled in the circumstances that psychology should be, and is being, given away. We all agree on the *fact* of the "giving." Psychology, as I have emphasized, had massively accepted George Miller's invitation many decades before he made it. But it seems to me that rather strange illustrations have been used to show that psychology is being given away effectively and fruitfully. The quality of these illustrations is highly reminiscent of what is involved when two years after an operation a surgeon is going back in search of a few sponges, scalpels, and so on, that have been left inside . . .

Williams: And charges you for it.
Koch: . . . the operative field after it has been sewn up. Because Mr. Williams made it very clear that the testing industry—as he calls it—is going through agonizing and crisp soul-searching with respect to the misuses of testing and related matters, and we can clearly attribute these misuses to the entire testing technology having been madly oversold throughout the century. I know Mr. Williams agrees with me on this because we've already discussed the matter.

Mr. White made, I thought, a telling analysis of the counterproductiveness of physical science emulationism. Whether I would be happy about referring to the "Fledermaus (as I like to call Habermas') tradition" as human *science* I don't know. I think science becomes a rather strained metaphor in this connection, but believe our positions to be largely consonant. But when Mr. White gave illustrations of modest things—and it was nice that they were at least modest—that psychologists could do by way of social welfare, again the illustrations, I thought, were rather thin. The aggregative information that we've been giving about groups, in our efforts to translate the mythic beasts that paper-pushers deal with into something close to reality, has throughout the century consisted of rather crappy caricatures of the aggregates in question. I think that Mr. White would agree with that, though he perhaps feels that matters are *now* getting a bit better by virtue of sophisticated, cognitive-developmental people (highly sensitive, loving, and so on) getting into this act. But again a thin, thin set of illustrations.

Now, when we come to Mr. Jackson, he talks about the AAP which could, I suppose, conceivably have noble aims, but when he talks about the kinds of advocacy that AAP is mainly concerned with, I get the impression that these follow in the line of the name of the organization. The advocacy is in the interest of institutionalized American psychology, by and large. And that kind of advocacy is not necessarily in the interest of human welfare; in some circumstances, it may be inimical to human welfare.

Jackson: Let me respond to that because I try to respond to that [criticism] more generally. And it has to do with the examples. I could start off in some way: Psychology has been irresponsible. Now let me start—very, very bold statements—let me make these statements. And it's irresponsible for this reason: because it has purported to be able to deliver something. All right? It says it has something to say about societal ills. We may do it in a laboratory, it may look farfetched, it may look this, it may look that, but it really doesn't. If only someone can only translate that into something. We've done that before. "Selling 'wolf' tickets" we used to call this, and psychology's been very, very big on it.

What I'm proposing is very simple. Psychologists should have become more responsible for what they say and what they do. If we really do believe, for example, that as clinical psychologists our interventions have something to say about individual welfare, have something to say about group welfare, have something to say about making changes with regard to people's lives, such that it makes people's lives better . . . all right, then we should be willing to live, fight for, argue for, make it psychology. Putting psychology in a position where it can indeed deliver those kinds of services. If indeed we can, then we want to make psychology an independent provider under national health insurance, for example, and so on.

Now, I'm an academic psychologist, and I'm arguing this from that particular perspective, looking at what goes on in the more applied areas of psychology. I really do believe that's true. I also believe, though, there are other things which we can do. When you start talking about advocating for a consumer's bill to create a Department of Consumer Advocacy, to be concerned about that, I don't think that has much to do with lining the pockets of psychology. I think it has to do with some . . .

Koch: That's the sole example you gave which was not essentially a professional vested interest.

Jackson: Well, I'm sorry. I didn't want to get involved in giving a whole long list of titles of stuff and so on, because we are involved in a whole series of bills and so on, some which have very, very meaningful things to do with psychology, but things that don't either. My feeling about the board as we go along, as we mature as an organization—I didn't want to get in a position here of defending an organization . . .

Williams: So he defends it.

Jackson: Oh, what the hell!

[*laughter—personal exchange*]

Jackson: You [Williams] got into that yesterday; I guess I can get into that today. I really don't want to, but the point is that my feeling about an organization which goes along . . . If psychology really has something to do about societal ills, at some point in time we should have a board which includes individual citizens from among those people we're supposed to be serving. At this present time we don't.

Williams: What you need is a board of directors like ETS.

Jackson: What can I say?! What can I say?!

Williams: That's what I said.

Jackson: I know. The board of directors of APA has absolutely all psychologists on it. It can be viewed as self-serving. But psychologists are quick to point—particularly academic, scientific type of psychologists—are quick to point out when the more applied types of psychologists say that we want this, we want that. They point to them to say that's self-serving. When we talk to them about their arguments for making sure that we get enough training grants, making sure the NSF is giving plenty of money for doing basic research, making sure that NIMH is giving money for departments and stuff, so we can research—which Scriven talked about feeding at the trough yesterday—they don't talk about it being self-serving. It certainly *is* self-serving. I mean nobody else can deny that; in fact, it's even more self-serving in some ways than what some of the applied people are talking about, and they sincerely believe that the kinds of things they're doing make a contribution to human welfare.

Koch: There's a very, very subtle . . .

Bevan: There is a simple piece of advice to follow up what . . .

Jackson: Sorry about that.

Bevan: . . . you just said. If you all . . . If the AAP is completely overtaken by guild issues, come in and join it and get in on the public side.

Jackson: Yeah, that's true.

Miller: May I say to the people who are quietly listening to this debate, that it takes me back ten years. It's exactly the quality of discussion that I remember at the meetings of the board of directors of the APA when I was privy to those meetings. These are exactly the issues . . .

Koch: Don't you agree that certain ideas are good enough to be timeless?

Miller: I'm amazed that in spite of the intellectual progress we've made in the intervening ten years in small-p "psychology," the problems of capital-P "Psychology" are still where they were ten years ago, and the range of opinions are still what they were ten years ago . . .

Koch: And in that you give us honesty.

Miller: . . . and the alternatives available to us are still what they were ten years ago.

Williams: That's reassuring.

Miller: Some things never change.

Williams: Let me say this before Sheldon, if I may . . . There's one part, Jim, that I want to pick up on.

Jackson [to Miller]: He [meaning Koch] should be able to say something, too.

Koch: Yes, would I be allowed one sentence of reply?

Williams: Yes, but when I . . . But I want to come back to something on the objectivity thing. It seems to me that we might do that with some caution, that is, giving up the objectivity when jumping into social policy matters. And if I could use one example, just to remove it from the American scene. And because it's a little crass and so doesn't provoke too much emotion we'll do it this way.

Once I was asked to be a consultant in a Mideastern country in which they had just recently passed a law to make education through the sixth grade mandatory; about three years—oh, I forget how long—ago that law was passed. So they're having people come out of the sixth grade, but there was no place for them to go after the sixth grade. One of the things they observed was they were moving from the rural areas into the cities, and then you had people who knew how to read, and they watched TV, and they were breaking all kinds of social rules and taboos, and the prime minister and leaders of the country felt, now we have another political bombshell. We'll have a riot, revolts, and make the government unstable, so what can we do? They have a number of alternatives. Psychologists, or someone, might suggest—well, you could build another school to put them in for another three years.

Jackson: That's the American solution.

Williams: You could, depending on how you look at it; you could put them all in the army. Start making little military types. Every so often you could start a war with your neighbor and kill them off. But there are these kinds of alternatives available. If I were to . . .

Miller: Send them back to the farm, as they do in China.

Williams: Send them out to the farm, but I'd have to impose certain kinds of monitoring things to be sure they were kept there, etc.

Now part of the objectivity notion as it's usually talked about is that one at least momentarily says, whatever my preference might be—my preference might have been to build some more schools and send them through—it does seem to me that one has a bit of an obligation to identify the other alternatives that might be a reasonable set within this solution domain. And I suppose that's all that's meant in the objectivity claim.

I think this is a part of the discussion about the unemployment picture in the United States. For example, where one can say you have a certain percentage or segment of a population that's unemployed. You can argue that unless something constructive is done it might lead to some social destruction with riots and so on and so forth; or you might say it's a residual which is quiescent at the moment. I don't have to worry about that; but I'm going to worry about some other economic sorts of things, and so the hell with it. In effect that's like saying I don't worry about the moral (whatever) issues at this point. What I want to do is to propose to

Jackson: you some possible alternatives to solve a problem at hand. But that becomes a political decision. I mean once there's, well . . .

Williams: I agree.

Jackson: Yeah, but you know, it's not so much the issue of somebody usurping the . . . whatever the political process may be. Again its become a kind of BS arrogance. I was really surprised—we talked about this before—about going to Washington and finding out that people don't even know psychology exists. Psychology? What's that? Is that a psychiatrist? We jump up and get mad because they want to cut off some of our training money. We wind up talking to people to find out what's going on. They have no intentions of getting at us at all. They were trying to get at psychiatry.

Audience: [*General confusion, laughing, more than one person talking*]

Jackson: Here we are the tail of the dog. They're trying to get the dog so the tail goes, too, you know. We have an arrogance about us, an arrogance about our profession, as I agree most professions probably do. And somehow . . . But it's even worse—because somehow we think that we really *do* have something to say about societal problems. Deep down inside almost all of us—even the ones who don't get involved with those problems directly—believe that somehow the work I do on learning, the S-R stuff I do or whatever, has really got something to contribute if somebody would just connect it. And therefore there's a certain arrogance of belief that people should listen to us when we go . . . when we go sit down in a hearing and this person says, "Well, what do you think, Dr. Jackson, you should do about this particular problem?" And I say, "Well, my opinion as a scientist is that we need to do x, y, and z." I expect that person to listen to me. I expect that person to do something. That person is not even listening to what I'm saying, let alone in some ways doing something with it such that there's going to be implementation.

Our role in the Great Society programs . . . I sat here and I heard about our role as a field in the Great Society programs. Political decisions! When Johnson decided we're going to have a Great Society, it really had nothing to do with eradicating poverty . . . It had something to do with eradicating poverty as related to the public welfare in some ways, or it's somehow related to good psychological outcomes? . . . If you think that, then you're a lot more naive than I think. It was nothing but a political decision. Let's prop [up] this thing, let's do this, let's do that. It has nothing to do with psychology. I think we have to come to some recognition of that because then it allows us to plug into the system properly, to try to have some effects upon the public welfare, and to try to have some positive benefits for society. Because I really do believe that we do have something to say about it. What it is exactly, I'm not sure . . . I'm talking too long. That was one sentence!

Miller: Would you like to give another . . .

Jackson: I got one thing to say; I'll be back now or later.

White: Go on, I'm sorry.

Bevan: He wanted to say something . . .

Miller: He wanted another word in edgewise.

Bevan: Well, his turn was next, though.

White: I wanted to . . . I guess I'm back with what Sig said about these small things that psychologists have really offered. I make some assumptions about the political process. Charles de Gaulle once said, "I've lived a long life and I've never seen a single problem solved." I believe that. That is, I don't . . .

Bevan: I believe that, too.

White: . . . I don't believe that big problems get solved. They get pushed or moved or something. And that's what I think George is alluding to when he says he has a feeling he was there ten years ago and it sounds the same. I do feel also that I think it's a mistake to look at policy as a kind of unitary thing. People assume that because the government is made up of people that policy represents an opinion. They anthropomorphize the government. They assume because government is made out of people that there's someone, somewhere out there who thinks the government's opinion. They apostrophize him. They say, change your policy—"Love children," or "Pay more attention to schools," or "Think scientifically"—as though there's anyone to listen.

I've given you this picture of this huge bureaucratic niche system because I feel it's an immensely differentiated group of unique individuals with unique and very limited capabilities of action. Policy happens when these people shift around a little bit. So the question is how, and when, and where do they shift around? My guess would be that one way they shift around is when their perception of the obvious changes. It's funny. Most of us don't think that the obvious ever changes. We just assume that what we see is obvious, and what we are told is suspect, but—and we don't believe the obvious really changes—but I can recall in my history of dealing with the government some changing perceptions of the obvious.

Let me give you an example: Jencks' book on inequality. When Jencks wrote his book analyzing the role of education on inequality, I don't think the book was very persuasive, but it adopted some statistical approaches that were favored before the book and reduced then to a reductio ad absurdum. People had for years been saying that correlations between education and income proved that education was good and Jencks sort of ran that through harder than anyone else, and he said education won't fix income inequality, whether or not that's true.

Alice Rivlin—who's really one of the sharpest commentators in the business—said in her review of the book, "You know the book is idle and empty because no one in his right mind ever believed that education would fix social problems"! Now, the only problem with that story is that I was with Alice ten years before and Alice believed that education would fix social problems. Not only that, Moynihan, who now says no one would have ever believed that education would fix social problems, left the government and amidst sixty different job offers took a job in a school of education because, he said, "Education is where it's at"!

So you can actually trace in the history of people—who now say that it is obvious that education could not have that leverage—votes with their feet ten years before when it seemed obvious to them that education was where it's at. Now there are interesting aspects of that—why the perception of the obvious changes—but I think we have to ask how and where and why the obvious changes.

Bevan: Or how you're going to make it change.

White: Well, I think the obvious changes for people each and every time they get together with a psychologist who looks at things with them.

Bevan: A psychologist?

White: A psychologist. I believe in exactly the same thing. And if he stands beside them, I said at the very beginning of my talk that I think that whenever a psychologist works with someone else on a common problem, some psychology is given away. And I think what's given away in a sense is a different way of looking at things. And, by the way, some non-psychology is given away. That is, psychologists become policymakers . . . Something like that.

Bevan: There's an intermediary process, it seems, that none of us have talked about and maybe we will later on. When we give psychology away or when we engage in intervention of one sort or another, we jump typically directly from research into application. On the physical side, you don't see that happen. We have left out the D in the R and D. When a weapon system is developed, there's a very long elaborate program of empirical testing and changing, empirical testing and changing, before the thing is put [totally] into effect. But we make a decision based on very approximate understandings and then go right to work for a full-blown program . . .

White: Sure.

Bevan: . . . And it falls on its face.

White: Well, of course the labs and centers in education were an attempt to create a "D." There are some interesting questions about whether you can create a "D," whether you can take something that's here, put and package it and test it in field tests and then sort of send it off through a delivery system. The whole question of whether you can make education into a thing that can be boxed and mass-produced and delivered is a very interesting question.

Jackson: This is the problem with that, though. I'll try to say this again. I guess I wasn't clear at all. Things that affect people, you know, oftentimes are large social programs. You can sit back with academic discussions about what good is that and how's that going to affect this and do that. But these things do impact upon people. I mean, the War on Poverty impacted upon people. It had effects. A bill designed to change educational things is going to have an effect upon the people. Bills designed for full employment, for example, versus not full, are going to have effects upon people. It's going to change somebody's life out there.

Williams: Well, I understood the question was whether it would have the intended effect? There's no doubt that there would be effects.

White: And why can't we find those effects?

Audience: Panel member (unidentified): Could you take something from out here for a second? You guys have been lying back. That's why we're doing this up here.

Audience: Something that Bel said about something that Shep was saying cues me to think about another kind of problem. And that is what happens when you give some psychology away and get committed to what you've given, and it turns out to be something other than what you thought? And we don't only find this problem in our lives of giving away psychology on the application side. We obviously get that commitment in everything we do—to a theory that we're hanging too long onto or something of that sort. But I was reminded of the problem when Bel gave the example in the Middle East. Then one of the alternatives he didn't suggest was we'd take away that sixth grade education. That may not be the idea, it may not be a good point, but essentially I'm saying this: We give something away. It's not working like we thought and instead of examining that, we tinker with it and want to give some more away, instead of taking a look where that's going . . . whether we should take back perhaps what's already there. I don't think I've heard that kind of a problem addressed, but how do we avoid that trap of an overcommitment . . .

Koch: Well, I would think that . . .

Audience: . . . to what we're giving may not be all so valuable after the fact.

Koch: Can I get in edgewise here because . . . I would think that, for instance, Mr. Williams' talk was addressed at precisely that kind of a problem—of in a way taking back part of what we've given away. And, by implication, many of the problems that your group [*gesturing to Jackson*] was addressing have exactly that force. But I would simply like, as a reprise, to say that there is a very important, if difficult to maintain, distinction which I would recommend very strongly and hopefully to your [Jackson's] group. On the one hand, one can image psychology in its relationship to public welfare as a repository—a scientific repository—of *information* into which at any given time you can reach to answer questions. This is closely wrapped up with the issue of delivering promissory notes that you know, in principle, you're not going to be able to take care of. On the other hand, if an organization like AAP seeks to facilitate putting not any psychologist, but the right psychologist, into contact with the right governmental or social problem, that is another thing. An organization which in effect is saying, "Well, this is what psychology is about and we have the answers, etc., etc.," is dreadfully unhappy in its effects. I know that that's a hard line to adhere to.

Jackson: See, again you hear this notion somehow that because you

Williams: enter a political process in some ways that somehow you give up some ethical . . .
He didn't say that.
Jackson: No, he didn't say that at all. I know exactly what you're saying, though—that it's unethical for us, no, for your own particular group to say you know that we indeed can deliver x, y, and z or can do x, y, z, when we don't know that to be the case; as a matter of fact, in a case where we know that *not* to be the case.
Williams: I was wondering whether you are arguing the stronger thesis and whether Shep was too, is that it might be impossible in principle. He raised that concern . . .
Jackson: That's what I was talking about.
Williams: . . . that it's impossible in principle to do it. I would really like to hear a bit of an elaboration on this especially when he gets to the things like the R and D centers, which was to be a vehicle through which you would begin to disseminate certain sorts of things out there in the real world.
White: Well, I think the R and D centers are a radical example of physics envy, to be quite honest about it. So let me . . . There's an interesting thing about this giving psychology away that I don't think we've talked about. You mentioned that they don't really know who psychologists are out there. Many people speak to the government in the name of psychology, and they have very mixed legitimacy and knowledge. You can't assume that the transmission of knowledge into practice is a very hi-fi process in which everyone who speaks either has a very good sense of what the data are, or of what they mean. You have to imagine a very loose process in which some of our colleagues—licensed, legitimate, good scientists—have a very dim notion of what to say on the basis of their warrant. And there's no way to censor this process.

An awful lot of stuff comes in that in my mind is noise, and that stuff is treated by and large on a par with the stuff that I would not call noise. And I don't know of any rules to correct this short of a fascistic, outrageous system for squelching what I would call wrong. I mean you just have to assume that you're one among many and the truth will win in the long run. But I think you have to recognize that the testimony in Washington includes people who tell congressmen that all kids should crawl on the floor in order to increase their brain size and their reading processes. It's a very funny process. Now, in general, Steven Leacock once announced the principle . . . I'll finish . . . that a half-truth . . .
Koch: The man is white [meaning Miller looks hungry].

Miller: I'm sorry Shep. I just want to get a little lunch in edgewise.

White: I'm not finished. He once said that a half-truth is like a half brick . . . it carries further. In actual fact, splashier claims, less solid claims really make much more splash in Washington than legitimate guys who come in and mumble something and say more research is needed. So in actual fact there is a balancing process by which the flamboyant stuff really travels further, gets heard better, and gets dealt with more than the less flamboyant stuff. And what that means is that as you go through this funny process—I think about it as a very slow evolutionary process—all steps forward are marked by, in effect, ridiculous claims by people overselling by a mile.

Koch: Don't be surprised when that little old lady who believes in the sun spots turns up as the chairman of your department . . .

Question and Answer: Miller and Jackson*

Miller: Dr. Jackson, you raised a number of fascinating issues. I should say—as you are well aware, but I'll put it on the

*Composed from exchanges occurring at the end of the second day as Miller analyzed each paper and redirected a question to each member of the symposium.

record—that I would prefer a non-legislative approach, that the sort of issues that you were discussing were just the kind that I felt had totally deadlocked the APA at the time. We were unable to get off and go. The vectorial resultant of all that discussion was just to sit on our broad back porch and do nothing.

So, one of the reasons that I tried to point out that psychology does change society in other ways than by activistic interventions was because I didn't see how to get us going. Now, with the AAP—Association for the Advancement of Psychology—I think we have an organization that can take some of that responsibility off of the APA which, in addition to advocacy, has a number of other important roles to serve. I think things are much better now than they were ten years ago.

I agree that legislation has been the major weapon used in our attempts, in the United States certainly, to solve social problems. It follows from that that if psychology is going to contribute to this attempt to solve social problems, psychology must contribute to the legislative process. And I also agree that familiarity with practical problems can often serve to focus and improve so-called basic research in psychology. But I too often found that the effectiveness of my own attempts to contribute to social policy had no correlation with the validity of the psychological dogmas that I was using at the time, but depended on my good luck in making connection with a politician who wanted to do what I wanted to advise him to do and who won the political battles.

So, the question is, What are your recommendations for having *real* influence, not merely serving as pawns in the political chess game? Not being asked to put the scholarly footnotes on the *Brown* decision, for instance, but actually get in and do something that makes the *Brown* decision go one way or another. Whichever way we feel it should have gone, on any piece of legislation. You know them better than I do now, certainly. If Senator X is in favor of this, he'll listen to you if you're in favor of it, too, and he'll maybe use your arguments to document his case. But the decisions aren't being made at that level. I don't see how at that point we can work without having laid the kind of general educational sympathy to our argument that I was arguing for in '69. But I'd like to draw you out on that, and I'm sure you're well prepared to do it.

Jackson: Let me move us away a little bit from . . . the kind of academic discussion which we can get into and try to respond to the question which Dr. Miller presented to me. The question he asked—one of the questions he put—was how can we avoid being pawns to powerful politicians? I guess there's a glib answer to that. If they do what we want them to do about a certain particular social policy, then what difference does it make? That's the glib answer.

The other answer is that I think we sometimes forget that politicians tend to have multiple motivations in terms of the things they do. While it may be true that Kennedy proposes a national health insurance because he believes that everyone in the society should have at least a guarantee to good health, it also doesn't hurt Kennedy's chances of getting re-elected. It indeed puts him into the public arena, and that's something that politicians like. They like the limelight. So they do indeed have multiple motivations as well.

I would think that what's of value—and I guess perhaps I tend to be very hopeful—is that we do play a kind of an educational role. I wasn't trying to play down this educational role when we indeed try to affect social policy. It's not so much that we're pushing a particular political orientation for ourselves as psychology, but instead that, based upon our psychology, we have a vision or view of what's good for society or some segments of society, or some large group in society. Our role as advocates is trying to persuade those who are responsible for developing and implementing social policy that this indeed is a reasonable perspective to have. And hopefully based upon, you know, the scientific evidence we have as psychologists.

So, I guess when I talked about advocacy, when I talked about dealing with and conversing with politicians and those people who implement social policy, I guess I'm talking about acting as an agent of the public. I see us giving psychology away by advocating certain sorts of legislation which we hope, in our vision, will have a certain sort of impact upon some particular social problem, some particular sort of societal ill which psychology is uniquely suited to make some statements about. And I did mention before that we can't make statements about everything. But there are certain sorts of societal problems I think that we are uniquely suited to make statements about. And when we can do that, I see no reason why we should not be willing to take the responsibility to stand in front of the public and say that we advocate this as a field because we think it's very, very important in redressing some particular societal ill. And that's a greater responsibility than we've been willing to take in the past, and I think it's something we should take. Is that a response to your question?

Miller: What you said would be very hard for me to disagree with . . .

Jackson: I wouldn't want you to.

Miller: . . . that we should voice our beliefs when we're given a chance. But the situation I see is that the politician has already made up his mind before you get to him. And all he wants you for—not you . . .

Jackson: No, no.

Miller: . . . *us*. All he wants us for is just to dress up his argument, and if he had made the opposite decision he would appeal to another group who would dress up the other side of the argument, you know. I want to know how we get in at the time he's making up his mind to put in a national health policy—or not to—and do something that really affects the course of things and doesn't just simply endorse what they're going to do anyway.

Jackson: Well, I know exactly what you mean. What Bill was talking about before . . . There's a whole host of attitude change, I think, that needs to take place with regard to psychology. When we start talking about giving psychology away we can talk about training the kind of people that Bill mentioned as involved with politicians by being in their offices. Social policy is oftentimes formulated at that particular level with congressional aids. Part of their role and their job is to think about those kinds of things a particular congressman ought to be involved with. Oftentimes the contacts that we make in Washington have nothing to do with the congressman. We never even see him and have no contact with him whatsoever. When we're dealing with Kennedy on national health insurance we rarely talk to Kennedy, although it happens every once in a while. The majority of the time we're talking to aides who in turn talk to the representative. If, indeed, we're able to place people who do have some understanding of science in these particular positions, I think we can start some kinds of meaningful dialogues on the kind of legislation that should be introduced. Well, often we're really starting late. One part of our task arises from the fact that there's a lot of legislation already on the books that affects society, and we have to be concerned about that. The other side of the coin, of course, is the matter of developing new legislation. And I think this can be done in the way I'm talking about.

Bevan: I would jump in, James, and George, at the risk of offending you. I think it's rather cynical to say that congressmen or politicians only want you to exploit you. I think as you get to know them you find that many of them have a deep sense of public commitment and are troubled by issues long before they ever promote them as legislation. And I know during the period of five or six years that I was involved with the Brookings Seminars for members of Congress where we weren't dealing with legislation immediately on the docket, but with issues that were going to come up, there was a deep—and, I think, genuine—concern to know more and to ask increasingly the right kinds of questions with regard to science-related policy issues.

Jackson: Yeah. Shep, I think, mentioned . . .

Bevan: When you get to know them, and they learn to trust you, then I think you . . .

Miller: Well, I've been on a lot of advisory committees, and I developed the Law of Seven. It was called Miller's Law of Seven, and it was that if seven committees in a row on a particular topic all recommended the same—yeah, plus or minus two!—if they all recommended the same thing, then somebody would do something about it. But then I did get cynical. You're absolutely right. I got tired of sitting on that many committees. It seemed to me that we had to say it often enough until eventually some politician saw it in his own self-interest to say, "Oh yeah, I wanted to do that anyhow so I'll make the recommendations of your committee." And if that worked out to be seven, you were lucky.

Audience: George, why haven't you observed that our symposium this year involves seven visitors?

White: Something medieval about this, George.

Miller: Minus one.

White: With an error. With an error.

Academic Science and the Federal Government

Miller's Introduction of Bevan

Our final speaker for this symposium if Professor William Bevan from Duke University. I knew Bill when we were both experimental psychologists. He's not only a fine experimental psychologist, he is a skilled administrator, a man who makes the right administrative moves by instinct, and that skill has gotten him into all kinds of trouble: departmental chairmanships, deanships, vice-presidencies, provostships, and even for four years executive officer of the AAAS. In the course of all that he spent considerable time in Washington preparing himself for what he's going to tell us today about "Academic Science and the Federal Government: Less Wed, More Locked." Professor Bevan . . .

Bevan's Opening Statement

Bevan: Thank you, George. As I take my turn at the podium I'm moved to say that I've known Sig Koch for thirty-six years I guess, and this is the first time I've ever been on a panel with him. I dare to hope now that I've come of age.

Koch: It's only an indication of the fact that I'm a failure, and you're a success.

Bevan: I remember an afternoon in the late fall of 1943, his leading a frightened 18-year-old through the litany of the oral preliminary examination—with incredible patience and kindness. I think if he can be accused of anything on that occasion it was bad judgment. Had he been less kind you all would have been spared this last hour and few minutes on these hard seats.

When Rick Kasschau wrote me inviting me to join this symposium and to speak to George's proposal that we give psychology away, I demurred. I guess I should say I copped out for a couple of reasons. While I recognize a strong Boy Scout streak in my constitution, with its attendant compulsion to do a good deed daily and to always think well of the future, I have in the decade since George issued his call become increasingly apprehensive about the matter of giving psychology away and particularly the proposition as Frank defined it yesterday. If we are indeed mindful of the public good, how much of which "psychology" should we then be giving away? I'm not prepared to say that it shouldn't be given away, but I do believe we must use greater discretion than we have sometimes in the past in deciding what we shall give, sell, or otherwise dispense to an unsuspecting public.

But I demurred for another reason. When I took note of the high-altitude intellectuals scheduled for the present bombing mission I concluded that a low-level mission on my part would add little to the total effect. Thus I decided to head off on a somewhat different vector. Instead of talking about psychology, I would direct my attention to the broader scientific community and at a matter that I think too few of us give attention to, namely understanding of the nature of our relationship with the federal government.

So that you might know what lies ahead of you I should say that I completed these remarks about ten days ago and decided to try them out on another university audience. When I completed my presentation, someone who I later learned was a professor of history got up and remarked that he detected a certain ambivalence in what I'd said, and I allowed that he was very perceptive, that I did feel some ambivalence about some of the things that I was talking about. He then said that I sounded like a young Barry Goldwater. This one caught me a little bit off guard. I had to admit that I had gotten more conservative as I got older, but hadn't realized that I had overshot the mark.

To complicate the matter further someone *sotto voce* observed that I really sounded like a repentant, middle-aged Communist. Now that one left me without any reply at all. The best I can do now after ten days is to absolutely declare that I didn't get to where I am through either route, and I won't bore you with how I did get there.

Academic Science and the Federal Government
Less Wed, More Locked?*

William Bevan
Duke University

The motivation for this essay originated in a conversation with a distinguished colleague in psychology some fifteen or sixteen years ago. The occasion was a site visit in connection with a request for a rather large grant, and I felt obligated to inquire about what importance his university placed on the proposed program and what it would do if funding were either not forthcoming or were to be cut back or terminated at a later date. His response was that my concerns need not be taken seriously nor were they particularly meaningful because his university was in fact a *federal* university and its priorities were set by the emerging national character of American science. But, I asked, wasn't he apprehensive that government functionaries, either as a matter of administrative mechanics, programmatic whimsey, or political necessity, might, willfully or otherwise, come to shape the academic character of his institution? "Oh," he replied, "that could never happen here." But, in fact, it has happened here. A whole host of events have indeed taken place, with scarcely any notice on the part of most members of the scientific community, that bids fair to have an utterly profound effect upon the future of science not only as an intellectual enterprise but—more fundamentally—upon science as an insti-

*This essay has evolved from themes presented in a series of talks during the course of the past year: in a symposium on public policy for children at the San Francisco APA meetings; at a symposium at the Albuquerque meeting of the National Conference on the Advancement of Research; as a public address at the College of Charleston, South Carolina; as the President's Invitational Address at the New Orleans meeting of the Southwestern Psychological Association; and as part of the Houston Symposium on Psychology and Society. I am grateful to Professors Norman Garmezy, Robert Gordon, and Henry Riecken for comments on an earlier draft. Obviously, some of this material will be less current upon publication.

tution of society as well. In not quite four decades American science, when viewed from the perspective of the individual practitioner, has become thoroughly professionalized. More than this, when it is viewed as a social entity, it is seen to have joined the long list of public-private complexes that have evolved as instruments of government purpose. We've come a long way, baby, as the current cigarette ads say, and the workaday scientist who still harbors the romantic myth that he rides forth alone each day to wrest knowledge from a recalcitrant Nature under the sponsorship of an admiring patron, cannot, if he understands what has really happened, be sanguine about the future outlook for his kind of scientific world.

For most of us the symptoms of change began to surface as a series of discordant themes after FY 1967, the peak year for the public support of science as we thought we knew and understood it: increasingly vocal protests, some from inside the scientific community itself, that science and technology were harmful; increasingly outspoken aversion for the perspective of conventional rationality on the part of certain philosophers and other humanists—the "New Dionysians," as Gerald Holton (1974) has recently called them; increasingly frequent challenges to the tradition of preemption in deciding issues of a scientific or technical nature; dramatic, if infrequent, reports of the falsification of research data; increasing impatience on the part of public officials for the philosophy that placed basic research at the cornerstone of the scientific edifice; the presidential science advisory apparatus being turned out of the White House; indications that scientific facilities are in disrepair and equipment obsolete; and, of course, less and less of the wherewithal to do the more-and-more of what we believe needs doing. After a decade of anxiety, the overall result within the community of academic science is a palpable sense of confusion and loss—loss of confidence, loss of direction, loss of purpose. A kind of numbing stasis has begun to set in. In 1967 our self-image was one of independence and of confidence about the importance and the rightness of what we were doing; in 1978 we are acutely conscious that we are, more often than not, a supplicant and a ward of the state. Steven Muller describes the situation between academic science and the federal government succinctly: "On the campus yesterday's partner now appears increasingly as today's oppressor, indispensable but stingy, and ever more intrusive" (1978, p. 33).

It would be both foolish and unfair of me to imply that all of the things that trouble us stem directly from the changed relationship of academic science to the federal establishment. Some among our problems are a reflection of the general condition of the times, others the result of our own improvidence during that earlier, easier era. However, if we are to achieve a more acceptable trade-off of costs and benefits than we now enjoy, it is essential that we understand more clearly than we now do how we have arrived at our present state of affairs and what the nature of our problems is. Let me quickly outline for you some of the more serious.

ACADEMIC SCIENCE IN THE LATE SEVENTIES, OR LIFE ON A SHRINKING RAFT

There are, I believe, four problems that overshadow all others in the seriousness of their implications for science in the American university of the future. The first two deal with the material welfare of science, the others with something more fundamental and significant. These are (1) the place of basic research in national science policy, (2) the question of technical obsolescence in the pursuit of basic science, (3) the problem of the renewal of human capital in the scientific enterprise, and (4) the changing role of professionals in the formulation of regulatory policy.

A New Deal for Basic Research?

With the presentation to President Truman of Vannevar Bush's recommendations (1945) on the role of government in post World War II science and the subsequent establishment of the National Science Foundation, the federal government undertook a formal commitment to support basic research. Pursuant of that commitment, the United States emerged over the next two decades as the world's undisputed world scientific leader. Basic research, of course, has always been the cornerstone of university science programs, and universities between the late forties and middle sixties prospered materially to an unprecedented extent with the aid of government grants and contracts. (Approximately 75 percent of all basic research done in this country is now done in universities.) Research funds were augmented eventually by training funds to facilitate the education of the next generation of researchers, and training funds in turn were followed by funds to improve the general understanding of science at all educational levels. Indeed, in all areas of basic science, but especially in fields like high energy physics where costs are extremely high, widespread participation by universities has been possible only because of generous government funding.

As a matter of convenience throughout this essay I shall from time to time make specific reference to the fortunes of the National Science Foundation, since the Foundation is probably the most reliable barometer that we have of the state of the relationship at any given moment between academic science and the federal government. The annual budget of the National Science Foundation has grown impressively over the past seventeen years from $500,000 in FY 1952 to what we may now anticipate with reasonable confidence will be close to a billion dollars for FY 1979. Despite this fact the fortunes of basic research, viewed in long-range relative terms, have not been overwhelmingly impressive. For example, in the last decade funds for basic research have been of the order of 0.15 percent of the Gross National Product and in fact until the last year or two had steadily declined in both relative and real terms. During the 1970s the proportion of R & D expenditures devoted to basic research has declined from 14 to 12 percent (National Science Foundation 1978). As Shapley, Phillips, and Roback indicate in their analysis of the FY 1978 R & D budget, funds for basic research, expressed in 1972 constant dollars, dropped almost 21 percent between 1967 and 1975. Only with this year's White House budget request, and only if it should survive the Congress intact, can they return to where they were twelve years ago (Shapley & Phillips 1978).

President Ford during his years in the executive branch consistently displayed a friendly interest in science, and during his brief administration he took special steps to improve the funding climate for basic research. President Carter has continued that lead. On August 15, 1977, Mr. Bert Lance, then director of OMB, sent a memorandum to all cabinet officers whose departments either conduct or support R & D, directing them to give attention to the funding of basic research as they prepared their budget requests. Subsequently, President Carter spoke in the most positive and direct terms about the importance of basic research to the nation when he made the National Medal of Science Awards in November 1977, again in his State of the Union message in January 1978, and still again in a June letter to all members of congressional committees that oversee basic research funding, appealing to them not to cut his recommended level of support.

The growth rate in R & D funding between FY 1976 and FY 1978 averaged a little over 11 percent. With an inflation level of 6 percent, this has meant actual growth in the support of basic science of about 5 percent. Based on the same assumed level of inflation, the proposed real increase for FY 1979 would again be approximately 5 percent, with the largest increases to occur in HEW, DOD, NASA, and EPA funding. Meanwhile, for the Biological, Behavioral and Social Science Directorate of NSF and the research directorates of ADAMHA, the sponsors to whom psychologists turn most frequently for research support, the requested increases would be 11 and 25 percent, respectively. (At the time of this writing, June 1978, an 8 percent assumed level of inflation appears more realistic. If it persists, real overall growth for FY 1979 would at best be 3 percent.)

For those who are interested in more detailed information on the administration's current budget request, particularly as it relates to those agencies of greatest interest to psychologists, the data are as follows: Overall, the proposals for basic research include about 300 million new dollars or, when expressed in 1972 constant dollars, about 100 million dollars of real growth. For NIH the overall increase requested is one of 69 million dollars (3 percent) with the only substantial proportional increase (20 percent) going to the National Institute of Child Health and Human Development. The ADAMHA request is for an overall increase of 40 million dollars, with NIMH's proposed increase of 23 million dollars representing a proportional increase of 21 percent. An additional 12 million dollars (35 percent more) has been included for the Drug Abuse Institute and 5 million dollars (31 percent more) for the National Institute of Alcoholism and Alcohol Abuse. Furthermore, initially proposed severe cuts in training funds for NIMH were restored, largely as a result of Mrs. Carter's reported personal intervention following the work of the President's Commission on Mental Health.

The administration proposed an overall increase of about 9 percent for NSF, an amount which would take the budget for FY 1979 to 941 million dollars. Among the largest proportional increases would be those provided for the social sciences (5.4 million dollars or almost 23 percent, for the behavioral and neural sciences (4.8 million dollars or 17 percent), and for research in science education (3.5 million dollars or approximately 43 percent). The budget of the new Directorate of Applied Science and Research Applications, about a fourth of whose projected program will be in the behavioral and social sciences, would be increased by 16 million dollars or about 27 percent. The proposed increase for the National Institute of Education is 10 million dollars or 11 percent.

One curious twist in the FY 1979 budget proposal that reveals how the attitude of the current White House bureaucracy feels toward support for basic science may be found in a decision on institutional grants for research. Forty-one million dollars has been included this year for the NIH Biomedical Research Support Grant Program, the first time in six years that the Office of Management and Budget has allowed such funding through the gate. These formula grants are prized by university administrations because they make possible a little flexibility in local research management—funds to help young, unestablished investigators, funds to take care of unanticipated equipment needs, and funds to help tide over established investigators for a short time between grants. The view of OMB during the Nixon and Ford years had been that these grants were local slush funds used for functions that universities could and should pay for out of their own resources. But lest the reader think there has been a wholesale conversion of OMB, it should also be noted that a similar but smaller-scale program (4.5 vs. 40 million dollars) at NSF, the Basic Research Stability Program has been canceled this year, one year after it was initiated, on the grounds that such a program would give a regional emphasis to the image of basic research support. The BRSP funds, if appropriated, will be used instead to fund cooperative university-industry research proposals.

Other agencies where behavioral scientists received favorable consideration in the planning of basic research support are the Department of Agriculture, the Department of Defense, and the New Department of Energy. In the latter case, a major matter for immediate emphasis is energy conservation, and while there are, as far as I know, no formal provisions for funding energy-related social and behavioral science research, it is clear that there is a genuine awareness on the part of the new Office of Energy Research that behavioral and social science are relevant to its mission.

If the Carter initiatives on behalf of basic research were a springtime source of joy in the camp of science, that joy could only be short-lived, for the House Appropriations Committee, sustained by the entire House, by late spring had essentially gutted the whole proposed program. Research at NSF was cut 44 million dollars, leaving the Foundation's resources about 3 percent ahead of FY 1978, an amount not even enough to meet inflation. Cuts in basic research totaled approximately 25 million dollars, with a 5.4 percent cut expressly targeted for social science. The remaining 19 million dollars came from the request of the new Applied Science and Research Applications Directorate, which has, as I have noted, a strong commitment to behavioral and social science. ADAMHA, where the final numbers reached an additional 75 million dollars, lost 10. In addition, the newly established competitive grants program of the Department of Agriculture was completely wiped out, the Department of Defense lost funds from its newly established Defense Science and Engineering Program, designed to support basic university science, and the Basic Energy Science Program of the Office of Energy Research suffered significant cuts. The only good news lies with NIH where the committee added 268 million dollars, with General Medical Sciences, the basic research arm of NIH, receiving 40 million. The Senate has yet to complete its work and it traditionally has been more generous with science than is the House. However, indications are that the ultimate levels that will come out of House-Senate conference negotiations will fall far short of the President's proposals for basic science (Smith 1978). Certainly, the most widely accepted version of the House action is that it is a reflection of its long-standing doubts about the value of basic research (cf. e.g., Roark 1978b). Instead of FY 1979 becoming basic science's best year in twelve, it could in fact represent a setback of several years. Furthermore, what we fail to achieve in FY 1979 we most likely will not achieve in FY 1980. W. Bowman Cutter (1978), executive associate director for the Budget of OMB, informed a recent conference on R & D policy that the fiscal 1980 budget will most likely turn out to be the tightest in a decade. This at a time when what basic science needs most of all from its federal partner, a policy that recognizes the inevitably slow and highly unpredictable unfolding of scientific knowledge with a commitment to stable long-range funding, remains as elusive as ever.

Why the largest number of our scientific colleagues persist in the Cartesian view of scientific patronage remains a fascinating mystery, for the support of science in this country, freely given or otherwise, has seldom if ever been motivated by a belief in the intrinsic value of knowledge for its own sake.

As Derek Price (1977) points out, there traditionally have been two conflicting views among scientists as concerns the justification of the public support of basic research: On the one hand, basic research is perceived to be a *consumption good* with direct value in the manner of the creative arts. On the other, it is seen as an *investment good* valued for its contribution to the economy or to the solution of some societal problem. Scientists have always insisted—or at least insinuated—the former; society has always bought the latter. And even with a benign administration, this circumstance has not changed. President Carter in his public testimonials for science has in every instance made reference to the importance of science for the nation's economic well-being and the solution of its pressing national problems. Similar arguments were heard from OMB (Cutter 1977) and from the Council of Economic Advisors (Nordhaus 1977) in their support of the FY 1978 science budget. What is only now beginning to surface is the conviction, emerging first in the scientific and technological communities and later spreading into government, that the quality of American science is not as good as it once was and needs to be, and that American technology is no longer an innovative technology (see Shapley & Phillips 1978). How this impression has come about and what will be done about it remains to be seen. Certainly money by itself can provide few cures. But whether or not we are about to enter a period of more enlightened mutual understanding in the science-government partnership must first of all depend to some certain degree upon scientists being capable of honest self-scrutiny, upon their ability to make better use of new resources, and upon their *firm* insistence that the partnership be a partnership of equals.

Impediment to the Future of Research: Obsolete Equipment and Deteriorating Facilities

Academic scientists have been increasingly aware that their options for research have become increasingly constrained by obsolete equipment and deteriorating facilities. This state of affairs is the result, among other things, of a curious form of benign neglect. As the attitude of the federal government hardened against university research, money became tight, and overhead levels went up, it was easiest for university investigators to opt for salary funds, for stipends for students, and for money for expendable materials and to gamble on the future for equipment. Similarly, when facilities grants were available, institutions scraped together their matching monies and gambled on finding the maintenance dollars later. The current physical state of science can easily be gauged from Shapley, Phillips, and Roback's discussion of the FY 1978 budget (1977). These authors report that between FY 1972 and FY 1976 overall funding for facilities remained constant at 600 million dollars a year with a 200 million dollar increase included between FY 1976 and FY 1978. However, an examination of this funding on an agency-by-agency basis makes clear immediately the fact that most of the facilities appropriations were for the support of large development projects with the recent increase going to meet the needs of one agency, the then Energy Research and Development Administration. In fact, NSF received considerably fewer facilities dollars in FY 1977 and 1978 than it had received in FY 1976.

Troubled by what it inevitably knew must be the unhappy physical state of American science, the Foundation several years ago proposed a firsthand review by disinterested parties. Such a study was carried out for the Foundation by two political scientists, Bruce Smith and Joseph Karlesky (1977). It took some eighteen months to complete and involved visits to thirty-six universities and extensive interviews with approximately 600 working scientists and 180 administrative officers. Their findings in the matter of instrumentation and facilities are clear. Physical resources of all sorts are indeed in short supply; equipment is indeed worn and in many cases obsolete; facilities are indeed in various stages of disrepair. The Smith and Karlesky report represents, as George Bonham (1977) noted when it appeared last summer, an advance sensor of what ails basic science in this country. More often than not science has passed on to a new generation of research technology and the universities by and large have been left behind. The report has been widely cited by editorial writers, by members of Congress, and, of course, by members of the scientific community. The White House took clear note of it, and its conclusions became the background for the President's budget message concerning basic research. At the same time, the White House made no special provison for equipment or academic facilities in the budget document itself, on the grounds that increased research grants would help to alleviate this problem through second-order effects. This reasoning is, I am sure, well intentioned, but it is also totally unrealistic. As Philip Abelson (1978) has pointed out, during the last twenty years the versatility and power of scientific instrumentation has advanced at the rate of a factor of ten every five years. Thus, for the most part, equipment that is ten years old is already obsolete. Abelson dramatically makes the case for chemistry, a field he knows at first hand. Last year NSF was able to supply 6.5 million dollars to the roughly 28,000 chemists involved in graduate education throughout the country. After allowing for an estimated number not actively engaged in research and the availability of funds from other sources, he concludes that for each professor and each graduate student doing research in chemistry there is about $1000 per year available for equipment. Yet many of the instruments needed for research at the cutting edge of chemistry cost $150,000 or more apiece. Peter Gwynne, writing in Newsweek, recently reported that the biomedical departments in one university alone (Iowa) needed 2 million dollars for equipment right now just to keep their programs operative. In the face of this great need, the NSF, if it is lucky, will be able to invest 3 million dollars of FY 1979 money to institute a program of regional instrumentation facilities. While the concept of regional centers is certainly commendable, the scale of the program, even if we assume that it will be allowed to expand, is totally inadequate to the need. If something more effective than this is not done, and done fast, the quality of graduate education in many, if not most, of the sciences may be irreparably harmed. One scientist with whom I am acquainted already has arranged to send as many of his graduate students as he can for a period of training in West Germany simply because the equipment they have access to there is not available to them anywhere in the United States.

Impediment to the Future of Research: Lack of New Blood

The most serious immediate problem faced by academic science is, however, not lack of money or of up-to-date equipment and facilities. It is the prospective lack of new blood. I refer to the fact that most colleges and universities are faced with extemely high proportions of tenured faculty members not scheduled to retire in significant numbers before the year 2000. (In a conversation about the problem of faculty turnover that I had with a senior government official the latter made specific reference to the very large proportion of our major institutions with tenure levels at 80 percent and identified one at 92.5 percent.) The data on the academic labor force for science and engineering are roughly as follows: By 1975 there were in the four-year colleges and universities of the United States approximately 148,000 science or engineering faculty members (NSF 1977). Of these, only an imperceptibly small number were below age 25, some 25 percent were between 25 and 34, roughly 62 percent were between 35 and 54, about 11 percent were between 55 and 64, and only about 2 percent were over 65. If all are retained until age 70, and the number of academic positions is held constant—neither of which is at all likely to occur—only about 38,000 college and university jobs will open up by the year 2000.

Furthermore, the problem of an aging, unchanging faculty will be further aggravated by federal legislation passed in the fall of 1977. You will recall that at the instigation of Representative Claude Pepper of Florida, the Congress amended the Age Discrimination in Employment Act of 1967, raising the commonly enforced retirement age of 65 to 70. In addition, several states have already removed all mandatory retirement-age limits as unconstitutional, and the federal government, again prodded by Mr. Pepper, the following spring took similar action with regard to federal career empoyees. Thus it is not at all inconceivable that we may soon see the elimination of all employment-age ceilings. When the Pepper legislation was first passed, colleges and universities were hopeful that they would be exempt, and a lot of legislative maneuvering took place to that end. But the situation is now perfectly clear. The most that colleges and universities can expect is an exemption until 1982, and I anticipate that we will see a range of plans devised on campuses across the country to compensate for the problem that will include an examination of traditional tenure policies. One question of extreme importance concerns whether or not tenure policy is yoked to retirement policy (Bartlett 1978). One plan that suggests itself immediately involves some form of early retirement. However, to accomplish this on a scale sufficiently large to be institutionally helpful would be prohibitively expensive, and, more than this, after the experience of a faltering stock market during the 1974 recession coupled with continuing uncontrolled inflation, older faculty members are understandably much more hesitant to consider early retirement than they might otherwise have been. Furthermore, administrations are not going to be able to force partial retirement, withhold salary increases, or otherwise reduce or terminate personnel benefits in any way in order to save money. The complex of regulations associated with ERISA, Equal Pay, Age Discrimination, and similar legislation will see to it that such economizing does not occur.

The problem of the faculty bottleneck emerges at a time when the demography of enrollment prospects leaves little room for optimism. The cohort of 18-year-olds from which we draw our entering classes is roughly 4.25 million and is as large now as it will be for some years to come. Indeed, by the mid-1980s it will have dropped to 3.6 million and by the early 1990s to 3.2 million, after which it will begin to rise again, reaching 4.1 million by the year 2000, which is still 125,000 below current levels. Enrollments are harder to predict, because of shifting patterns in what young people decide to do after high school, geographical shifts in population, etc. However, the American Council on Education expects that the 1985 college and university level will be about 4.5 percent below that for 1975, although in some states it will be down by as much as 25 percent (Henderson 1977.)

There has been, to my knowledge, little systematic thought given as to how to achieve safe balance in supply and demand in the scientific labor market. Indeed, the information that we have on unemployment is largely anecdotal. Four years ago, Congress moved to exercise some control over the production of Ph.D.s in the biomedical and the behavioral sciences through one of the provisions in the National Research Service Awards Act of 1974. This act separates the authority for the funding of research training in the biomedical and behavioral sciences from the older Public Health Service Act which provides support of clinical training in the several fields related to medicine. In so doing, it takes cognizance of the question of the national need for research personnel. One requirement of the act is that Congress receive informed recommendations each year concerning the national requirements for trained researchers in the biomedical and behavioral sciences. The responsibility for formulating these recommendations falls upon the National Academy of Sciences. In the light of its best guess concerning future job markets, the Academy in 1976 recommended a gradual transition during the period 1975 to 1982 from an educational support policy that would provide a predominant number of predoctoral students to one that would provide a predominance (70 percent) of postdoctoral students, meanwhile maintaining the ratio of traineeships to fellowships at the current 82 percent to 18 percent (National Research Council 1976). This policy position falls squarely between that of NIMH and ADAMHA, which have favored immediate termination of predoctoral training, and that of the university departments, which want more support for the status quo. But this status quo refuses to accommodate to the hard truth about enrollments, about stasis in the faculty, and about escalating costs. Furthermore, academic departments typically will only reluctantly give thought to what the future may hold for them unless they are forced to do so through the mechanisms of the budget. It is my personal view that we need to spend less time resisting the realities of the future and more in seeking out additional and new career options for our students and adapting our programs to better prepare them for such options. Meanwhile, the National Research Council staff has begun to accumulate some solid data on the job market, academic and otherwise. For example, the number of behavioral science Ph.D.s graduated annually in 1976 was 4.5 times the number graduated in 1960 and more than twice that for 1969. However, the number with firm plans for employment upon graduation dropped from about 82 percent in 1969 to about 71 percent in 1976, with roughly only 45 percent of the 1976 class scheduled to enter academic life. While total unemployment among behavioral scientists is still minimal (2.4 percent), the statistics on graduate enrollments suggest that Ph.D. output will be sustained for at least the next three or four years, and there is no clear indication that this level will be matched by available positions in research settings (National Research Council 1977; Ebert-Flattau 1978). The NRSA legislation came up for renewal in May and was extended for at least three more years.

The problem of new blood for the immediate future of science is exceedingly complex and difficult, and no single solution will suffice. Rather we shall need to seek a combination of solutions—both short-range and long-range and short-term and long-term—if the future is to be protected. This means creating a wider spectrum of career options and roles for both younger and older scientists, the availability of an increased range of work settings, and new institutional mechanisms for the conduct of research, in addition to exploring such matters as incentives for early or partial retirement of senior scientists. Certainly we must look to a more liberal use of the postdoctoral training program; special working arrangements between university and government and between university and industry; new non-academic roles both in industry and in government, particularly state and local government; and, of course, to the creation of a wider variety of autonomous research institutions, university related or otherwise. But whatever the combination of strategies, we most certainly must exercise greater imagination than we are now exercising in order to ensure that those bright and dedicated young people who are best suited for the laboratory of the future get there.

Impediment to the Freedom and Responsibility of Scientists: The Federal Government's Penchant for Regulation

We live in a litigious age. Nowhere is this clearer than in our government's rapidly growing zeal for creating regulations. Not only has the professional bureaucracy found its metier, but Congress now resonates to the same themes, and regulations float out of Washington about as easily as soap bubbles from a pipe—and in at least the same profusion. Don't get me wrong. I am not an "autonomy freak." I long ago stopped believing in the romanticized notion that science operates in splendid isolation, generating its own incentives and initiatives. Nor do I buy the more dangerous fiction that scientists are morally superior people who must be left totally to their own devices in order that humankind may ultimately benefit. The doctrine of absolute self-regulation (cf. e.g., Polyani 1962) belongs to an earlier and more innocent age. We've seen enough of falsified data and indifference to human welfare in the scientific community to know that self-regulation is not working exactly perfectly. For example, one need only recall the incident at Sloan Kettering several years ago of animals doctored to give the appearance of significant results in a cancer experiment (Culliton 1974a, 1974b), the more recent report of widespread sloppiness in toxicity testing carried out in both university and industrial laboratories (Smith 1977), or the alleged multiple violations by the Psychology Department at SUNY-Albany of both federal and state policies governing the treatment of human subjects (Lowman 1977). I firmly believe that some public oversight and accountability is absolutely essential if democratic values are to be realized. But the calculus of oversight is not precisely formulated, and it is easy to drift from the essential to the intolerable. In my opinion we have in the last decade done exactly that, and in the absence of a clear definition of essential constraint I find myself thrown back to Carlyle's phrase, "anarchy plus a constable," as the protective principle.

That we are overregulated is self-evident to the thoughtful observer of university-government relations, and one doesn't need the elaborate arguments advanced by philosophers of science over the last two decades to understand this fact (Bozeman 1977). One needs only to look at the scale of regulatory practice and the cost to those regulated.

There are eighty-seven federal agencies with regulatory powers, employing 100,000 people. The top thirty have combined operating expenses of 2.9 billion dollars per year. The Commission on Federal Paper Work has estimated that together they generate enough paper to fill fifty-one major league baseball stadiums (Anonymous 1978a). For example, the Dupont Corporation each year must spend 5 million dollars and 180 man-years in generating some 15,000 reports, not only concerning its own activities but also those of every vendor from which it purchases $2500 or more of goods or services. With patience, Dupont will probably survive, for it is big enough and strong enough to resist, and it can, I assume, pass on the financial cost of both compliance and resistance to its customers. Colleges and universities are in a more precarious position. They have fewer resources with which to resist and they are less able to pass on costs to their clientele. Meanwhile, they bear the brunt of the full range of public regulatory activity. In a study of six representative institutions (one large state university; two private universities with hospital complexes, one large and one medium sized; two small private colleges offering up to the master's degree; and two large public community colleges) costs of compliance were found to have gone up between 100 and 2000 percent during the decade 1965 to 1975 (Fields 1975b). At the large private university studied, the increase was from $110,000 to $3.6 million; at the medium-sized institution, from $2000 to $300,000; and at the large public university, from $438,000 to $1.3 million. These estimates, furthermore, are probably quite conservative, for they do not adequately include the costs of time spent by countless department heads, general administrative officers, and faculty members who serve on compliance committees, etc. One institution estimated that if it were to achieve full compliance, it would have to spend some 25 million dollars (Fields 1975a). Some notion of the real magnitude of these costs is obtained from the fact that they represent from 5 to 18 percent of net tuition revenues.

Even more alarming than the exorbitant cost of compliance, however, is the motivational psychology of the regulatory process. Regulation seems somehow to have become an end in itself. Two years ago Duke University was required by OSHA to spend some several hundred thousand dollars to install metal guide rails on virtually all of its external steps although there is no record of any serious accident through falling in the fifty-year history of the campus. Similarly, a North Carolina construction firm was recently required to provide a portable toilet at a construction site even though the company had arranged to use the bathroom at a filling station fifty yards away and the workers were quite content with this arrangement. Indeed, it has even been reported that OSHA has been persistent in the matter of providing portable toilets for cowboys doing range work, apparently totally innocent of life styles in the great outdoors! Nor is OSHA the only agency whose rulings have bordered on the absurd. An action recently threatened by the Justice Department in the interest of fair housing practice was such that had it been carried out, Brigham Young University would no longer be able to operate legally separate men's and women's dormitories (Anonymous 1978b). Not only do colleges and universities become burdened beyond belief by the sheer volume of regulatory activity; they not infrequently find themselves forced out of compliance with one agency by virtue of its attempt to comply with another. The experience of the University of Pennsylvania is representative. Although its cost of compliance in 1977 was 3.2 million dollars, it is being forced to spend an additional 2.5 million dollars to meet new regulations aiding the handicapped. The Department of Health, Education and Welfare has ruled that the university install a $100,000 elevator in College Hall. However, if the university makes any structural change in this 100-year-old building, it will be required to spend 1 million dollars to bring the entire structure up to the standards set by the local building code (Anonymous 1978a).

But the impact of the government's penchant for regulation is far more profound than something that is reckoned in terms of precious dollars and an unconscionable demand upon time and energy. It is in fact changing the very character of our institutions. Neither the persons who make the laws nor those who translate them into regulations appear to have even the slightest understanding of the tradition that dictates how colleges and universities both organize and govern themselves. Most federal regulations appear to have been written for hierarchical corporate organizations, and when they are imposed upon academic institutions in the fashion that they have been, the operational structure of the latter is inevitably forced to become increasingly that of the former. Robert Scott (1978) has chosen to describe the change in terms of the sociologist's Gemeinschaft-Gesellschaft typology. Educational institutions are being changed from communities of colleagues who work together because they share interests, values, and goals to collections of individuals that function as groups through formal controls and contractual arrangements.

The greatest concern of all, however, must be reserved for the increasing intrusion of government into what are not only the traditional freedoms of the college and the university, but the rights of their individual citizens as well. Agencies of the federal government, as Senator Daniel Patrick Moynihan not long ago pointed out on the floor of the Senate, are "mandating practices which would have appalled us a decade ago, practices which mindlessly violate the most fundamental principles of this nation as set down in the Constitution" (Anonymous 1978a, p. 50). Twenty-one years ago, Mr. Justice Frankfurter identified the four essential freedoms of the university as "the right to determine for itself on academic grounds who may teach, what may be taught and how it shall be taught, and who shall be admitted to study" (Culliton 1977). It is ironic that while Mr. Frankfurter was delineating our freedoms, some of us were busily giving them away—on that occasion, in the name of national security. I refer to contracts for classified research held by universities in the 1950s and 1960s, under which the government assumed the prerogative of specifying who would be permitted to work on the research, and under what conditions, and what would be communicated of the research results, if, indeed, anything. This situation came about because it never occurred to any of us at the time that we could or should resist such external control. What we should have learned, as Rosenzweig has recently observed (1978), is that when the government—whoever that may be—has decided that it is in its own interest to do so, it will set aside the ordinary rules that relate the governing and the governed in a democracy. When universities found that they could resist and did, ways of declassifying projects were quickly found. When Aneurin Bevan, that both best-loved and best-hated of British politicians, was asked thirty years ago how he would prevent the medical profession of England from resisting nationalization, he is reported to have replied that the government would stuff their throats with gold. While I am not so cynical as to think the American government deliberately set about to compromise its universities, that has been the ultimate effect of its funding policies.

If the reader is inclined to doubt this consequence, I need only point to the recent history of capitation grants for medical education. With the passage of Medicare and Medicaid legislation in the early 1960s, Congress assumed that questions concerning the number of physicians to be trained by American medical schools were to be matters of national policy and accordingly in 1965 passed the Health Professions Educational Assistance Amendment. This legislation provided institutional grants as an incentive to increasing the size of entering medical classes. The grants have accomplished what Congress had intended them to. Since their inception, the number of physicians in training has approximately doubled. At the same time, the number admitted to medical schools has been for some years only a minor fraction of those seeking admission and, indeed, about 5,000 of those not admitted are currently doing their pre-clinical training at institutions outside the United States with the hope of eventually transferring to an American school. In fact, these 5,000 do more than hope, for they have become a persistent pressure group for the Congress. Thus it was not surprising that when the Health Professionals Educational Assistance legislation came up for renewal in 1976 it contained a section which directed the Secretary of Health, Education and Welfare to establish a register of those Americans studying abroad who had passed the initial part of the National Medical Board Examination. The secretary, furthermore, was to indicate for each medical school a quota to be filled from this register, with no student to be denied admission because of failure to meet regular local admissions standards. Failure to comply with this quota would result in withdrawal of capitation funds and denial of eligibility for federally funded student aid to the students of schools not in compliance. This time universities recognized the implications of the string placed on subsidy. Should the government be able this easily to prescribe admission standards for medical schools, then they could just as easily intrude in other fundamental ways upon the autonomy of the Academy. Thus educational leaders strongly urged President Ford to veto the act. When this strategy failed, university representatives made their unhappiness known to members of Congress in the hope that the requirement of admission quotas would be withdrawn before the act took effect. Initially four and ultimately eighteen medical schools asserted that they would forego capitation supplements rather than allow external direction of their admissions policies (Roark 1978b;) Anonymous 1978b). After embarrassment on both sides and no little irritation on the part of Congressman Paul Rogers of Florida, who had authored the section on quotas, a compromise measure was passed by both House and Senate which requires schools accepting capitation to make a good-faith effort to increase their third-year classes by 5 percent for one year, with the understanding that the 5 percent would be selected from Americans in foreign medical schools, but without any prejudice as far as local admission standards are concerned. Meanwhile, the government will have the final word. The Department of Health, Education and Welfare's FY 1979 budget proposal, while keeping capitation funding for schools of public health at their 1978 levels, reduced those for medical, osteopathic, and dental schools by a third and totally eliminated such funding for all other health professions. In addition, the Assistant Secretary for Health has underway a study to determine whether or not the program of capitation grants should be totally eliminated (Anonymous 1978c). Meanwhile, the GAO (Roark 1978a) has begun an audit of capitation expenditures in eleven medical schools—including the four leaders of the rebellion—that, in its timing, has all the earmarks of bureaucratic harassment.

But resistance comes late and only slowly. The new GI Bill also passed in 1976 with no resistance from the academic community contains provisions that govern classroom attendance, the proportion of veterans in individual classes, the scheduling of classes, policies on grading, on the assignment of credit, and even on the reporting of information on non-veteran students whose records are supposed to be protected by recent legislation on privacy.

If I appear uptight about government regulations, let me remind the reader that during the last thirty years American colleges and universities have increasingly abandoned their fundamental role as preservers and transmitters of the humane tradition and have become Big Business. More than anything else, the higher education–government relationship which has evolved during those thirty years is responsible for this change.

ACADEMIC SCIENCE: INTELLECTUAL PLAYGROUND OR NATIONAL RESOURCE?

What has brought us to our current uneasy relationship with the federal government? The answer is obviously not a simple one. There are a number of plausible reasons, all of which, in one way or another, could conceivably have made their contribution to the present state of affairs. One is the sheer size of the federal financial involvement with colleges and universities. If the FY 1979 budget proposals were to survive congressional action in our most-hoped-for condition, the federal government woud have set aside in excess of 3.5 billion dollars for research and development activities in colleges and universities. This generally is for high-risk work, something that typically makes any sponsor—particularly a public sponsor—nervous. Furthermore, this budget figure says nothing about monies for training and other research-related activities. When totals reach a certain visible level in the federal budget they become targets for politically motivated scrutiny. It is in the nature of public sponsorship. Furthermore, if we now pay the price of size, we also suffer from the effects of excessive dependence on federal dollars, and the psychology of chronic overdependence, whether it involves individuals or nations, does not usually make for a cheerful outlook in the dependent partner. Overdependence is not something that typically comes about overnight. It results from a long series of transactions where the attractiveness of the benefits obscures the burdens of the relationship until involvement has passed the point of easy control. Frailty of resistance, to use Muller's (1978) phrase, becomes a characteristic posture.

In addition, there are ingredients in the relationship between government and the Academy that are a reflection of a broader set of changes in American public life. The role of the professions in the evolution of public policy that had obtained for the past hundred years has changed markedly during the last ten. We no longer can claim preemption in a way that we have heretofore. We no longer have prior claim to a fenced-off turf. This change in status, Yarmolinsky (1978) believes, results from three conditions. The first we have brought about ourselves. Membership in particular professions has grown so rapidly and is, at present, shared by so many people that the public at large no longer recognizes the role as distinctive. Second, the bureaucracy has reached such size that it includes significant subsets of the several professions and has simply appropriated many of the functions earlier exercised by the private sector. And third, as a consequence of the issues surrounding the Vietnam War, participatory democracy has gained in ascendency in almost every sphere of public life. Indeed, in some instances so many people get into the act that the consolidation of a policy position is virtually impossible. Congress is a good case in point. In the old days there was a clearly understood division of labor among congressional committees, with each becoming expert in its specific area of interest. As a consequence of its particular expertise, each committee thus acquired the "right" of decision-making for its area of responsibility. Things are no longer that simple. The new breed in Congress, disdainful of the seniority system, shaped by the styles of participatory democracy, and increasingly pressed by the public, wants a piece of every action. As a result, passage of even the simplest bill has become a highly complex, uncertain, and protracted affair (King 1978).

But the complexity of the current legislative process and the legislative load reflect something far more fundamental than the temperament of the new breed in Congress. They are the reflection of the inevitable fact that the politics of a participatory democracy is an issue-specific politics and one that goes far beyond the politics of special privilege—that motivated by the financial interests of business, labor, the guilds, other sectors of the economy—that we have had with us probably since the invention of government. Indeed, as Richard Rovere (1978) has suggested, it is really like nothing we have seen before. The issues—environmental pollution, nuclear power, euthanasia, drug abuse, endangered species, abortion, old age, women's rights, to name a few—are issues that legislatures have never before had to confront. Indeed, they vary fom the real and significant to the downright frivolous (Matthews & Walcott 1978). The activists involved appear as individuals, for the most part, not to be persons seeking either money or political power. Their political concerns are narrowly focused and they do not risk compromise by allegiance with other special interest groups. Their strategy, in the beginning at least, is more likely to be one of opposition than of advocacy—generally the more difficult kind with which to deal. They are effective money raisers. People are typically more prepared to contribute funds in support of particular, concrete, clearly understood projects and causes than they are for general purposes and goals. Former Representative William Brock, now chairman of the Republican National Committee, has recently publicly complained that his party is being seriously hurt financially by the efforts of specific-issue fund raisers. Furthermore, specific-issue politics is taking away more than money from the parties. It is taking away loyalty and participation as well. Increasingly, issues tend to be bipartisan, and individual citizens can pick and choose. They no longer need "to buy a package" in order to take part in the political process. The rise of specific-issue politics is dramatized by Rovere's report than in the last few years alone over two thousand new lobbies have come into existence.

All this then is the reflection of a marked shift from private to public ways of meeting social needs that began with the New Deal and that snowballed during and after the Johnson Administration. And if this shift has brought a sometimes bewildering fragmentation to the working of the Congress, it has also meant a disturbing centralization of political power in the executive branch. More and more things are being run from Washington. Specific-issue politics results in more legislation. For example, Rovere has noted that in 1977 there were more than 700 recorded votes in Congress as compared to about 100 fifteen years ago. With such a growth in amount and diversity of legislation, it follows that there must be both a growth in the bureaucracy and ultimately in its powers, for while Congress is both answerable to and must ultimately respond to the electorate, no such control exists upon the bureaucracy. This later fact, more than any other, is responsible, I suspect, for the centralization of power I have just mentioned. Changes in HEW with the arrival of Secretary Califano are instructive. Acting on the ground that administrative consistency is enhanced by limiting the responsibility for decisions to fewer persons, the Secretary relieved the ten HEW regional directors of all but a modicum of their authority and is now apparently calling the shots personally from Bethesda. With such a consolidation of power comes the attitude that any institution of society, either public or private and whether it likes it or not, shall be exploited as an instrument of government purpose when the government decides to so view it.

The question of medical capitation funds is important right now precisely because it is so instructive on this point. Senator Edward Kennedy and Senator Adlai Stevenson, both good friends of academic science, each has made the situation utterly clear in public statements to the scientific community during the past several years. Senator Kennedy, speaking to members of the Yale Medical Center at the end of 1974 on what he characterized as the national health care crisis, made reference to the use of federal funds as levers for change. "Not to use the levers," he said, "would be a violation of public trust. . . . It would allow you [Here he was referring to persons in academic medicine] to set your own course exclusively on your own terms. It would allow you to turn inward, to perfect what you already do well, and to neglect the problem that now seems peripheral to your mission and a threat to your competence" (Rosenzweig 1978, p. 62). Senator Stevenson, speaking at the 1977 AAAS Conference on R & D in the federal budget, reminded scientists of their inclination to avoid the diffcult questions that relate to the roles of science and technology in achieving broad societal goals. Referring to the relationship between the aims of government and the needs of society, he observed, "Among the 17 specific powers of Congress enumerated by the founding fathers in Article 1, Section 8 of the Constitution is one 'to promote the Progress of Science and the Useful Arts.' Beyond this constitutional mandate is the obligation of the Subcommittee [He was referring to his Subcommittee on Science, Technology, and Space of the Senate Science, Technology, and Transportation Committee] to exercise vigorously its legislative and oversight responsibilities for science and technology. *This will be done.* [Italics mine] Our efforts will be guided by the 13 goals for R & D contained in the Science Policy Act enacted last year" (Stevenson 1977, p. 74). When American universities stopped being simple, scholarly communities and became a national resource, they lost the luxury of self-determination.

THE POLITICS OF PROFESSIONALIZED SCIENCE

To fully understand the nature of the present science-government relationship it is necessary to trace its changing character, particularly over the last forty years, as Marland Blissett (1972) has done. According to Blissett, the institutional development of American science has been intimately linked to the emergence of three distinct but overlapping systems of political power, what he calls respectively the liberal state, the bureaucratic state, and the post-industrial state. The emergence of science as a profession in the United States, he contends, resulted from the fact that government initially had only a limited interest in the promotion and development of scientific knowledge. Government powers in general were narrowly defined and carefully circumscribed, and science, like the other professions, consequently developed in the private sector. While there certainly are isolated instances of the American government's early interest in scientific matters, formal involvement was virtually nonexistent until the federal chartering of the National Academy of Sciences in 1863 in order to acquire technical advice through public service. Level of involvement, however, remained limited until the eve of World War II.

Meanwhile, the beginnings of major-scale industrialization in late-nineteenth-century America meant the creation of regulatory instruments and the beginnings of the bureaucratic state. With the move toward public ownership during the era of the New Deal, the bureaucratic state matured, the bureaucracy became well established, and the scope of the regulatory function was widely expanded. Although the government had previously established scientific bureaus, its serious engagement with the scientific community did not occur until the World War II period. Its strategy of engagement at that time was the traditional one for the bureaucratic state. It mobilized scientists to work on its behalf, supplied funds, but otherwise left the direction of science largely to the decisions of its panels of scientific advisors from the private sector. And because research and development represented meaningful goals for many bureaus, the public-private system that evolved was necessarily pluralistic in form. This period is what many older members of the scientific community remember as the good years.

As the system grew and the need for coordination increased, this situation was met through the eventual creation of several administrative mechanisms within the White House: the Office of Science and Technology, the Federal Council for Science and Technology, and the President's Science Advisory Committee. But growth brought another change. While decision-making for science still lay largely in the hands of scientists, its site began to shift from the private sector into the federal agencies as these latter committed increasingly large sums from their budgets to the scientific enterprise. The ostensible reason for any agency's support of basic research was, of course, to facilitate meeting its mission, but in fact there was typically little immediate and direct relation between the basic research supported by an agency and the concrete problems associated with that agency's mission. Meanwhile the institutional purpose served was clearly one of augmenting resources—dollars, equipment, markets, and budget leverage. As levels of funding grew, and with them both the size of the science-related bureaucracy and the attention of individual members of the political community, increasingly broad considerations, many extending well beyond the domain of science, entered into allocation decisions. And, as one would expect, as scientists became increasingly dependent upon particular agencies for the future of their work, they were increasingly drawn into the policy politics of these agencies.

Within the last decade, scientists have found themselves facing yet another shift in political power. Out of the brokering activities of the bureaucratic state there are emerging institutional complexes that constitute new clusters of influence. These spheres of influence, while not always readily apparent, are broader in scope and the decision-making apparatus associated with them a much more complex and far-ranging one. By way of illustration, Blissett has tallied the institutions at present involved in pesticide policy: the large chemical companies, the Department of Agriculture, the Department of the Interior, the FDA, the Public Health Service, the EPA, and, increasingly, public interest groups as well. As Bronowski points out in his Silliman lectures (1978, p. 130), the founding principle of the modern state is that knowledge is the means to power. Thus in the post-industrial state, these emerging institutional complexes become the units of political power. They maintain their status by accumulating resources and by using them for their own protection and growth. Under such circumstances, science becomes just another instrument for accumulating power.

Some years ago Alvin Weinberg (1967) suggested that basic research constituted the overhead that kept scientists happy in the institutional complex. Stephen Toulmin (1966) has gone even farther. He suggests that in the post-industrial state science constitutes what he calls a tertiary industry the social purpose of which is the employment of institutional resources, a view echoed in Derek de Solla Price's more recent extrinsic value theory of research (1977). In contrast to primary industries which produce new materials, and secondary industries which produce salable commodities, science, along with other tertiary industries, functions primarily to produce jobs. If, in fact, this is the case, then we may expect science to become integrated increasingly into the purposive institutions of society, to be tied closer to technology, and consequently, along with technology, to be subjected to a still greater range of political pressures. At such a stage of political involvement, programs to implement public policy will replace grants and contracts as the mechanisms for allocating public resources. Indeed, we already see this trend increasingly in both the legislative actions of Congress and the lists of targeted projects promulgated each year by the agencies of the executive branch. Furthermore, the fact that academic science is being institutionally transformed by the post-industrial state at the same time that its long-term exponential growth appears to have come to an end (Price 1963; Walsh 1978) makes the whole issue of its extrinsic value as compared to its value as an investment good, as well as its identity separate from technology, an extremely important policy question to persist in raising.

WHERE DO WE GO FROM HERE?

As academic science contemplates its future relationship to the mechanisms of government, it is imperative—if it is to ensure its own continued integrity as well as to meet its essential responsibility as a social institution—that academic scientists give greater attention to identifying effective strategies for engagement with the process of public-policymaking. And to do so they must have a better understanding than they have had in the past concerning the assumptions, both about the policy process and about the social character of science, that underlie such participation. I would suggest the following five points, noting parenthetically that I will say nothing about the increasingly international character of modern science, although I do recognize that this will have a necessary and significant impact on the American science of the future.

First of all, it is important to recognize that government is, before everything else, a state of mind that reflects the human search for order and continuity. By its very nature, however, it will, short of total disintegration, continue to grow, to become more complex, and thus to intrude, to monopolize, and to centralize. In short, it seems always to be, in Tussman's phrase (1977, p. 6), "on the verge of becoming an evil." It is therefore incumbent upon the governed, in their own best interest, to harbor a healthy distrust of the elaboration of the machinery of government, to insist constantly on the distinction between legitimate need and demand, and, in other ways, to resist growth that exceeds the rate required to realize government's proper purpose. In a democracy the basic function of government is the constant balancing of special interests. Thus its processes are fundamentally adversarial in character and the protection for the governed resides in an essential pluralism.

Second, the existence of complexes—the military-industrial complex, the communication complex, the service and regulatory complex, the techno-science complex—is real. Though only rarely in plain view, such complexes are becoming each year more elaborate, and with this growth, the apparatus for policy decisions becomes broader, grows more complex, and incorporates more diverse elements. Yarmolinsky is right in his hypothesis about the monotonic decline in the status of the professional in America (if you doubt him ask yourself what happened to the political clout of the so recently powerful AMA) and nothing will be gained by yearning for the good old days (Was it Sean O'Faolain who asked rhetorically, "Will you understand that the good old days are right now?"). Certainly, no one who is fair-minded can take exception to the principle that in a democracy those who are the objects of a decision are entitled to share in that decision. Technical knowledge has clearly become an increasingly important prerequisite to sound public decisions, and this fact requires more public roles for both the laboratory scientist and the science-based technologist of the future as well as a better understanding of the intellectual structure—methods, perspectives, values—of science and technology on the part of the public as a whole.

Third, human beings are political animals and I refuse to buy the premise (Bozeman 1977) that scientists are unsuited by both training and disposition for the policy arena. We can do as well as any other subset of the human community if only we will develop the heart and the stomach for it. Further, we must recognize the need to balance our requirement for autonomy in the pursuit of knowledge with our need to participate in those processes that will ensure the socially responsible application of that knowledge. The model for the scientist of the future must more closely resemble Francis Bacon than René Descartes.

Fourth, the federal government will continue to be the major patron of science. However, I am pessimistic about any expectation that basic science can be justified as a consumption good on a significant scale in the foreseeable future. It is therefore important that justification be sought on some alternative ground, and Derek Price's extrinsic value-overhead theory (participation in basic research is necessary and important preparation for various essential jobs in society) warrants serious examination. Whether valid or not, it does make a certain psychological sense for the future. The survival of academic science requires that colleges and universities recognize that thorough training in the basic sciences is essential for a far greater variety of intellectual roles and occupations than simply those of research and teaching. Indeed, scientists must confront their own need for greater diversification of career roles within the scientific community itself. We would do well to give greater attention than we now do to the question of how one educates for such diversity. All this adds up to our needing to strike a sounder internal balance among our educational strategies and goals than now exist.

Fifth and finally, we need to contemplate a new relationship between academic science and the federal government, one in which we are willing to assert a greater independence, recognizing that if science must depend upon government as its ultimate patron, so also must government understand that it has needs that only science and its attendant technology can meet. It must be a partnership of equals, one in which neither member can afford to take the other for granted. This means that we in the universities have to be prepared to hold the federal government at arms length when we perceive that the integrity of our enterprise may be compromised. We need courage to draw the line, as the medical schools did in the capitation issue, and to draw it more frequently than we have in the past. We need to explore new mechanisms for the science-government relationship of the future. The military establishment long ago developed strategies for ensuring continuity of support; the scientific establishment needs to occupy itself with a similar exercise. And, what we must understand most of all, if we are to feel comfortable in a more assertive posture vis-à-vis the government, is that the "golden years" between 1941 and 1966 were an abnormal period, a perturbation that in fact signaled that we were arriving at the inflection point of the exponential curve of scientific growth (Price 1963, pp. 23–30). Furthermore, as we contemplate the new relationship between academic science and the federal government to which I have just referred, it is important to adopt a new metaphor. For a long time academic scientists, when commenting on their agency sponsors, have been fond of speaking in terms of the accommodations of a marriage. I would suggest that it is more advantageous to think in terms of the negotiated treaty. Successful marriages are said to be built on mutual trust. Successful treaties are based on mutually recognized self-interest.

ON THE NATURE OF POLICY

For those of us in the academic community who are motivated to participate in the shaping of public policy, it is imperative that we understand clearly what policy and the policy processes are and are not. In the interest of time let me make a series of short declarative statements:

The creation of policy is a highly complex, highly focused, and at the same time, highly variable sequence of events. Involvement in one sector does not render one an expert in another.

It is the exception rather than the rule for policy to exist as a totally explicit, completely rational, clearly formulated, and fully comprehensive set of statements. Indeed, in the final instance, public policy is more often than not what the relevant bureaucracy elects to do about a particular matter at a particular time. A policy then can be any principle, plan, or course of action and the bottom line is course of action.

Policies are almost always trade-offs between benefits and liabilities, and more often than not the margin of benefit is small.

Don't waste your time debating about who *should* decide a policy question. The proper question is who *will* decide. Given the way we govern ourselves in this country, it will be some combination of persons who are willing to assert their interest in an issue and who, through dint of persistence, skill, and political influence, are able to exercise an impact on the direction that the policy resolution of that issue takes. If an area of policy formulation concerns you, get involved. No one is going to take the trouble to invite your participation.

Finally, since, as I have just suggested, policy is almost always the end-product of an adversary process, the crucial aspects of a policy question almost always lie in the realm of values, not of facts. While the mechanisms devised to achieve the ends of a policy decision may depend upon the advice of particular experts, the goals of the policy can only be set by the resolution of questions of political and social vale.

WE ARE THE GOVERNMENT—YOU AND I

If academic science is going to achieve a new and qualitatively different social contract with the federal government and one that at the same time is going to be more satisfying than its present arrangement, a significantly larger number within our community is going to have to seek active roles at the interface. These roles will need to be both institutional and individual. Universities as universities are simply going to have to involve themselves in a way and to an extent that they heretofore have avoided in the day-to-day activities of the federal policy apparatus. Our scientific associations must do the same. But in my personal view the bottom line is individual participation. While I'm neither so naive nor so evangelistic as to insist that *every* scientist become a born-again political activist, I would insist that as a community we must put our let-Jack-do-it philosophy behind us. There is no free lunch in a democracy.

Before universities seek to take an effective policy role in science policy they would do well to put their houses in order. More than anything else they need to rediscover their own identity, make clear to themselves what their goals are in the late seventies and eighties and seek strategies for pursuing them with both reasonable confidence and seriousness of purpose. At the same time, they need to create mechanisms that will allow them to assess the legislative climate continuously and to take rapid action in their own behalf when it is appropriate. I would suggest for each university a full-time legislative affairs officer, and a small but active Council on Federal and State Relations, staffed by the Legislative Affairs Office chaired by a senior university officer such as the president or provost, and made up of experienced and knowledgeable members of the faculty and administration. Finally, universities must band themselves together to act rapidly and in concert. Our greatest weakness in the past is that we have insisted too often on going it alone. Thus I would suggest a National Council on Academic Science Policy that is prepared to coordinate policy positions and to arrange to communicate these to the Congress both in the context of the formal hearing and informally in the setting of a congressman's office.

There are a range of useful activities that our scientific societies, particularly the larger societies, can initiate. They can organize workshops on the policy process for those of their members who wish to acquire a background for participating in public affairs. They can, on a larger scale than is at present the case, organize sessions at their annual meetings for the discussion of particular legislative questions of importance to their fields. They can set up special seminars to allow for the more extended discussion of major legislative issues. (For example, each year for the past several, AAAS has conducted a two-day conference on R & D in the budget that eventuates in a very useful paperback that is available to the public at large.) They can arrange person-to-person advisory services for individual members of Congress (the American Society of Biological Chemists initiated such a program several years ago [Sullivan 1974]). They can conduct regularly scheduled seminars for members of Congress and their legislative aides that deal with technical issues relating to pending legislative proposals. And they can create staff and committee machinery to produce in-depth studies of scientific and technological issues relevant for current legislation. (This would mean a function similar to that of the Office of Technology Assessment and the recently proposed Institute for Congress.) They can maintain a Legislative Reference service that can help prepare testimony and provide qualified persons to appear before legislative committees on short notice. Finally, they can form nationwide networks for the grass-roots expression of policy positions.

One note of caution: When universities and societies join in the process of policy formulation, they are faced with two complementary roles, education and advocacy, that must under all circumstances be kept distinctly separate. This is easier said than done. Even the most "neutral" statement of fact may contain implicit value judgments. Mixing educational and advocacy roles is the easiest way to lose a hard-earned reputation for trustworthiness. Perhaps the easiest way to keep educational and advocacy roles separate is through different institutional mechanisms. In my view, the American Psychological Association used excellent judgment when it decided to create the Association for the Advancement of Psychology. The APA is for education; the AAP for advocacy, I have proposed a special council for advocacy on behalf of higher education. This should free organizations like the Association of American Universities and the Association of American Colleges to pursue an educational role with policymakers.

If there are any among the readers of this essay who are moved to take up the cause of better science policy, let me suggest the following rules of thumb:

First, become thoroughly familiar with the institutions for policymaking and how they work. Give special attention to the budgetary process and its relation to policy. (I would strongly urge that science departments in this day and age develop a special seminar or course to be taken by all graduate students before completing their doctoral requirements that would provide a practical knowledge of the relationships that obtain among the several worlds of science, politics, and government.)

Second, maintain an up-to-date knowledge of legislative issues. Situations change with striking rapidity.

Third, get to know your representatives in the Congress and in your state legislature. Their offices can provide copies of legislation and other useful documents. Indeed, it is extemely important for you to understand that any advice that you may proffer political decisionmakers will receive prompt attention to the extent that you are known and trusted by them. Stay strictly nonpartisan in any educational role you may assume with regard to legislation. Academics generally start with an advantage; decision makers tend to view professors as above petty self-interest. But don't limit your contacts to politicians; get to know their legislative aides. Legislative aides play a significant role in the preparation of legislation.

Fourth, when working with lay persons, for goodness sake shed all jargon. Write and speak about your science in plain English. Learning to do this may be a lot harder than you realize. It is a skill one has to cultivate deliberately.

Fifth, when you give advice, provide background, or present testimony, make clear in simple language the confidence you place in your own opinions. At the same time, don't equivocate. Policy makers want answers and an "on the one hand, A; however, on the other hand, B" won't help them very much. This does not mean that you should let them lead you beyond your own prudent levels of confidence in the validity of your advice. That will do no one any good.

Sixth, treat the facts with great reverence. When you are caught up in an issue, it is easier to bias their interpretation than you may realize.

Seventh, learn patience and persistence. Neither Rome nor Washington was built in a day. Involvement with the political process—whether in educational or advocacy roles—is no activity for the one-shot artist. Develop a thick skin and learn to control your temper, if you haven't already learned to do so.

Eighth, keep your educational and advocacy roles clearly separated.

And finally, give serious consideration to the ultimate role as citizen, that of seeking public office. Government sorely needs people who can look beyond assertions to assumptions and beyond mechanisms to objectives. Above all, it needs people who can resist the temptation to impose simple solutions upon complex problems.

The title of the present remarks is "Academic Science and the Federal Government: Less Wed, More Locked?" I suppose one might think of it as a kind of projective device. If one's major preoccupation is with the functioning of research and training programs, then it may remind one of the early days of uncritical funding. If one thinks of recent attacks by members of Congress on the intellectual content of science, then it must arouse nostalgia for the time when the scientist was everybody's darling. If one is made anxious by the advent of the post-industrial state, then one will remember the freedoms that we have either lost or traded away in the past quarter century. But whatever aspect of those good old days that are so often part of our current talk, it is essential to understand that they are just that—good old days that are gone forever. It is now urgent that academic scientists take the initiative in creating a new science and government relationship within which we can make clear our own inviolate conditions for participation. In doing so we must be prepared to draw the line whenever the government intrudes upon essential academic prerogatives. And we must be eternally vigilant to the possibility that it will do so. Being willing to say no means also being willing to give up, if necessary, what we would have received for saying yes. The late Mr. Chief Justice Earl Warren, in his little book, *A Republic, If You Can*, published shortly after he retired from the Supreme Court, quotes Benjamin Franklin, twenty years before the Bill of Rights: "Those who would give up essential liberty to purchase a little temporary safety deserve neither liberty nor safety" (Warren 1972, p. 158). This is not, I would suggest to the academic science community, a bad aphorism for our times.

References

Abelson, P.H. Obsolete instrumentation at universities. *Science,* 1978, *200,* 1111.
Anonymous. Rage over rising regulation. *Time,* 1978, *111*(1), 48–50. (a)
Anonymous. Federal aid: Too many strings. *Time,* 1978, *111*(17), 73-74. (b)
Anonymous. Budget shrinks manpower bureau; capitation sliced for medical schools. *Drug Research Reports,* 1978, *21*(4), 8. (c)
Bartlett, T.A. Federal relations agenda, 1978. Washington, D. C.: Association of American Universities, January 1978.
Blissett, M. *Politics in science.* Boston: Little, Brown, 1972.
Bonham, G.W. Is American science good enough? *Change,* 1977, *9*(6), 10–12.
Bozeman, B. A governed science and a self-governing science: The conflicting values of autonomy and accountability. In J. Haberer (Ed.), *Science and technology policy.* Lexington, Mass.: Lexington Books, 1977.
Bronowski, J. *The origins of knowledge and imagination.* New Haven, Conn.: Yale University Press, 1978.
Bush, V. *Science, the endless frontier: A report to the President on a program for postwar scientific research.* Washington, D.C.: U. S. Government Printing Office, 1945 (reissued by the National Science Foundation, 1960).
Culliton, B. J. The Sloan-Kettering affair: A story without a hero. *Science,* 1974, *184,* 644–650. (a)
Culliton, B.J. The Sloan-Kettering affair (II): An uneasy resolution. *Science,* 1974, *184,* 1154–1157. (b)
Culliton, B. J. Four medical schools draw the line on capitation. *Science,* 1977, *197,* 1066.
Cutter, W.B. Opening address. In D.I. Phillips, C.C. Cleare, & M. Patterson (Eds.), *Research and development in the federal budget.* Washington, D. C.: American Association for the Advancement of Science, Report No. 77-R-4, 1977, 11–18.
Cutter, W.B. Remarks. Third Annual AAAS Conference on R & D Policy. Washington, D. C., June 20–21, 1978.
Ebert-Flattau, P. Implications of a changing market for federal research training support in the behavioral sciences. Paper presented at the Annual Meeting of the American Association for the Advancement of Science, Washington, D. C., February 1978.
Fields, C.M. Analyzing campus costs of federal programs. *Chronicle of Higher Education,* 1975, *9*(8), 12. (a)
Fields, C.M. Government asked to share cost of compliance. *Chronicle of Higher Education,* 1975, *11*(10), 13. (b)
Gwynne, P. A growing R and D gap. *Newsweek,* 1978, *92*(1), 89.
Henderson, C. Changes in enrollment by 1985. Washington, D. C.: Policy Analysis Service Reports, American Council on Education, 1977, *3,* no. 1.
Holton, G. On being caught between Dionysians and Appolonians. *Daedalus,* 1974, *103*(3), 65–82.
King, J.A.S. Why Congress doesn't work. *Newsweek,* 1978, *91*(2), 9.
Lowman, R. Court closes case on SUNY fuss. *APA Monitor,* 1977, *8*(12), 9.

Matthews, T., & Walcott, J. On to Washington! *Newsweek,* 1978, *92*(4), 34–37.
Muller, S. A new American university? *Daedalus,* 1978, *107*(1), 31–45.
National Research Council. Personnel needs and training for biomedical and behavioral research. Annual Report of the Committee on a Study of National Needs for Biomedical and Behavioral Research Personnel. Washington, D.C.: National Academy of Sciences, 1976.
National Research Council. Personnel needs and training for biomedical and behavioral research. Annual Report of the Committee on a Study of National Needs for Biomedical and Behavioral Research Personnel. Washington, D.C.: National Academy of Sciences, 1976.
National Science Foundation. *Characteristics of doctoral scientists and engineers in the United States, 1975.* Washington, D.C.: National Science Foundation, NSF Document 77–304, 1977.
National Science Foundation. *National R and D spending to exceed $50 billion in 1979.* Washington, D. C.: National Science Foundation, NSF Document 78–304, 1978.
Nordhaus, W. Opening address. In D.I. Phillips, C.C. Cleare, & M. Patterson (Eds.), *Research and development in the federal budget.* Washington, D.C.: American Association for the Advancement of Science, Report No. 77-R-4, 1977, 19–32.
Polanyi, M. The republic of science: Its political and economic theory. *Minerva,* 1962, *1*, 54–73.
Price, D.J. de S. *Little science, big science.* New York: Columbia University Press. 1963.
Price, D.J. de S. An extrinsic value theory for basic and "applied" research. In J. Haberer (Ed.), *Science and technology policy.* Lexington, Mass.: Lexington Books, 1977.
Roark, A.C. Eleven medical schools face federal audits. *Chronicle of Higher Education,* 1978, *15*(20), 9. (a)
Roark, A. C. House slashes spending for basic scientific research. *Chronicle of Higher Education,* 1978, *16*(16), 1, 11. (b)
Rovere, R. Affairs of state. *The New Yorker,* May 8, 1978, 139–146.
Rosenzweig, R. M. An end to autonomy: Who pulls the strings? *Change,* 1978, *10*(3), 28–34, 62.
Scott, R.A. More than greenbacks and red tape: The hidden costs of government regulations. *Change,* 1978, *10*(4), 16–23.
Shapley, W.H., & Phillips, D.I. *Research and development AAAS Report III. R & D in the federal budget: FY 1979 R & D, industry, and the economy.* Washington, D.C.: American Association for the Advancement of Science, 1978.
Shapley, W.H., Phillips, D.I., & Roback, H. *Research and development in the federal budget: FY 1978.* Washington, D.C.: American Association for the Advancement of Science, 1977.
Smith, B.L.R., & Karlesky, J.J. *The universities in the nation's research effort.* New Rochelle, N.Y.: Change Magazine Press, 1977.
Smith, R.J. Creative penmanship in annual testing prompts FDA controls. *Science,* 1977, *198*, 1227–1229.
Smith, R.J. Budget-cutting mood in Congress begins to hit science. *Science,* 1978, *201*, 330–332.

Stevenson, A.E. Dinner address. In D.I. Phillips, C.C. Cleare, & M. Patterson (Eds.), *Research and development in the federal budget.* Washington, D. C.: American Association for the Advancement of Science, Report No. 77-R-4, 1977, 67–76.

Sullivan, W. Scientists plan to aid Congress. *New York Times,* June 5, 1974.

Toulmin, S. The complexity of scientific choice. II. Culture, overheads, or tertiary industry? *Minerva,* 1966, *4*(2), 155–169.

Tussman, J. *Government and the mind.* New York: Oxford University Press, 1977.

Walsh, J. Historian of science states case for catching up on basic research. *Science,* 1978, *199,* 1188–1190.

Warren, E. *A republic, if you can.* New York: Quadrangle Books, 1972.

Weinberg, A. *Reflections on big science.* Cambridge, Mass.: MIT Press, 1967.

Yarmolinsky, A. What future for the professional in American society? *Daedalus* 1978, *107*(1), 159–174.

General Discussion of Bevan's Paper

Miller: We have fifteen minutes for discussion.

Williams: I'd like to ask Bill just a quick question about all of you academics here assembled. It would seem to me that you covered it in one of your remarks near the end that there are certain things that might be included in the courses for psychologists, etc. that would acquaint them more with the policymaking governmental processes. As a matter of fact, I jotted down a note about that, and it's related a little bit to what Jim had said earlier. That is, the model that we tend to follow for pursuing the truth is one of objective inquiry with a lot of rules and things implied, but we tend to eschew the adversary-like one which is a part of the legal profession of intense debate and questioning and impeaching not only evidence, but motive and everything else which is more frequently found in the legislative process. So I was sort of wondering in your opinion whether there might not be some other models designed for graduate training in psychology to the extent that almost all of us—whether experimentalist, statistician, or phonetician, or somebody else again—get involved at one time or another in the grant seeking and working with government, or consulting, or expert witnesses, or whatever, which would begin to expose us to wider models of sort of gaining evidence or seeking the truth or whatever the case might be, which is a little bit different from the classical models that many of us have known in the past.

Bevan: Well, I give such a seminar, and it's an ideal part of the general education of science for the modern world. I've been continuously . . . continually appalled at how limited the knowledge of young scientists is, when they get outside of their area of special substantive interest, and so I do give such a course and I've found the response to be a very good one. There's good interest on the part of young people in learning more about the nuts and bolts as well as the philosophical issues behind some of these questions.

I have another program to propose. Let me open it up for a minute and make a sales pitch, I guess. I feel very strongly about the need for alternative career options. I would like to see a person with good scientific training who's not going to be necessarily a good laboratory person find another fulfilling kind of role, and I have a postdoctoral program for young behavioral scientists who spend a year with me dealing with the issues of how policy gets made and who the players are and how the system works and then spend a year with a committee of the Congress working as an administrative staff officer.

This is the expansion, actually, of a program I got underway when I was at the AAAS. At that time with the roughly 5,000 professional legislative aids operating in the Congress there were only one or two who had any formal training in any branch of science. We started that program five years ago. There are now some fifty alumni of the program working in one way or another with the legislative process either as a staff officer for members of the Congress or for congressional committees or with various agencies like the OTA or the Library of Congress and so on. This has provided an increasing resource, and it puts a scientist in different relationships with members of the Congress. Instead of being involved in the adversary relationship across the

	table where the congressman is only confused by two scientists with equally impressive credentials saying the opposite things, he has someone to turn to who plays a relatively neutral role.
Williams:	Bill, the problems of exposing in a graduate program—which was your specific suggestion—people to these processes are much more difficult because you say you're appalled at how naive the young scientists are. You should be equally appalled at how naive the old ones are.
Bevan:	Since the future of science depends on the young and not on the . . .
Audience:	There are very few of us around who could even begin . . .
Bevan:	. . . To do that.
Audience:	. . . to do that to the extent that you can; that have that knowledge of how that process works. And how does one get it started?
Bevan:	Well, the best way is to involve oneself. I said a while ago, nobody invites you into this game. You get in yourself because you find it of interest. I've—through circumstance, in terms of the kinds of roles I've had in recent years, jobs I've had—I've been forced into it and found I liked it.
Audience:	This is very long-term.
Bevan:	Sure. Sure. I think it's an alternative way to spend a sabbatical year for a member of the faculty who has a strong interest in this kind of activity and would like to know more about it in a first-hand way. And again, it's the kind of thing that one could find in the AAAS program.
Jackson:	That's becoming more and more common by the way.
Bevan:	Sure.
Jackson:	Many faculty members are now taking sabbaticals and actually becoming involved in this, and a lot of organizations are . . .
Bevan:	And one doesn't have to limit oneself to thinking in terms of the federal government. One has one's own state government, and then local government. And there's usually a crying need, or at least a strong desire, for help on the part of the people in local government. In fact, some thirty-five states now have established offices of science and technology either attached to the state legislature or to the executive offices of the governor. So scientists are beginning to take these roles in an official way, but again at the state level or the local level, funds are typically short for this kind of thing and volunteer help is always greatly welcomed. But I would

Koch: again point out the advice one gives in this role. One has to be very, very careful about being criticized and keeping the educational role and the political role separate.

Koch: Bill, since we're both former academic officers, let me get your viewpoint on one issue that's very much concerned me. I take it that you are somewhat appalled over certain of your experiences on the line as a high-echelon administration person. I certainly am over some of mine.

     I was much impressed by the strength and detail with which you documented the supine attitude of universities (based on a misplaced estimate of self-interest) in relation to encroachments by bureaucratic and postindustrial pressures. However, it seems to me that most of the remedies you suggested, which are very good ones, are defensive. I have long been impressed with the sense that it may be too late. But at some point we should have gone on the offensive in a certain way.

Bevan: Absolutely!

Koch: And I think that, in general, American university administrators have been totally derelict in redefining the intellectual basis . . .

Bevan: That's right.

Koch: . . . for the university.

Bevan: That's absolutely right.

Koch: This society, it seems to me—and here's where I'm not so cynical—is at least sophisticated enough to understand the social cost of not having intellectually free universities which are plugged in . . .

Bevan: That's right.

Koch: . . . to the tradition of the university as it has been known in the West.

Bevan: That's right.

Koch: No one has tried to advance that policy in the academy.

Williams: So I'd say it's somewhat a function of an attitude or view not so much of . . .

Bevan: I think it's a function of a number of things, Bel, and I think Sig might agree with me on this. First of all, I would also agree with what he said, that the ultimate role in policy formation is the active role and not the defensive role. And that's another problem with the AAP, I think, as James would have said. They've been so busy reacting defensively to the special interests of our various constituencies that they haven't taken that next step, which they're going to have to do if they're

	really going to make it count. I think part of the problem comes from the fact university leadership is no longer academic leadership.
Koch:	No, exactly.
Bevan:	We have presidents who are businessmen or crisis managers or whatever who don't understand the values of the university and don't exercise a positive leadership role inside the university as well as outside. And I think that's the critical problem facing universities right now. Setting aside . . .
Koch:	The enemy is within.
Bevan:	That's precisely the point.
Williams:	It seems to me . . . [*General confusion*]
Williams:	We need to have a university president or some officer of the university who does understand these businesses . . .
Bevan:	That's right.
Williams:	Because it is a big business.
Bevan:	But you don't have many that really do.
Williams:	Well, maybe you don't. But I'm just saying that it seems to me that you . . .
Jackson:	We've got to be able to appreciate some of these political kinds of things that you're saying . . .
Koch:	But that alone is not enough . . . [*General confusion*]
Bevan:	Another thing is that our professional associates of higher education like the ACE again have not taken imaginative and aggressive roles in these matters, and, in fact, some thirty universities have now banded together to form what I refer to as a proposal . . . an ad hoc Committee on Science Policy, and I happen to represent Duke in that consortium where we essentially are now moving to take positive and direct and aggressively active roles.
Jackson:	Well, look at the decade which we have just come out of in terms of what's been going on with regard to university presidents and so on. Suddenly some university presidents have been hanging on by their fingernails trying to keep the lid on with regard to the university where there have been all kinds of demands being made—some of them diametrically opposed to each other. At the same time we're saying that this university president ought to be reiterating the values of the economy.
Bevan:	No. What I'm saying is that we've come to a new era for higher education, and the time in which the crisis management or the fund raising—primarily fund raising—is the essential role has changed. And we are now in effect faced in

	many institutions with presidents who are obsolete from the point of view of the requirements of the institution.
Williams:	Sure. Well, let me ask a question on that, though. It seems to me that the academy has been very comfortable in forming relationships with government and very uncomfortable in forming relationships with the business community in the main. As a matter of fact, when you get a person like Henry Ford who resigns from the Ford Foundation because they somehow turn their back on American industry, it seems to me it says something. I'm interested in why the academy doesn't form more relationships with big business, with labor unions, with the whole set of other people in the community in order to keep the complexes, if you please, very dynamic in their involvement.
Bevan:	I think the academy is making do, and certain sectors of the academy have always done that. For example the business schools and . . .
Williams:	The business schools, yes.
Bevan:	. . . in the big university. That's where their strong financial support comes from.
Williams:	Sure. Sure. I agree with that.
Bevan:	And this whole program in the NSF which really is replacing the NIH institutional grants program which the OMB killed. What happened was that one sector of the OMB moved it into the budget while Huey Long had his back turned and was looking after the little program at NSF and he got that one put to sleep while the big one from NIH got on the docket. But that NSF money is now going to be diverted to presumably encouraging university-industry relations on the ground that industry—at this particular period in the economy—is very, very apprehensive about spending high-risk capital on science and therefore hopes to encourage this kind of thing in a partnership. When there's peace. In fact, one of the problems in medical school is the whole question of conflict of interest, for example in the relationship with the drug industry in the testing of drugs and so on.
Williams:	Sure.
White:	I'd just like to say that a couple of problems may work themselves together. Early in the talk you mentioned the fact that the research and teaching job market was vanishing. Now in my experience in the last five years a good number—I think of at least four or five—of the developmental psychologists have gone through an honorable training [and] are now positioned somewhere in the governmental complex. That is,

	by virtue of some interest they had before the doctorate. But by virtue of the job they've taken afterwards, they've assumed interfaced positions capable of representing both scientific values and some sophistication of understanding. I think that kind of thing is going to increase as the academic market shrinks, and that in a sense there's something natural about building that kind of relationship to social policy.
Bevan:	Indeed, I think if we are brave enough to face the facts of life a lot of things can really happen.
White:	Yeah.
Jackson:	People who take those kinds of positions have to be looked on by academicians as being full participants in the discipline as much as anyone else. And I think that's very important, really.
White:	They're not. They're now . . . Well, to take just local history. They're now regarded as having moved beyond the pale. But at the same time the Society for Research in Child Development has rather nervously formed an arm that is supposed to have something to do with social policy. And I got a call from an office they set up in Washington asking which way is Northwest! But they're there and they're beginning to look around. And I think since more people are going to be interested in that kind of thing, it has to grow.
Williams:	I've been curious why one doesn't find more psychologists involved in labor negotiations for conflict resolutions. Typically, people who do that are arbitrators, lawyers, or some such background, but not psychologists. We're supposedly fairly expert at looking at conflicts between and among people—interpersonal conflicts.
Bevan:	It's just a guess on my part, but I think, again, as an insecure science we are very much concerned about respectability, and respectability means being tied very close to academe. Physicists are much more relaxed about moving in and out of academe, and it's a peculiar, it seems to me, American misconception that intellectual . . . a vigorous intellectual life involves being tied to the academy and that's certainly not true at all.
Koch:	It's rather more monastic—the assumption here—than in Europe.
Bevan:	That's precisely right. In Europe these lines don't exist. In fact some of the important contributions come from outside the academy, and the academy is full of very dull people, as you know.
Koch:	Present company excepted.

Jackson: You ought to know about that.
Bevan: Some, *some* very dull people.
Miller: I think that's probably a good note on which to take a short break. Let's try to get going again at 3:15.
Bevan: I hope you're not going to publish all this!

Question and Answer: Miller and Bevan*

Miller: Whether I agree with Bill's talk or not is totally irrelevant. It doesn't agree with me. It's overwhelming. These items come in, this week in *Science,* next week in the *New York Times,* and the week after that in some other form, and you don't line them all up in one massive dose and extrapolate the clear direction that things have been taking.

As he was talking, I was thinking of my own career. I began graduate study in psychology in 1940, and the period from the beginning of World War II until—I would have dated it 1970, but I'll accept your date of 1967, twenty-five years—was a [period] of constantly growing research budgets, and, for me, as an individual, the natural state of affairs was a growth rate of about 15 to 20 percent per year. And that meant you bring more students in, you constantly expand, you do all kinds of wonderful things, and it was really great. And after twenty-five years of that you begin to think that that's the normal state of affairs. Whereas when you look at it in a longer perspective, we now realize that was a very abnormal period in the history of science in this country or

*Composed from exchanges occurring at the end of the second day as Miller analyzed each paper and redirected a question to each member of the symposium.

any other. And the fact that it just happens to coincide with my own active scientific career is one of the most lucky things that could ever have happened to anybody, and I'm enormously grateful.

So, the fact that we have three and a half billion dollars a year for science, I find it difficult to really moan about how poor we are and how little you can do with three and a half billion dollars. Now, if we don't fight for that three and a half billion dollars, you're obviously telling us—and for our own intellectual freedom, and our own social conscience, and our own moral health—it's going to be taken away from us. And that's the real message, that's more important than the budgetary message, I think. And it does seem to me to be inevitable that we're somehow going to have to take a more active role in defending ourselves; perhaps as Sig says, "A good offense is the best defense."

But, I got into the academic world because that was just what I didn't want to do! If I'd wanted to do that, I'd have gone into business. I had several opportunities through my family, and I'd be a much wealthier man, and I wouldn't be here in Houston now. I might own Houston.

But, this worries me, you know. It isn't what I want to do. I heard you say that maybe we can get a few of our friends who don't do what I want to do, and let them take care of it. I just want to know, when am I going to have time to do my science? These things intrude on me more and more. I feel I'm being run by accountants, controlled by lawyers, ordered about by bureaucrats, and spit upon by my university administration. But I'll take all that if they'll just leave me alone long enough to get my head into a problem that fascinates me, long enough to go into that special trancelike state where you feel, whether it's true or not, you feel you are being creative. That's the motor that runs the whole bloody three and a half billion dollars, after all. If we can't arrange our defense with some room in it for an awful lot of that, we're in trouble. I wondered what your thoughts were: In advocating advocacy, how are we to protect what we are advocating?

Bevan: I'm relieved that George didn't ask me a profound question, but he did ask me an important one. Let me say, first, I'll apologize if I was obfuscating with a lot of budget data. In my earlier chats with Rick I got the impression that was something you might be interested in.

I can't agree with George. While three and a half billion

dollars is a lot of money, I can't agree that's something we need not be concerned about when we face the eroding effects of inflation on a fixed income, if you will. And when we see the costs of compliance going up as much as 2000 percent in ten years, the real dollars we have to work with indeed *are* getting fewer. And while I'm sure it's not—at the moment at least—a completely worrisome matter for, say, *your* university, it is for many where they have . . . they find themselves with 50, 60, 70, 80 percent of their operating budgets based on federal dollars, and where they have staff commitments on soft money and they have tenured people, and they have to worry about, in effect, meeting a long-term institutional obligation to those people, and those dollars aren't there any longer. So I think that the budget thing is a matter at least of concern, if not to the individual investigator, then certainly to his institution.

But I think George raised a very important and troubling question for all of us. That is, how are we going to continue to be scientists if we've got to keep ourselves busy fighting the battle? Actually, before some of us got to Washington, we were busy doing that; trying to keep accounts and make "effort reports" and all the other things that involved complying with regulation. Nothing was free, and there was no free lunch. It just took us a long time to find that out.

Now, George is an extremely creative and productive person, and I think he should stay in the laboratory. And for those of us who may not be as productive, we have an obligation to see that he does, and do the other thing. I guess what I'm saying is that in a community of 150,000 academic scientists—and when I talk about the scientific and technical community generally, two and a half million people—not all of us are going to be George Millers. And there is room for a division of labor.

I think a division of labor in two senses. I think it's more . . . I have the personal bias that it's more important for a person to do well certain things on behalf of the scientific community. I'd rather see a person doing policy work well than doing third-rate science in the laboratory, so that even our young people are involved where they may not be. And after all, we all know that the productivity within the scientific community is not measured by how many Ph.D.s there are. There are many people who take degrees and who never make major contributions or any contribution at all from the point of view of the intellectual progress of the field. So that I do think that there is room for a division of labor and for career change. The question of measuring the effective and productive life, the scholarly life of a person, is a hard one, and I suppose it sometimes gets to be a matter of individual judgment on the part of that person, but I think it's important for those who have the courage to recognize that they may be peaking out to seek other kinds of productive roles on behalf of the scientific community.

Miller: I remember talking to a game theorist who said, "In life the reward for winning at one game is the right to play in another game." Then you add to that the Peter Principle . . . [*Laughter*]

Frankly, I'm afraid that if I tried to switch games at this point I'd wind up totally incompetent, but as long as there are people like you . . .

Bevan: George, those of us who've survived in administration know that that's part of the game . . . making switches . . . trying to get switches.

Koch: But you've just given up being a prophet, so you have room to do something else now.

Miller: A prophet without honor.

Koch: With much honor.

Conclusions

Miller's Closing Statement

Miller: I started us off yesterday morning by indicating that I was going to listen for a note of hope in the speeches at this symposium because I really believed that if I gave up hope that psychology would be of some benefit to mankind, I would probably give up psychology. But most of what I've heard here is that my hopes have been too high, that our needs are more complex and the ideas that we have available to meet those needs are weaker than I imagined in 1969.

    Perhaps, operating as I was at that time as a spokesman for the profession, I was too inclined to give my constituency the benefit of any scientific doubts I might have had. But what I've heard here has not managed to cure my optimism. I don't believe that our basic research is socially irrelevant, or that we can't continue to improve the services that we offer to individuals and groups, or even—and this is a point that was very important to me in 1969—that we can't promote reforms on the basis of more realistic public appreciation of the eternal compromise between what's humanly desirable and what's humanly possible. So I hold on to my hopes for psychology only slightly chastened by all the difficulties that these speakers have said lie in our path. I would point out that I never promised you it would be easy.

Kessel: I certainly don't want the last word, but you should remember that Rick Kasschau is responsible more than anybody else for what went on today and yesterday, and amongst thanks he deserves the most.

Koch: Yes.

Afterthoughts
George A. Miller
The Rockefeller University

I was unprepared for the response to my address to the American Psychological Association in 1969. Some of the stir may have resulted because the position I advocated was not one I would have been expected to advocate. As an experimental psychologist, I was not expected to advocate anything—I was expected to report on my research. But if I did choose to set aside my own work in order to address more pressing concerns, most who knew me would have expected a conventional defense of the experimental approach to the problems of psychology. Unexpected, unpredictable behavior tends to attract attention.

I was prepared for criticism from my experimental colleagues, but little developed. Some of them agreed with me; those who did not apparently decided to ignore it. What I was not prepared for was a flood of appreciative mail from psychologists of all varieties who felt that they had been "giving psychology away" for years and were gratified at last to have a spokesman; I have been told that my choice of that metaphor elevated me to the rank of a minor saint in the calendar of counseling psychology. Apparently I had formulated a point of view that many others had been groping toward.

That echoes of my address are still being heard, however, is less testimony to the wisdom of the views I advanced than to the importance of the issues I addressed. Although it took the tumultuous events of the sixties to force those issues to the top of everyone's agenda, they have remained there ever since. Indeed, conflict between the scientific and the professional roles of psychologists had been festering for years, with the prestige of the scientists pitted against the numbers of the professionals in many bitter debates at all levels, from departmental meetings to national conventions, from curriculum decisions to federal funding policies. It was inevitable that those arguments would erupt into the open eventually; the contentious atmosphere of the sixties merely hastened the event and focused our attention on it.

Although public debate might have led to some general consensus, the proceedings of this conference make it clear that no such consensus has emerged. If there is any agreement at all, it is that we have a problem that runs far deeper than the old quarrels between the laboratory and the clinic. Nowhere is that problem more clearly revealed than in our efforts to obtain federal funding for our work.

The exponential growth of science could not continue indefinitely, and during the sixties it became obvious that no longer could every worthwhile project be funded. It became necessary to choose, and in Washington the bureaucrats and politicians turned to scientists for priorities in terms of which intelligent choices could be made. It was not a question that scientists could answer. It was not merely that a scientist's definitions of "interesting" and "trivial" are so different from a layman's, although that was part of the difficulty. Science in this country is simply not organized to speak with a single voice on such matters—no one can say how many dollars spent on biochemistry are worth one dollar spent on astronomy. So Washington turned next to accountants and to notions of cost-effectiveness, leaving each discipline to make its own case however it could.

How should the case for psychology be presented? The question could not be avoided, but it could not be answered by a profession divided between its scientific and its professional aspirations. The professionals seemed to be providing services that the public wanted, but their case was weak as long as the scientists maintained that the base on which those services rested was pretentious or fraudulent. The scientists seemed to be in the best position to make intellectually serious claims, but their case was weak as long as the professionals maintained that the scientific results were trivial or irrelevant. As long as both sides insisted on sharing the label "psychology," they needed each other. The debate that came out into the open in the late sixties was a self-conscious attempt to resolve our internal differences and to present a unified, coherent image to the world.

The public pressure would not have been so powerful, however, if our disciplinary ambivalence had not reflected a personal ambivalence in many psychologists on both sides of the debate. Karl Lashley once said that in psychology we face a choice between being vague and being wrong; Lashley preferred to be wrong. For most psychologists, however, the choice seemed to be between being right and being relevant. No scientific psychologist enjoyed being irrelevant; no professional psychologist enjoyed substituting hunches for data. It was not enough to present a unified, coherent image to the world. Psychologists wanted, and still want, an image of their discipline that they can live with from day to day.

The search for such an image of psychology is reflected in each of the presentations at this conference. I will not comment on the different aspects of our common problem that each speaker addressed, except to say that the hope for a single image now seems to me an impossible dream. I wish the American Psychological Association could reform itself as the Federation of Psychological Sciences. But that, too, seems an impossible dream.

Nor will I try to present any new opinions, or any new defense of my old opinions. For the record, however, I can put down here some reflections on my situation and my behavior in 1969, in the hope of clarifying what I really had in mind.

At this point in time I cannot recall my personal reasons for entering the debate on the social responsibilities of psychologists, but I can reconstruct some of the considerations that led me to take the line I did. At the heart of it was a simple contrast I felt between institutionalized and personalized social action, between passing high-minded resolutions at professional meetings and helping people to help themselves. If psychologists were to become activists—and many were clearly determined to do so—I had no doubts about which kind of activism I favored. My preferences today are the same as they were then.

Around this nucleus I began to build my message. Advocating personalized social action had several virtues in my eyes. For one thing, helping people help themselves did not require the intervention, or even the blessings, of the American Psychological Association. It could take place without those heated and often pointless arguments among the members of the association, arguments that I felt often distracted us from duties that only the association could perform. For another, it enabled me to focus attention on the differences between two forms of social action, rather than on the differences between research and professional practice. I did not then, nor would I today, endorse any slackening in our efforts to expand the scientific base of psychology. Moreover, it suited an ill-formed notion I had about how democracies ought to work. If, by helping people help themselves, we could educate public opinion concerning the value of psychology, our message would reach the politicians in the most effective possible way—through their constituencies. On this point I am less optimistic today. I am less confident how to educate the public about the value of psychology, and I am less confident that politicians pay as much attention to voters as to lobbyists.

Nevertheless, on such grounds as these I felt I could follow a narrow line through most of the disputes of that time and deliver a useful address without having to choose between positions that were all, in my view, equally wrongheaded. As I began to develop these ideas, however, my basic theme became entangled with a second theme: I felt it necessary to argue that psychology really has learned something that could help people help themselves. If (heaven forbid!) I were to make the speech again today, I would probably choose different examples. But I should confess that I was surprised that so many psychologists objected so strenuously to my contention that psychological research has yielded many generalizations relevant to real human problems. I had assumed that my audience would take the truth of that claim for granted, that what was at issue was the most effective delivery system.

I have always believed that psychology is a revolutionary science. By that I mean that if the stated goals of scientific psychology—the understanding, prediction, and control of mental and behavioral phenomena—were to be realized, the social and personal implications would far outrun the implications of atomic energy or recombinant DNA. Indeed, the implications are so frightening that many people (including, apparently, many psychologists) deny that those goals, as stated, are realizable. That would be a comfortable solution to an Orwellian problem, but it would leave us with another problem, namely, defining new goals that are realizable. Personally, I am content to work toward understanding and prediction—the difficult social issues surrounding control still seem premature to me. It may turn out that people are like the weather: much easier to understand and predict (within limits) than to control.

How far we have come toward any of our goals does not strike me as a profitable topic for discussion in this forum. Let me return, therefore, to my original premise, that the social responsibilities of psychologists can best be discharged by learning how to help people help themselves—the idea that inspired my metaphor about giving psychology away.

My convictions on this score did not arise from any great practical experience in helping people, much less from any principaled devotion to a populist political ideology. They arose from my own experience in the dual role imposed by the demands of a modern university, the role of teacher-researcher. The most satisfying experiences I have had as a teacher were not in indoctrinating students with my beliefs, but in helping them develop the implications of their beliefs. I did not begin teaching in that spirit. I spent years lecturing to bench-bound victims, covering (rather than uncovering) the information I expected them to repeat to me on examinations. As the years passed and I gained self-confidence, however, I began to have more faith in learning and less faith in teaching—no doubt my research interest in the acquisition of language by children contributed to this gradual change in my teaching philosophy.

My idealism, therefore, has a rather different source from those attributed to me. My ideal is for teacher and students to work as a team dedicated to giving all members (and never think that teachers do not learn as much or more than students) the knowledge and skills they want to master. Like all ideals, I have seldom realized this one, but at least it helps me to recognize success if I see it.

When I tried to find within myself a model for psychologists in their professional roles, my conception of a good teacher shaped my ideas. I searched through my limited knowledge of psychological practice to find examples that seemed to parallel the goals I had set myself as a teacher. Robert White's notion of a need for competence fitted well with my idea, but perhaps the other examples I pointed to were less appropriate. I am less concerned to defend them than to clarify my intent in choosing them.

It has been interesting to have this excuse to revisit the questions that occupied so much of my time and thought in the sixties, and to see the spectrum of opinions on those questions that has emerged in the seventies. I must confess, however, that time and events have done little to alter the basic beliefs that I drew upon in 1969. If I have any regrets, they relate to my closing exhortation to my colleagues to give psychology away. The ideal I really had in mind could better have been phrased as an exhortation to help people help themselves. I still believe that that is a goal all psychologists can subscribe to, however much we may disagree on the best way to achieve it.

Postscript to the Symposium

Frank S. Kessel
University of Houston

The principal themes of this symposium were obviously twofold: First, George Miller's APA address, and second, arising out of that address and serving as a focus at another level, the set of issues I sketched in the Introduction. Given Miller's graceful personal coda on the theme of his address, what of the issues? What of the variations sounded by the six participants on the elements of that theme? How are their variations related to one another and to those of other voices?

SCIENCE AND SOCIETY

In keeping with the spirit of my Introduction it is worth noting initially that the climate surrounding these general issues shows no sign of becoming more temperate and comfortable for the scientific community. Pressures on the relationship between science and its public have not dissipated; changes in that relationship continue, as do simultaneous efforts to understand and shape its future course. For a clear, compelling confirmation one need look no further than Bevan's contribution here, dealing as it does with the relationship between science and in many respects its most important public, the federal government. With a characteristic combination of analysis and factual detail (albeit too much budgetary detail for Miller's taste!), he demonstrates how uneasy the relationship has become, considers the roots of the unease, and suggests both where we might go and how we might get there. As institutions and individuals we could do worse than to reread and pay heed.

One of Bevan's major worries is the "government's rapidly growing zeal for creating regulation." His illustrations do not, however, cover the question of regulation of the processes of scientific inquiry itself but they might well have. Increasingly, that has become a critical question and, in several guises, there is debate about society's means of encouraging or restraining the search for knowledge. This debate is covered well in an issue of *Daedalus* bearing the title "Limits of Scientific Inquiry" and appearing around the time of this symposium. In his epilogue Holton (1978) adds weight to Bevan's analysis:

> The vigorous public discussion about constraints on scientific research seems to have come upon us with startling suddenness. For decades, scientists had proudly accepted the well-known operational definition, "The scientific method is doing one's damndest, no holds barred." Now they are asked to add "except as laid down in guidelines issued by the Department of Health, Education and Welfare." The old image of science as the endless frontier is giving way in some quarters to the notion of science as the suspected frontier. . . . If the debate is of such recent origin, can it last? . . . Are we dealing here, too, with a highly visible but short-lived excitement? The answer seems to be a clear "No". . . . We have only begun to struggle with such problems. Whether one likes it or not, it seems to me, the "limits of scientific inquiry" disputes have been inevitable and overdue. Depending on the specific cases that clamor for attention of the parties, the intensity of the discussions may wax or wane,[1] but they have a certain pre-ordained character, and in maturing form will remain with us for a long time.

An important and anything-but-faddish debate therefore, but from how widely within the scientific community are its participants drawn? The answer is mixed. On the one hand, the overall field of "science, technology, and society" is growing rapidly in many areas of American higher education, building on contributions from many disciplines. And the field's pedagogy rests, in turn, on an increasing range of papers, books, and conferences that signal the spreading interest.[2]

On the other hand, it is unclear what proportion of active researchers (as opposed to historians, sociologists, and philosophers of science) go beyond a general awareness of the debate and reiteration of the classical "science-as-endless-frontier" position. Of course, saying that amounts to no disservice to those who are seriously concerned and involved. The single greatest source of recent controversy has been the "recombinant DNA affair," and several researchers were themselves responsible for opening up that debate. But then why is it that a recently published history of the discovery of DNA, written by two scientists, says almost nothing about that ongoing affair? Why does such a history betray a "lack of any perceptible social consciousness"? The questions and phrases are not mine but Toulmin's (1978) in reviewing the book. His answers underscore Bevan's contribution here and serve as a significant summary of where we stand now on the major sub-theme of science and society:

> For more than a decade there has been a shift in the historiography of science. The focus is now much more on the social and institutional context of scientific research. . . . Would it not have been worth putting this intellectual narrative [of DNA discovery] into a slightly broader context? Though the outcome of scientific research is rarely determined by its social infrastructure, its direction and priorities certainly are. . . . The

tantalizing impression remains that Portugal and Cohen did not address these further issues simply because it never occurred to them to do so. Like so many scientists, they were content to take their intellectual problems as they found them, and to discuss them apart from all wider questions about the social and institutional context of the research, or anything else.[3] . . . If many of the scientists involved were so taken aback by the recombinant DNA affair, the reason is clear enough. It never occurred to them that anyone would seriously imagine they wanted anything except to go on solving these fascinating theoretical problems. . . . Why should they be personally concerned with the technological applications of their results? By the time those had any practical reality the scientists themselves would be far away, caught up in some quite other set of intellectual issues. And in the meantime *of course* they could be trusted not to be careless in their research methods. What a thought! Indeed, it is probably their single-minded indifference to larger issues—philosophical, social, or whatever—that will ultimately condemn research scientists (not only in this field, but more generally) to some form of social and political accountability, even to public regulation. . . . From one point of view, it is a marvel that pure scientific research has gone on for so long, in an age of political questioning and skepticism, without any kind of formal public regulation. But it should be clear by now that, as a result of the recombinant DNA affair, the scientific research community is, at best, on probation. The starry-eyed innocence of a book like [this] can hardly go without comment. This is said without any hint of anti-scientific feeling on my part. On the contrary, my own long-standing loyalties to science . . . incline me to nostalgia for those earlier days, when science could go its own monastic way without fear of public attention. Still, if the joys and values of those days are to be preserved and appreciated, scientists are going to have to pay more attention to the social and political conditions that make a truly independent and self-directed science a viable part of the larger commonwealth. . . . The days when the political innocuousness of science could be taken for granted have—alas, maybe, but undeniably—gone forever.

PSYCHOLOGY AND SOCIETY

That psychology and psychologists are part of, or at least, sensitive to the overall science-society picture is demonstrated clearly enough by this symposium. So too by some of the symposia and papers on the program of APA's 1978 convention: "Social scientists' attempts to influence public policy"; "Bridging psychologists and policymakers"; "Policy implications of psychology"; "Theory and practice"; "Is relevance irrelevant?"; "Psychologists in political arenas"; "Psychological testing after Larry P.: Legal implications"; "Psychological testimony in court."

Naturally such titles do not say terribly much about the breadth of involvement and concern within psychology itself, nor about the extent of psychology's influence in wider outside arenas.[4] But it is my impression that these sorts of titles are appearing more frequently on convention programs. In any case, there is little doubt the Association for the Advancement of Psychology (AAP) has now been accepted by a sizable number of psychologists as an organization playing an appropriate advocacy role in the public policy domain. Which signals, in turn, that the guiding philosophy of AAP enthusiastically espoused here by Jackson—what he terms the "activist/collaborator model"—has at least struck a responsive chord.

Which is naturally not to say that such a model is beyond qualifications and questions. Indeed, several arise in relatively short order at points in the symposium discussions: Koch wonders whether the "advancement of psychology" and "promotion of human welfare" are necessarily synonomous, arguing that "guild interests" predominate when Jackson gets down to specifics. Miller, for his part, repeats a slightly earlier caution (1978) that "brilliance in science is no guarantee of superior wisdom in worldly affairs"—hence, on what grounds is the "scientific advocate" resting his case?—and also wonders how to avoid being a pawn in the political chess game.[5] To Jackson such questions have an escapist ring, especially if they are based on misplaced assumptions (about "value-free science," for example) that he deals with in the early parts of his paper, and more especially if the overall net effect is lack of involvement in pressing issues of the day. But the spirit of the questions remains, springing to life when Jackson suggests, in discussion, that we act as "agents of the public" advocating positions *"hopefully* based upon the evidence we have as psychologists" (my emphasis). Trouble is, as Jackson knows full well, and as White points out, in the political world one scientist's "truth" or "facts" can all too easily be countered by another's "truth."

And yet the spirit of Jackson's position survives and flourishes, and so it should. Allied to such a spirit the sort of debate represented here, but writ large across psychology, can only bring the science and profession closer to the kind of state envisaged by Bevan: where its representative societies initiate a variety of policy-related activities, where the distinction between psychology's educational and advocacy roles is nonetheless sharpened and honored, where understanding of the nature of the policymaking process is deepened. And all this can only enhance the contribution of psychologists, at least those so inclined, to that process and, thence, one assumes, to society.

"GIVING PSYCHOLOGY AWAY": THEORY-AND-PRACTICE/BASIC-AND-APPLIED

Although Miller (in his Afterthoughts) expresses some misgivings about the "giving psychology away" metaphor, it served as a convenient shorthand for the specific issue of how psychology can, does, and should influence society, of how best to conceive of the link between knowledge and practice, between basic and applied science. The policy-related arguments of Bevan and Jackson provide one view of these issues. There were, of course, others.

Scriven, bemoaning psychology's "failure to break free of the Newtonian fantasy," proposes an alternative model (as exemplified by "OWT" and "IQ") of the theory-practice dimension. The matter of psychology's fantasy (and related states of mind) is best left to the next section, but the model itself should give us pause. Scriven is scrutinizing some of the fundamental presuppositions psychologists have held regarding "application," and his questions make eminently good sense to me. While one can and should celebrate theoretical insights on intrinsic intellectual grounds (and doubtless Scriven would do so himself), it is worth asking why we "can't conceive of practical research that doesn't involve applying a theory." A Zen turn of mind may be necessary, but it is worth examining the possibility that atheoretical, purely practical problem-solving "*is* the intellectual content" and can have "high yield." Scriven's paraphrase of Lewin, "there's nothing as theoretically important as a good practice," is not a bad starting point for serious examination of the conventional theory-praxis position.

Whether Scriven's examples of the OWT/IQ model at work in psychology carry much weight is another question. But he could argue that it has not been given much of an opportunity. Suffice it to say that some turn of mind leads one to start noting views that reinforce his basic position. For example, after spending a year in a bilingual public school program as teacher and not researcher, Cazden (1976) writes on "how knowledge about language helps the classroom teacher—or does it?":

> Of course, research knowledge about language isn't the only basis for improved action. I think it's fair to say that there is a general trans-Atlantic contrast at this point. Whereas Americans like me have worked "down," trying to derive implications for education and theories about language and its development, colleagues in England have worked "up" from instances of the best classroom practice.[6]

Perhaps, therefore, we need turn our minds east but no further than across the Atlantic! As another example, consider the Study of Mathematically Precocious Youth (SMPY) conducted by Stanley and colleagues, a study that has had wide impact and about which Wallach (1978) says the following in a recent review:

> What is particularly striking here is how little that is distinctly psychological seems involved in SMPY, and yet how fruitful it appears to be. It is as if trying to be psychological throws us off the course and into a mire of abstract dispositions that help little in facilitating students' demonstrable talents. . . . But all this in fact is not unpsychological; it simply is different psychology.[7]

White's view of what it means to give psychology away is more poetic in style but no less "practical" in substance, having been prompted in part by extensive experience in entering the worlds of practitioners and policymakers. The phrase "entering their worlds" is apt, of course. For what he provides, building on the anthropological concept of myth,[8] is a compelling picture of how, say, the event of "Johnny learns to read" is viewed in the heterogeneous symbolic worlds of all those involved in that event. "These people," says White, "this heterogeneity, is practice," and giving psychology away means attempting "to benefit this practice system with knowledge." How? By shaping their symbolic worlds, a process which occurs, in any case, whenever the psychologist communicates with the non-psychologist.

As should be apparent, White's account is far richer than conveyed by a bare summary, not least of all because his analysis of the giving-away process is embedded in a consideration of psychology's historical and sociological contexts along the "historiographical" lines advocated by Toulmin. In discussion, White acknowledges that not everything about psychology-into-policy-and-practice can be said to involve the carrying forward of myths. But it should be clear that in speaking in such illuminating fashion about "psychological findings . . . offered as components of mythic stories" White presents us with a view as far removed from the classical "three-zones" notion as Scriven's, though in a very different direction.[9]

In one interesting respect, and at one level, Koch takes a position not at all dissimilar to White's. Having called on us, in characteristically colorful and compelling fashion,[10] to take psychology back, he presents an alternate view of psychology which implies an alternate giving-away process (if there is to be one at all!). Psychology is best regarded, not as a repository of facts and findings waiting to be put into practice, but as a body of psychologists with "rich and specialized sensibilities relevant to the particular phenomenal domain at issue." Thus, as Koch argues in later discussion, we give away not psychology but psychologists. Not psychologists who are "technicians under the cloak of scientific impeccability" but psychologists who are "disciplined connoisseurs of ranges of human experience," who have "rich and specialized sensibilities relevant to the particular phenomenal domain at issue." And what such psychologists do vis-à-vis the non-psychologist is to employ such sensibilities to assist the latter in "making sense of things," in avoiding misleading simplisms, in deepening their understanding of the matter at hand. In a word, or in White's words, the psychologist seeks to add depth and insight to the non-psychologist's "symbolic world." Nor is the psychologist the "expert." The non-psychologist is regarded as a full and even more-than-equal partner in the process, in keeping both with Williams's central sentiment that the psychological measurement community be committed to the integrity of the individual[11] and with the underlying spirit of Miller's original address (as enunciated in his Afterthoughts).

Again, there is far more to Koch's view than this, and numerous questions are worth pursuing. For one thing, since he concedes that the pool of "disciplined connoisseurs" will ever be limited, his position is, in some ways, quixotic.[12] Nonetheless, what is significant in the present context is that the essential character of his position is consistent with the views of Scriven and White and, to a somewhat lesser extent, Bevan and Jackson. As different and yet complementary positions they all provide alternative and, to my mind, liberating perspectives on the theory-practice, basic-applied issue. In addition, standing on a foundation of these kinds of analyses, "helping people help themselves" can amount to as elevated a structure as Miller rightly believed, and believes, it is.

PSYCHOLOGY AS "SCIENCE"

One major thread running through the positions I have reviewed thus far is the argument that psychology's mistaken views of the basic-applied link have had their source in the adoption of the physical science model of that link. And that, the speakers agree, is but a reflection of psychology's attempts to mimic the physical sciences in all matters "scientific." To Bruner's "methodolatory" and my introductory comment about a "fossilized model" has now been added a rich store of like-minded phrases: From White, "physics envy,"[13] the reminder that Wundt—our father of experimental psychology—felt that "a fully experimental psychology would be 'trivial'," and the contention that we have not one discipline but "a multiparadigmatic, pluralistic set of inquiries." From Scriven, "the Newtonian fantasy" and "the dead hand of an irrelevant model," argument about why and how we are "theory junkies," and discussion of "the great fiasco of the value-free commitment" as a repeat of his earlier writing (see the Introduction). And lest it be thought that Scriven is expressing a minority or extreme view, consider a recent AAAS address by Max Black (1978) on "scientific neutrality":

> On the whole, the thesis of the gap between "is" and "ought," although it has had enormous appeal and widespread currency, deserves to be regarded as one of the most debilitating dogmas of contemporary Western civilization. . . . The "neutrality thesis" becomes particularly pernicious when coupled with a correlative view about the alleged "subjectivity" of normative and evaluative judgments, and especially so when the realm of rationality is exclusively identified with that of scientific discourse.

It is Koch, however, who provides the most wide-ranging and concentrated critique of the conventional conception of psychological science. He repeats and extends earlier arguments that we need "a sensible alternative to the absurdities of the definitional schemata of logical positivism and operationalism," that the view that "psychology can be an integral discipline is [a] nineteenth-century myth,"[14] that we do far better to think in terms of "the psychological studies"[15] employing "methods [that are] contextual and flexible" and "conceptual ordering devices [that are] perspectival, sensibility-dependent relative to the inquirer, and often noncommensurable." Which leads, in turn, to the suggestion that "psychology must finally accept the circumstance that extensive and important sectors of psychological study require modes of inquiry rather more like those of the humanistics than the sciences," and that the knowledge or "epistemically rich concepts" already embedded in the humanities and the natural language can serve as a touchstone for knowledge—claims made in the psychological studies: hence his "classificatory test for conceptual frameworks" employing what I might call "ontological validity" as its key criterion.

That the natural language of Koch's own paper—why bother to paraphrase?—calls for more than casual, one-time reading goes without saying. So too the fact that his language points toward an ontology anything but familiar or initially comforting to most psychologists. As one example, the subjective-sounding argument that we use "high-order, refined, and relevantly specialized sensitivity" to understand human functioning on the surface flies in the face of what is generally considered science's publicly shared, "objective" character. But then, Koch might argue, is "objective" necessarily synonymous with the lowest common denominator of scientists' observational and analytical capacities? Would we want to place any store in what tone-deaf individuals had to say about the harmonic qualities of a Beethoven sonata?

In any event, what is worth saying is that neither the need for re-reading nor the challenge of an unconventional ontology can justifiably preclude serious examination of Koch's point of view.[16] For his ontology is not only unfamiliar but, to my taste, rich; and rich not only on its own terms but in the perspectives it offers for a psychology genuinely disposed toward growth beyond "physics envy."[17] Whether the discipline is so disposed is an open question. Scriven, for one, confesses to having been driven by psychology's inertia to simply "poking fun at the Newtonian fantasy with a good strong stick"! But then perhaps the collective weight of the ideas in this symposium is substantial enough to help effect a change of direction, although that is the very last metaphor I should be employing in this context!

EDUCATING PSYCHOLOGISTS

Although the issue of educating psychologists was barely explored during the symposium, the kinds of positions taken on other issues, notably that of science-society relations, all point in the same general direction, namely, agreement with Bevan's argument (mentioned in the

Introduction) that psychological scientists need to be prepared for diverse roles in diverse settings. Says Scriven, "One might as well face the fact that training psychologists for practical contributions will mean quite a reform in the *curriculum* (and not just the orientation) of psychology departments." White points to the now obvious fact of life that the research and teaching market is hardly bright and that graduates are going to move into non-academic settings whether one likes it or not. Whereupon Bevan and Koch remind us that it is a largely American, and largely American psychology, misconception that "vigorous intellectual life only exists in the academy,"[18] while Bevan suggests that there is surely room for division of labor in the larger community of 150,000 scientists.

This is again a theme being widely sounded. Saks (1978), for example, reflecting on his experience as a social psychologist on a state legislative commission, is led to this conclusion (framed, you will note, in terms of the conventional basic-applied, theory-practice view):

> Knowing empirical findings and theory is not enough. One does not then automatically see the connections between the psychological principles and the social problem. I would argue that the psychological knowledge is applicable, but application requires some skill, some practice, to make the transfer, to reconceptualize the facts of a problem within the framework of psychological knowledge, to see what otherwise would not be seen. There are learnable skills, but they are taught in few, if any, graduate programs. . . . I did not feel qualified to chair a legislative subcommittee. I was trained to conduct research and to communicate knowledge; that is what my professional role models did. I was not prepared to lead a committee planning social policy. Since that time, I have been preparing myself to assume such roles when called upon. I suggest that we prepare some of our students to do the same. . . . How to do all this preparing [is] a radical departure from the way most of us presently conceive even the applied social psychologist's role.

And some new forms of training and preparation are emerging. In the area of developmental psychology, for example, the Bush Foundation has recently established four university centers for training individuals interested in child development and social policy (at UCLA, Michigan, North Carolina, and Yale), while at the Society for Research in Child Development's 1979 biennial meeting an extensive workshop was devoted to creating training programs in the same area.

A related sign of the times is the convening of conferences at which basic researchers and practitioners explore common ground, for example, "Implications of Basic Speech and Language Research for the School and Clinic." This is an instructive case in point because of both the conference's fundamental purpose and some of its outcomes:

> Central in importance in planning the conference was the conviction that we could find knowledgeable basic researchers who could summarize the state of the art in each of the various segments of speech and language

research we had designated. We asked each of these investigators to survey a particular segment of the field and to look forward to potential areas of application of this basic knowledge. . . . [But] neither the state-of-the-art papers nor their discussions were particularly rich in examples of knowledge that could be exported immediately to the applied fields. There appear to be two reasons for this: First, as is apparent from a study of the papers, the authors tended to concentrate on the problems most on their minds, namely the current, vexing issues in speech and language research. They were more likely to point to problems, controversies, and unsettled issues than to describe what is known in an even-handed, textbook-like manner. This was probably inevitable, although we thought we had taken care to minimize current issues in designing the conference. When researchers get together they tend to talk about what they are doing, regardless of their assignments. (Jenkins 1978)

Before laying a charge of gross egocentrism at the basic researchers' door we should note Jenkins' second reason, namely, that in the language and speech domain many findings are already "in the field" (in itself an interesting state of affairs). Hence, "there seemed to be no great urgency in moving basic findings" into practice. Nevertheless it seems reasonable to expect that when researchers get together with practitioners they do *not* "talk about what they [the researchers] are doing, regardless of their assignments." More broadly, it seems appropriate to conclude that a greater sensitivity to and understanding of the "symbolic worlds" and needs of practitioners and policymakers is one quality essential for working in nonacademic settings; and that the education of psychologists, or at least some psychologists, will have to be modified to foster this quality and others.[19]

PERSONAL STYLES AND QUALITIES

To speak of "at least some psychologists" is to introduce a more general qualification. Despite their shared emphasis on psychology's need for a broadened view of the issues under review and on the specific value of moving beyond basic academic research in new ways, the symposium participants undoubtedly agree that there are "dangers in an unduly utilitarian view" (as I put it in the Introduction). Appropriately, it is Miller who, having helped to set the ball rolling in the direction of giving psychology away,[20] sounds the warning loudest. To Bevan's conclusion that "the good old days are gone forever" and that scientists are going to have to join the political fray in various ways, Miller replies that he got into academic life in the first place because he did not want to be involved in business or politics. He asks when he would have time "to do my own science" and makes a plea, best described as passionate, to be "left alone by lawyers, accountants, bureaucrats, and university administrators long enough to do creative work. . . . If we can't arrange our defense with concern for lots of that [creative work] . . . we're in trouble." Bevan's own reply, in equally personal and arresting terms, is that the problem of "how to continue to be scientists if we have to fight the battle" is undoubtedly critical but not all that new. What we now need is to acknowledge and value a division of labor: "George is extremely creative and productive. . . . We have an obligation to see that he [can do] his thing. Others who are less productive [in the conventional basic-research sense] can do the other." Thus celebrating psychology's—better, the psychological studies'—pluralism means both enhancing it by more widespread involvement outside academia *and* celebrating the value of creative basic research, much as in "the good old days"; and where the criterion of creativity does not rest solely, if at all, on pragmatic considerations, on immediate or even distant "payoffs."

I have cited the Bevan-Miller exchange because it conveys so well some of psychology's and psychologists' conflicts,[21] as well as the means of their resolution. Both its substance and tenor also bring me to two sets of concluding comments. One, about the personal qualities of scientists in general, reinforces Miller's view and comes from an unlikely source; the other is about the personal qualities of those involved in this symposium.

On scientists in general: In the *New York Times Book Review*, on the very day after the end of the symposium, John Leonard devoted his column to the images of scientists projected in contemporary literature. In a coincidence too curious to go unnoted here, Leonard's comments focus on what he refers to as "an engaging new book called 'Spontaneous Apprentices: Children and Language' [by] George A. Miller, a professor of psychology at the Rockefeller University." The convergence of his comments and some of Miller's sentiments the previous day is striking:

> What makes "Spontaneous Apprentices" so agreeable is its portrait of scientists at work in the everyday, unencumbered by crash programs, doomsday deadlines, malice, greed, the specter of Alfred Nobel, the appetite of war for the technology of death, and so on. . . . It is a civilized activity, this science, even when—as is most often the case—it is boring. It is also a social activity. . . . And it is rather dreamy, an innocent ambition to know and explain on the part of not-so-spontaneous apprentices. . . . In my experience, the kind of science and the kinds of scientists described by Dr. Miller are typical: curious and civilized. To be sure, the mandarins of physics got out of hand, and the geneticists ought not to be allowed to do the same. But most scientists go about their business of trying to understand the way it all works. I do not, however, find this science and these scientists in the pages of contemporary literature. I meet evil and monsters instead. Not teachers and healers, but black magicians and wicked witches. Not Prometheus or Faust, but Frankenstein and Dr. Strangelove. Science, according to the dominant literary sensibility, seems entirely morbid and manipulative, power-hungry and amoral. It seeks mastery. Anything it can do, it will do, just because it can. . . . Why are our writers so hard on the case of science? Surely the desire for elegance, the sense of wonder, the experience of mystery and the uses of inspiration belong as much to science as to art.

On this symposium: Leonard would doubtless have found this symposium similarly "agreeable." Here too were scholars/scientists "at work in the everyday," exhibiting in full measure the quality of being "curious and civilized," of being "teachers and healers," of both desiring and exhibiting "elegance" and "inspiration." They did so each in his individual way, in styles discernible in their papers and perhaps conveyed by some of my comments here.

Some of these styles, at least on the surface, might actually make some pause before speaking of "healers"! But running through the symposium was a spirit of warmth, wisdom, and wit that deserves to be noted and celebrated. Though such a spirit is seldom adequately conveyed in print, its presence is signaled at small points in the introductions and discussions, some of which I have referred to already. Amongst others:

> Miller's casual relevation that he was nominated for the presidency of APA at precisely the time he was contemplating resigning from the organization!
>
> His deadpan introduction of Jackson, mentioning, almost in passing, that they had met but once before some nine years earlier; this followed by Jackson's own "true story" of the fateful day and manner of that meeting, just as Miller was to deliver the very address the present symposium was examining.
>
> And Bevan's opening reminiscences of the day of his preliminary oral some thirty-five years earlier, when a certain Sigmund Koch sat on his committee.
>
> In discussion, White gently reaching out to Koch and Koch reciprocating on the matter of respecting every individual's efforts to make sense of his or her world.
>
> White also voicing tentative and quietly compelling thoughts about truth and beauty in science.
>
> Jackson taking on all comers in a spirited defense of his paper.
>
> And Koch, ever at the ready with the pithy, penetrating phrase, even at the low point in his daily cycle and even as a means of turning his own error into audience hilarity: ". . . teacher in a small New England school . . . Didn't I say New Zealand? I said New England? There *are* no inspired teachers in New England! Very, very definitely New Zealand!"

At some point during the symposium a colleague buttonholed me with the comment, "Well, this is all very exciting and challenging stuff but what are we left with? What are you going to tell the graduate students on Monday?" I don't know what I replied that day, but now I would say that the symposium was indeed exciting and challenging; that the excitement and challenge came from the intellectual and personal qualities of the participants; and that psychology (and society) is richer for the fact that six of them are bonafide, committed members of the discipline and one a philosopher with strong ties to it. Thus, as psychology moves into its second official century, confronting enduring and new issues,[22] the chances of creative and symbiotic growth are all the greater for the reach of such men and their ideas. *That* is what I would say to the graduate students.

NOTES

[1] Since this symposium human *in vitro* fertilization has had a successful outcome for the first time—a case that certainly clamors for the attention of all parties and creates a distinct waxing of the discussions' intensity!

[2] Here, as elsewhere, how to keep up?! Probably the single best source is the quarterly review of *Science, Technology, and Human Values* published under the auspices of Harvard's Program on Science, Technology, and Public Policy.

[3] Ironically, James Watson himself was not one of the many. His "personal account of the discovery of the structure of DNA" (the actual subtitle of *The Double Helix*) is a striking example—if not *the* example—of one form of the broadened historiographic approach. For many scientists, of course, Watson's account of the personal and interpersonal factors at work in the DNA search was far too broad and candid. See Stent's (1978) enlightening reconsideration of the book, and the views of its critics, in the light of subsequent events (including the unlikely return, some nine years later, of some of the central characters, this time to the scene of the recombinant DNA affair).

[4] One has to search long and hard to find the contributions of psychologists in the reasonably extensive bibliographies in each of the *Science, Technology, and Human Values* reviews. (See note 2.) This may be due in part to an editorial and readership bias towards the physical and biological sciences, but, to my mind, in only small part.

[5] In so doing Miller promulgates a new version of his famous "magical number seven" principle! More importantly, he suggests that psychologists played a far more peripheral role in the *Brown* Supreme Court decision ("provided scholarly footnotes") than I had argued in the Introduction. Gottlieb (personal communication) has made the same point. On that matter my sketch was not only sketchy but misleading! For extended treatments see Rosen (1972) and Saks (1977, 1978), the latter speaking of how judges and decisionmakers use empirical research "as a hook on which to hang their presuppositions."

[6] Without consideration, at some point, of variation from country to country the overall picture of science-society relations misses an important dimension. See Nelkin (1978).

[7] See Stanley's (1978) own reflections, even though they are framed largely within the conventional basic-applied formula.

[8] White's meaning is conveyed by Sagan (1977): "I am not here employing the word 'myth' in its present popular meaning of something widely believed and contrary to fact, but rather in its earlier sense, as a metaphor of some subtlety on a subject difficult to describe in any other way."

[9] Jackson and Kieslar (1977) employ terms that are "non-mythic," and hence perhaps more palatable to some, in presenting a position similar to White's.

[10] As Koch himself indicates, on occasion his "fashion" or style is hyperbolic. Which leads to the observation that psychologists—better still, scientists in general—do

not routinely encounter or value a diversity of intellectual and writing styles (in *scientific* work, of course), let alone a full-blown effort in "new literary criticism"! An "unconventional" piece therefore runs the risk of having its substance less than fully appreciated for the wrong reasons.

[11] By and large, Williams chooses—perhaps understandably—not to "pluck the rose" I had placed before him in the Introduction. See Scarr (1979) for a related analysis.

[12] That is, "impractical." After all, what are the rest of us to do in the meanwhile?! Another simile, however, is "visionary," which to my ears has a more appropriate, positive connotation: "A person who is given to audacious ideas."

[13] Stop the presses! A more diligent reading of the discussion transcript would have revealed that a "member of the audience" used this fine, felicitous phrase first. George Howard, on the Houston faculty, deserves both credit for the phrase and my apologies!

[14] Koch's "myth" is intended, I suspect, to convey both the neutral, anthropological, and the more common, "fictitious" sense.

[15] Note Miller's afterthought that "the hope for a single image [of psychology] now seems to me an impossible dream. I wish the American Psychological Association could reform itself as the Federation of Psychological Sciences."

[16] See note 10 on the wrong reasons for not fully appreciating or for dismissing an argument.

[17] It may be worth reiterating that the "physics" envied is itself out of date. Nor do those envied seem to have as much difficulty with the flavor of at least some of Koch's arguments: "Amusingly, psychology is one of the few fields in the community of scholars in which it could still seem heretical to suggest that a germ-proof curtain cannot be erected between science and the humanities. The appalling threat upon intellectual hygiene thereby created has been weathered quite heroically by the physicists, mathematicians, biologists, historians of science, and philosophers (among others)." (Koch 1976)

[18] See note 6.

[19] In a personal communication Jenkins has indicated that, at Minnesota, "We're not putting out any routine experimentalists any more." Graduate students there are required to become involved in some "applied" area, a practice now probably widespread across the country. How they are involved and whether their training is explicitly directed towards the types of sensitivities and skills I am alluding to here are, of course, the interesting questions. Incidentally, Jenkins et al.'s (1978) refinement of the conventional theory-practice dimension in the light of their conference experiences is worth examining.

[20] Again the Newtonian metaphor!

[21] Note Miller's Afterthoughts on disciplinary and personal ambivalence.

[22] Appropriately enough, the Second Houston Symposium, held in May 1979, bears the title "Psychology's Second Century: Enduring Issues."

References

Black, M. Scientific neutrality: Between truth and irresponsibility. *Encounter*, 1978, (2), 56–62.

Cazden, C.B. How knowledge about language helps the classroom teacher—or does it: A personal account. *The Urban Review*, 1976, 9, 74–90.

Holton, G. Epilogue to the issue, "Limits of scientific inquiry." *Daedalus*, 1978, 107 (2), 227–234.

Jackson, P. & Kieslar, S.B. Fundamental research and education. *Educational Researcher*, 1977, 6 (2), 13–18.

Jenkins, J.J. Implications of basic research: Thoughts behind the conference. In J. F. Kavanagh and W. Strange (Eds.), *Speech and language in the laboratory, school and clinic*. Cambridge, Mass.: The MIT Press, 1978.

Jenkins, J.J., Liberman, A.M., & Curtis, J.F. Problems and promise in applying basic research. In J.F. Kavanagh and W. Strange (Eds.), *Speech and language in the laboratory, school and clinic*. Cambridge, Mass.: The MIT Press, 1978.

Koch, S. Language communities, search cells, and the psychological studies. In W. J. Arnold (Ed.), *Nebraska symposium on motivation, 1975*. Lincoln: University of Nebraska Press, 1976.

Leonard, J. Science, virtuous villain. *New York Times Book Review*, April 9, 1978.

Miller, G.A. Review of J. Bronowski, *A sense of the future*. *Human Nature*, 1978, 1 (2), 20–26.

Nelkin, D. Conference on the social assessment of science. *Science, Technology, and Human Values*, 1978, No. 25, 6–7.

Rosen, P.L. *The Supreme Court and social science*. Urbana: University of Illinois Press, 1972.

Sagan, C. *The dragons of Eden*. New York: Random House, 1977.

Saks, M.J. *Jury verdicts*. Lexington, Mass.: D.C. Heath, 1977.

Saks, M.J. Social psychological contributions to a legislative subcommittee on organ and tissue transplants. *American Psychologist*, 1978, 33, 680–690.

Saks, M. J. Psychologist as policy-maker. Paper presented to the American Psychological Association Convention, Toronto, August 1978.

Scarr, S. From evolution to Larry P., or what should we do about IQ tests? *Intelligence*, 1978, 4 (2), 325-342.

Stanley, J.C. Is relevance irrelevant? Invited address to the American Psychological Association Convention, Toronto, August 1978.

Stent, G. S. Reconsiderations of J.D. Watson, *The double helix*. *Human Nature*, 1978, 1 (8), 92-96.

Toulmin, S. Review of F.H. Portugal and J.S. Cohen (Eds.), *A century of DNA*. *Human Nature*, 1978, 1 (6), 18–23

Wallach, M.A. Review of J.C. Stanley, et al. (Eds.), *The gifted and the creative*. *Contemporary Psychology*, 1978, 23, 616–617.

Appendix A
Psychology as a Means of Promoting Human Welfare *

George A. Miller
Rockefeller University

The most urgent problems of our world today are the problems we have made for ourselves. They have not been caused by some heedless or malicious inanimate Nature, nor have they been imposed on us as punishment by the will of God. They are human problems whose solutions will require us to change our behavior and our social institutions.

As a science directly concerned with behavioral and social processes, psychology might be expected to provide intellectual leadership in the search for new and better personal and social arrangements. In fact, however, we psychologists have contributed relatively little of real importance —even less than our rather modest understanding of behavior might justify. We should have contributed more; although our scientific base for valid contributions is far from comprehensive, certainly more is known than has been used intelligently.

This is the social challenge that psychologists face. In the years im-

---

*Presidential address to the American Psychological Association in Washington, D. C., September 1969. It is customary on this occasion to summarize one's own research. Although that would be a more comfortable role, I have decided instead to take this opportunity to express some personal opinions about the current state of our discipline and its potential role in meeting the human problems of our society. This departure from tradition is intended to honor the theme of the 1969 convention, "Psychology and the Problems of Society." I am indebted to several friends, and especially to J. A. Varela, for critical comments on earlier drafts.

Requests for reprints should be sent to George A. Miller, The Rockefeller University, New York, N. Y. 10021.

Miller, G.A. Psychology as a means of promoting human welfare. *American Psychologist*, 1969, 24, 1063–1075. Copyright 1969 by the American Psychological Association. Reprinted by permission.

mediately ahead we must not only extend and deepen our understanding of mental and behavioral phenomena, but we must somehow incorporate our hard-won knowledge more effectively into the vast social changes that we all know are coming. It is both important and appropriate for us, on occasions such as this, to consider how best to meet this social challenge.

In opening such a discussion, however, we should keep clearly in mind that society has not commissioned us to cure its ills; a challenge is not a mandate. Moreover, there is nothing in the definition of psychology that dedicates our science to the solution of social problems. Our inability to solve the pressing problems of the day cannot be interpreted as an indictment of the scientific validity of our psychological theories. As scientists we are obliged to communicate what we know, but we have no special obligation to solve social problems.

Our obligations as citizens, however, are considerably broader than our obligations as scientists. When psychological issues are raised in this broader context, we cannot evade them by complaining that they are unscientific. If we have something of practical value to contribute, we should make every effort to insure that it is implemented.

I believe that the majority of American psychologists have accepted this broader interpretation of our responsibilities and have been eager—perhaps, sometimes, overly eager to apply our science to social problems. We have not been aloof or insensitive; the bulk of our profession works full time on exactly such problems. And I do not wish to discount the many and often successful efforts toward application that we have made already. Yet I cannot escape the impression that we have been less effective than we might have been. "Why" and "what more might be done" are questions that have troubled me increasingly in recent years.

First, however, I would like to raise a somewhat parochial question.

ROLE OF THE AMERICAN PSYCHOLOGICAL ASSOCIATION

If we accept this challenge to use psychology to solve social problems, what role should we expect the American Psychological Association to play? I raise this question because my experience as an officer of APA has taught me that many of our members look to their national organization for leadership in insuring that our scientific and professional activities have greater social relevance.

Psychologists have been well represented among those who sign petitions of political protest (Ladd 1969), and they have not failed to make their opinions heard in their own national headquarters. Scarcely a meeting of the board of directors in recent years has not featured one or more petitions from concerned members, committees, boards, divisions, or state associations requesting some action related to public affairs. These matters range all the way from the proper use of psychological tests, where APA usually has something to say, to the endorsement of particular political candidates, where APA usually does not.

These demands have imposed considerable strain on the association, which was not created to be an instrument for social action and which responds hesitantly to any suggestion that it should become something more than a scientific and professional organization. But it does respond. I was surprised to discover how seriously APA regards any legitimate request from its membership, and how sensitive it is to the social implications of its actions, policies, and communications. Some members wish APA would do more, some less. On balance, I think APA has reflected reasonably accurately the general consensus of its members with respect to its role in public affairs.

It is not my intention to raise here any of the specific issues of public policy that have concerned the board of directors and the Council of Representatives, or even to offer a general formula for deciding what the public role of the APA should be. Procedurally, I am willing to stand on the thoughtful recommendations of the ad hoc Committee on Public Affairs (Tyler 1969).

A point of general interest, however, and one that relates more directly to the theme I wish to discuss, is the frequently heard argument that APA should take some action or other because the first article of our Bylaws states that the association shall have as its object to promote human welfare, a goal that is echoed in our statement of the *Ethical Standards of Psychologists*.

This argument is usually made by those who recommend that APA should publicly advocate some particular social reform. When these recommendations are appropriate, the action is adopted—the necessary letters are written, public statements are released to the press, etc. But not every recommendation is acceptable. It has been my impression that the less related the issue is to the scientific and professional interests of our membership, the greater is the likelihood that the promotion of human welfare will be invoked in the course of the discussion.

In most cases this argument has not persuaded me; I have traced my skepticism to two sources.

First, even the most cursory study of welfare economics will show that human welfare has never been operationally defined as a social concept. If there is such a thing as human welfare in the general sense, it must be some kind of weighted average. In difficult cases, where disagreement is most probable, something that advances the welfare of one group may disadvantage another group. The problem is to decide whose welfare we wish to promote. The APA is committed to advancing the welfare of psychologists, of course, but we dare not assume blindly that whatever is good for psychology must always be good for humanity.

Vague appeals to human welfare seldom answer specific questions because we seldom have sufficient information to decide which actions will have the desired result. And even when we do have sufficient wisdom to know in advance which actions will promote human welfare most effectively, we still face the ethical question of whether such actions are morally permissible.

My first reason for distrusting appeals to human welfare, therefore, is that they do little to clarify the logical, informational, or ethical bases for making difficult decisions. Something more is required than a sincere declaration that our heart is in the right place.

My second reason has to do with the fact that the phrase is usually quoted out of context. At the risk of losing your attention, therefore, I would like to state Article I of our Bylaws in full:

> The objects of the American Psychological Association shall be to advance psychology as a science and as a means of promoting human welfare by the encouragement of psychology in all its branches in the broadest and most liberal manner; by the promotion of research in psychology and the improvement of research methods and conditions; by the improvement of the qualifications and usefulness of psychologists through high standards of professional ethics, conduct, education, and achievement; by the increase and diffusion of psychological knowledge through meetings, professional contacts, reports, papers, discussions, and publications; thereby to advance scientific interests and inquiry, and the application of research findings to the promotion of the public welfare. (APA 1968, p. xii)

As I understand Article I, our corporate aim is to promote psychology. We justify that aim by our belief that psychology can be used for the public good. I do not understand Article I as a general license to endorse social actions or positions, however meritorious on other grounds, that do not advance psychology as a science and as a means of promoting human welfare. The APA is our own creature, of course; we can change our bylaws any way we like. As presently conceived, however, APA does not have a charter to intervene on behalf of every good cause that comes along.

There are many things of social value that APA can do, and many that it has already done. If your officers have not always seemed hungry for innovation, eager to reshape APA to meet every new social issue, they have certainly been open to constructive change within the scope of our charter. I believe they have reflected the wishes of the bulk of the membership, and I feel no need to apologize for what has been accomplished. The APA has been doing what its membership wanted to do, and doing it rather well.

Of course, the membership has been far from unanimous in these matters. For example, there has been a running debate in recent years concerning the proper role for individual psychologists to play in the initiation of social reforms. We have been divided as to whether psychologists should remain expert advisers or should take a more active, participatory responsibility for determining public policy. An adviser is expected to summarize the arguments pro and con, but to leave the policy decisions to others; a participant wants to make the policy decisions himself.

Those who favor more active participation by individual psychologists tend to argue that APA should also become directly involved in advocating particular social policies. This whole debate seems to presuppose, however, that social reforms can occur only as a result of policy decisions by government or industry. This presupposition should not go unchallenged. Perhaps our options for promoting human welfare are broader than this debate would suggest.

It was E. G. Boring who first impressed on me the importance of a clear distinction between Psychology with a capital P and psychology with a small p. Capital-P Psychology refers to our associations, departments, laboratories, and the like. Small-p psychology refers to the discipline itself. Capital-P Psychology can do little to promote human welfare, outside of its faithful promotion of small-p psychology. We should not, through impatience or bad judgment, try to use capital-P Psychology where only small-p psychology could succeed. Let us by all means do everything we can to promote human welfare, but let us not forget that our real strength in that cause will come from our scientific knowledge, not from our national association.

In my opinion, our association can never play more than a supporting role in the promotion of social change. I do not conclude from this that APA has become irrelevant or useless, or, even worse, that it has tacitly endorsed a political bureaucracy that presides over the inequitable distribution of health, wealth, and wisdom in our society. The fact that APA has not reformed society does not mean that it approves the status quo; it means simply that there is relatively little such an association can do. When one considers the magnitude and urgency of the problems mankind faces, the question of what positions APA takes is, after all, a minor matter.

The important question, to my mind, is not what APA is doing, but what psychologists are doing. What Psychology can do as an association depends directly on the base provided by psychology as a science. It is our science that provides our real means for promoting human welfare.

So let me turn now to broader aspects of my topic.

REVOLUTIONARY POTENTIAL OF PSYCHOLOGY

I will begin by stating publicly something that I think psychologists all feel, but seldom talk about. In my opinion, scientific psychology is potentially one of the most revolutionary intellectual enterprises ever conceived by the mind of man. If we were ever to achieve substantial progress toward our stated aim—toward the understanding, prediction, and control of mental and behavioral phenomena—the implications for every aspect of society would make brave men tremble.

Responsible spokesmen for psychology seldom emphasize this revolutionary possibility. One reason is that the general public is all too ready to believe it, and public resistance to psychology would be all too easy to mobilize. Faced with the possibility that revolutionary pronouncements might easily do more harm than good, a prudent spokesman finds other drums to march to.

Regardless of whether we agree that prudence is always the best policy, I believe there is another reason for our public modesty. Anyone who claims that psychology is a revolutionary enterprise will face a demand from his scientific colleagues to put up or shut up. Nothing that psychology has done so far, they will say, is very revolutionary. They will admit that psychometric tests, psychoanalysis, conditioned reflexes, sensory thresholds, implanted electrodes, and factor analysis are all quite admirable, but they can scarcely be compared to gunpowder, the steam engine, organic chemistry, radio-telephony, computers, atom bombs, or genetic surgery in their revolutionary consequences for society. Our enthusiastic spokesman would have to retire in confused embarrassment.

Since I know that rash statements about the revolutionary potential of psychology may lead to public rejection and scientific ridicule, why do I take such risks on this occasion? My reason is that I do not believe the psychological revolution is still pie in the sky. It has already begun.

One reason the psychological revolution is not more obvious may be that we have been looking for it in the wrong place. We have assumed that psychology should provide new technological options, and that a psychological revolution will not occur until someone in authority exercises those options to attain socially desirable goals. One reason for this assumption, perhaps, is that it follows the model we have inherited from previous applications of science to practical problems. An applied scientist is supposed to provide instrumentalities for modifying the environment—instrumentalities that can then, under public regulation, be used by wealthy and powerful interests to achieve certain goals. The psychological revolution, when it comes, may follow a very different course, at least in its initial stages.

Davis has explained the difference between applied social science and applied natural science in the following way:

> Applied science, by definition, is instrumental. When the human goal is given, it seeks a solution by finding what effective means can be manipulated in the required way. Its function is to satisfy human desires and wants; otherwise nobody would bother. But when the science is concerned with human beings not just as organisms but as goal-seeking individuals and members of groups—then it cannot be instrumental in this way, because the object of observation has a say in what is going on and, above all, is not willing to be treated as a pure instrumentality. Most

so-called social problems are problems because people want certain things or because there is a conflict of desires or interests. (1966, p. 26)

Davis goes on to argue that once conflicts of interest have developed, applied social science is helpless; that it is only when people are agreed on their goals that our information can be usefully applied.

Although I agree with Davis that behavioral and social sciences cannot be applied to people and institutions in the same way physical and biological sciences are applied to objects and organisms, I do not agree with his view that we must remain impotent in the face of conflict. We know a great deal about the prevention and resolution of conflicts, and that information could certainly be put to better use than it has been. Indeed, sometimes what is needed is not to resolve conflict but to foster it, as when entrenched interests threaten segments of the public that have no organizational identity. And there, in turn, we know a great deal about the creation of appropriate constituencies to defend their common interests. Behavioral and social scientists are far from helpless in such situations.

More important, however, I believe that the real impact of psychology will be felt, not through the technological products it places in the hands of powerful men, but through its effects on the public at large, through a new and different public conception of what is humanly possible and what is humanly desirable.

I believe that any broad and successful application of psychological knowledge to human problems will necessarily entail a change in our conception of ourselves and of how we live and love and work together. Instead of inventing some new technique for modifying the environment, or some new product for society to adapt itself to, however it can, we are proposing to tamper with the adaptive process itself. Such an innovation is quite different from a "technological fix." I see little reason to believe that the traditional model for scientific revolutions should be appropriate.

Consider, for example, the effect that Freudian psychology has already had on Western society. It is obvious that its effects, though limited to certain segments of society, have been profound, yet I do not believe that one can argue that those effects were achieved by providing new instrumentalities for achieving goals socially agreed upon. As a method of therapy, psychoanalysis has had limited success even for those who can afford it. It has been more successful as a method of investigation, perhaps, but even there it has been only one of several available methods. The impact of Freud's thought has been due far less to the instrumentalities he provided than to the changed conception of ourselves that he inspired. The wider range of psychological problems that Freud opened up for professional psychologists is only part of his contribution. More important in the scale of history has been his effect on the broader intellectual community and, through it, on the public at large. Today we are much more aware of the irrational components of human nature and much better able to accept the reality of our unconscious impulses. The importance of Freudian psychology derives far less from its scientific validity than from the effects it has had on our shared image of man himself.

I realize that one might argue that changes in man's conception of himself under the impact of advances in scientific knowledge are neither novel nor revolutionary. For example, Darwin's theory changed our conception of ourselves, but not until the past decade has it been possible to mount a truly scientific revolution based on biological science. One might argue that we are now only at the Darwinian stage in psychology, and that the real psychological revolution is still a century or more in the future. I do not find this analogy appropriate, however.

To discover that we are not at the center of the universe, or that our remote ancestors lived in a tree, does indeed change our conception of man and society, but such new conceptions can have little effect on the way we behave in our daily affairs and in our institutional contexts. A new conception of man based on psychology, however, would have immediate implications for the most intimate details of our social and personal lives. This fact is unprecedented in any earlier stage of the Industrial Revolution.

The heart of the psychological revolution will be a new and scientifically based conception of man as an individual and as a social creature. When I say that the psychological revolution is already upon us, what I mean is that we have already begun to change man's self-conception. If we want to further that revolution, not only must we strengthen its scientific base, but we must also try to communicate it to our students and to the public. It is not the industrialist or the politician who should exploit it, but Everyman, every day.

The enrichment of public psychology by scientific psychology constitutes the most direct and important application of our science to the promotion of human welfare. Instead of trying to foresee new psychological products that might disrupt our existing social arrangements, therefore, we should be self-consciously analyzing the general effect that our scientific psychology may have on popular psychology. As I try to perform this analysis for myself, I must confess that I am not altogether pleased with the results.

I would like now to consider briefly some of the effects we are having and where, in my view, our influence is leading at the present time. Let me begin with a thumbnail sketch of one major message that many scientific psychologists are trying to communicate to the public.

CONTROL OF BEHAVIOR

One of the most admired truisms of modern psychology is that some stimuli can serve to reinforce the behavior that produces them. The practical significance of this familiar principle arises from the implication that if you can control the occurrence of these reinforcing stimuli, then you can control the occurrence of adaptive behavior intended to achieve or avoid them. This contingency between behavior and its consequences has been demonstrated in many studies of animal behavior, where environmental conditions can be controlled, or at least specified, and where the results can be measured with some precision.

Something similar holds for the human animal, of course, although it is complicated by man's symbolic proclivities and by the fact that the disparity between experimenter and subject changes when the subject is also a man. Between men, reinforcement is usually a mutual relation and each person controls the other to some extent. This relation of mutual reinforcement, which man's genius for symbols has generalized in terms of money or the promise of money, provides the psychological basis for our economic system of exchange. Psychologists did not create this economic system for controlling behavior, of course. What we have tried to do is to describe its psychological basis and its limits in terms sufficiently general to hold across different species, and to suggest how the technique might be extended to educational, rehabilitative, therapeutic, or even political situations in which economic rewards and punishments would not normally be appropriate. Once a problem of behavior control has been phrased in these terms, we may then try to discover the most effective schedule of reinforcements.

My present concern has nothing to do with the validity of these ideas. I am concerned with their effect on the public at large, for it is there, if I am right, that we are most likely to achieve a psychological revolution.

In the public view, I suspect, all this talk about controlling behavior comes across as unpleasant, if not actually threatening. Freud has alrady established in the public mind a general belief that all behavior is motivated. The current message says that psychologists now know how to use this motivation to control what people will do.When they hear this, of course, our scientific colleagues are likely to accuse us of pseudoscientific claims; less scientific segments of the public are likely to resent what they perceive as a threat to their personal freedom. Neither reaction is completely just, but neither is completely unjustifiable.

I believe these critics see an important truth, one that a myopic concentration on techniques of behavior control may cause us to overlook. At best, control is but one component in any program for personal improvement or social reform. Changing behavior is pointless in the absence of any coherent plan for how it should be changed. It is our plan for using control that the public wants to know about. Too often, I fear, psychologists have implied that acceptable uses for behavior control are either self-evident or can be safely left to the wisdom and benevolence of powerful men. Psychologists must not surrender the planning function so easily. Humane applications of behavior control must be based on intelligent diagnosis of the personal and social problems we are trying to solve. Psychology has at least as much, probably more, to contribute to the diagnosis of personal and social problems as it has to the control of behavior.

Regardless of whether we have actually achieved new scientific techniques of behavior control that are effective with human beings, and regardless of whether control is of any value in the absence of diagnosis and planning for its use, the simple fact that so many psychologists keep talking about control is having an effect on public psychology. The average citizen is predisposed to believe it. Control has been the practical payoff from the other sciences. Control must be what psychologists are after, too. Moreover, since science is notoriously successful, behavior control must be inevitable. Thus the layman forms an impression that control is the name of the road we are traveling, and that the experts are simply quibbling about how far down that road we have managed to go.

Closely related to this emphasis on control is the frequently repeated claim that living organisms are nothing but machines. A scientist recognizes, of course, that this claim says far more about our rapidly evolving conception of machines than it says about living organisms, but this interpretation is usually lost when the message reaches public ears. The public idea of a machine is something like an automobile, a mechanical device controlled by its operator. If people are machines, they can be driven like automobiles. The analogy is absurd, of course, but it illustrates the kind of distortion that can occur.

If the assumption that behavior control is feasible in some precise scientific sense becomes firmly rooted in public psychology, it could have unfortunate consequences, particularly if it is coupled with an assumption that control should be exercised by an industrial or bureaucratic elite. Psychologists must always respect and advocate the principle of *habeas mentem*—the right of a man to his own mind (Sanford 1955). If we really did have a new scientific way to control human behavior, it would be highly immoral to let it fall into the hands of some small group of men, even if they were psychologists.

Perhaps a historical analogy would be appropriate. When the evolution of species was a new and exciting idea in biology, various social theorists took it up and interpreted it to mean that capitalistic competition, like the competition between species, was the source of all progress, so the great wealth of the new industrialists was a scientifically necessary consequence of the law of the survival of the fittest. This argument, called "social Darwinism," had unfortunate consequences, both for social science and for society generally (Hofstadter 1944).

If the notion should now be accepted that it is a scientifically necessary consequence of the law of reinforcement that industrialists or bureaucrats must be allowed the same control over people that an experimenter has over his laboratory animals, I fear that a similar period of intolerable exploitation might ensue—if, indeed, it has not already begun.

The dangers that accompany a science of behavior control have been pointed out many times. Psychologists who study motivation scientifically are usually puzzled by this widespread apprehension that they might be successful. Control is not something invented by psychologists. Everyone is "controlled" all the time by something or other. All we want is to discover how the controls work. Once we understand that, society can use the knowledge in whatever manner seems socially advantageous. Our critics, on the other hand, want to know who will diagnose our problems, who will set our social goals, and who will administer the rewards and punishments.

All that I have tried to add to this familiar dialogue is the observation that the social dangers involved need not await the success of the scientific enterprise. Behavior control could easily become a self-fulfilling prophecy. If people generally should come to believe in the scientific control of behavior, proponents of coercive social programs would surely exploit that belief by dressing their proposals in scientific costumes. If our new public conception of human nature is that man's behavior can be scientifically controlled by those in positions of power, governments will quickly conform to that conception. Thus, when I try to discern what direction our psychological revolution has been taking, some aspects of it disturb me deeply and lead me to question whether in the long run these developments will really promote human welfare.

This is a serious charge. If there is any truth to it, we should ask whether any other approaches are open to us.

Personally, I believe there is a better way to advertise psychology and to relate it to social problems. Reinforcement is only one of many important ideas that we have to offer. Instead of repeating constantly that reinforcement leads to control, I would prefer to emphasize that reinforcement can lead to satisfaction and competence. And I would prefer to speak of understanding and prediction as our major scientific goals.

In the space remaining, therefore, I want to try to make the case that understanding and prediction are better goals for psychology than is control—better both for psychology and for the promotion of human welfare—because they lead us to think, not in terms of coercion by a powerful elite, but in terms of the diagnosis of problems and the development of programs that can enrich the lives of every citizen.

PUBLIC PSYCHOLOGY: TWO PARADIGMS

It should be obvious by now that I have somewhere in the back of my mind two alternative images of what the popular conception of human nature might become under the impact of scientific advances in psychology. One of these images is unfortunate, even threatening; the other is vaguer, but full of promise. Let me try to make these ideas more concrete.

The first image is the one I have been describing. It has great appeal to an authoritarian mind, and fits well with our traditional competitive ideology based on coercion, punishment, and retribution. The fact that it represents a serious distortion of scientific psychology is exactly my point. In my opinion, we have made a mistake by trying to apply our ideas to social problems and to gain acceptance for our science within the framework of this ideology.

The second image rests on the same psychological foundation, but reflects it more accurately; it allows no compromise with our traditional social ideology. It is assumed, vaguely but optimistically, that this ideology can be modified so as to be more receptive to a truer conception of human nature. How this modification can be achieved is one of the problems we face; I believe it will not be achieved if we continue to advertise the control of behavior through reinforcement as our major contribution to the solution of social problems. I would not wish to give anyone the impression that I have formulated a well-defined social alternative, but I would at least like to open a discussion and make some suggestions.

My two images are not very different from what McGregor (1960) once called Theory X and Theory Y. Theory X is the traditional theory which holds that because people dislike work, they must be coerced, controlled, directed, and threatened with punishment before they will do it. People tolerate being directed, and many even prefer it, because they have little ambition and want to avoid responsibility. McGregor's alternative Theory Y, based on social science, holds that work is as natural as play or rest. External control and threats are not the only means for inspiring people to work. People will exercise self-direction and self-control in the service of objectives to which they are committed; their commitment is a function of the rewards associated with the achievement of their objectives. People can learn not only to accept but to seek responsibility. Imagination, ingenuity, and creativity are widely distributed in the population, although these intellectual potentialities are poorly utilized under the conditions of modern industrial life.

McGregor's Theory X and Theory Y evolved in the context of his studies of industrial management. They are rival theories held by industrial managers about how best to achieve their institutional goals. A somewhat broader view is needed if we are to talk about public psychology generally, and not merely the managerial manifestations of public psychology. So let me amplify McGregor's distinction by referring to the ideas of Varela, a very remarkable engineer in Montevideo, Uruguay, who uses scientific psychology in the solution of a wide range of personal and social problems.

Varela (1970) contrasts two conceptions of the social nature of man. Following Kuhn's (1962) discussion of scientific revolutions, he refers to these two conceptions as "paradigms." The first paradigm is a set of assumptions on which our social institutions are presently based. The second is a contrasting paradigm based on psychological research. Let me outline them for you very briefly.

Our current social paradigm is characterized as follows: All men are created equal. Most behavior is motivated by economic competition, and conflict is inevitable. One truth underlies all controversy, and unreasonableness is best countered by facts and logic. When something goes wrong, someone is to blame, and every effort must be made to establish his guilt so that he can be punished. The guilty person is responsible for his own misbehavior and for his own rehabilitation. His teachers and supervisors are too busy to become experts in social science; their role is to devise solutions and see to it that their students or subordinates do what they are told.

For comparison, Varela offers a paradigm based on psychological research: There are large individual differences among people, both in ability and personality. Human motivation is complex and no one ever acts as he does for any single reason, but, in general, positive incentives are more effective than threats or punishments. Conflict is no more inevitable than disease and can be resolved or, still better, prevented. Time and resources for resolving social problems are strictly limited. When something goes wrong, how a person perceives the situation is more important to him than the "true facts," and he cannot reason about the situation until his irrational feelings have been toned down. Social problems are solved by correcting causes, not symptoms, and this can be done more effectively in groups than individually. Teachers and supervisors must be experts in social science because they are responsible for the cooperation and individual improvement of their students or subordinates.

No doubt other psychologists would draw the picture somewhat differently. Without reviewing the psychological evidence on which such generalizations are based, of course, I cannot argue their validity. But I think most of you will recognize the lines of research on which McGregor's Theory Y and Varela's second paradigm are based. Moreover, these psychologically based paradigms are incompatible in several respects with the prevailing ideology of our society.

Here, then, is the real challenge: How can we foster a social climate in which some such new public conception of man based on psychology can take root and flourish? In my opinion, this is the proper translation of our more familiar question about how psychology might contribute to the promotion of human welfare.

I cannot pretend to have an answer to this question, even in its translated form, but I believe that part of the answer is that psychology must be practiced by nonpsychologists. We are not physicians; the secrets of our trade need not be reserved for highly trained specialists. Psychological facts should be passed out freely to all who need and can use them. And from successful applications of psychological principles the public may gain a better appreciation for the power of the new conception of man that is emerging from our science.

If we take seriously the ideas of a peaceful revolution based on a new conception of human nature, our scientific results will have to be instilled in the public consciousness in a practical and usable form so that what we know can be applied by ordinary people. There simply are not enough psychologists, even including nonprofessionals, to meet every need for psychological services. The people at large will have to be their own psychologists, and make their own applications of the principles that we establish.

Of course, everyone practices psychology, just as everyone who cooks is a chemist, everyone who reads a clock is an astronomer, everyone who drives a car is an engineer. I am not suggesting any radical departure when I say that nonpsychologists must practice psychology. I am simply proposing that we should teach them to practice it better, to make use self-consciously of what we believe to be scientifically valid principles.

Our responsibility is less to assume the role of experts and try to apply psychology ourselves than to give it away to the people who really need it—and that includes everyone. The practice of valid psychology by nonpsychologists will inevitably change people's conception of themselves and what they can do. When we have accomplished that, we will really have caused a psychological revolution.

HOW TO GIVE PSYCHOLOGY AWAY

I am keenly aware that giving psychology away will be no simple task. In our society there are depths of resistance to psychological innovations that have to be experienced to be believed (Graziano 1969).

Solving social problems is generally considered to be more difficult than solving scientific problems. A social problem usually involves many more independent variables, and it cannot be finally solved until society has been persuaded to adopt the solution. Many who have tried to introduce sound psychological practices into schools, clinics, hospitals, prisons, or industries have been forced to retreat in dismay. They complain, and with good reason, that they were unable to buck the "System," and often their reactions are more violent than sensible. The System, they say, refuses to change even when it does not work.

This experience has been so common that in my pessimistic moments I have been led to wonder whether anything less than complete reform is possible.

Deutsch has made an interesting case that competitive and cooperative social relationships tend to be mutually exclusive. He summarizes the result of considerable research in the following terms:

> The strategy of power and the tactics of coercion, threat, and deception result from and also result in a competitive relationship. Similarly, the strategy of mutual problem solving and the tactics of persuasion, open-

ness, and mutual enhancement elicit and also are elicited by a cooperative orientation. (1969, p. 4)

Each orientation has its own internal consistency; elements of one are not easily injected into the other.

Perhaps a similar pressure toward internal coherence lies at the root of public resistance to many of our innovative suggestions. It often seems that any one of our ideas taken alone is inadequate. Injected into the existing social paradigm it is either a foreign body, incompatible with the other presuppositions that shape our social institutions, or it is distorted and trivialized to fit the preexisting paradigm.

One of the most basic ideas in all the social sciences is the concept of culture. Social anthropologists have developed a conception of culture as an organic whole, in which each particular value, practice, or assumption must be understood in the context of the total system. They tell terrible tales about the consequences of introducing Western reforms into aboriginal cultures without understanding the social equilibria that would be upset.

Perhaps cultural integrity is not limited to primitive cultures, but applies also to our own society here and now. If so, then our attempts at piecemeal innovation may be doomed either to fail or to be rejected outright.

I label these thoughts pessimistic because they imply a need for drastic changes throughout the whole system, changes that could only be imposed by someone with dangerous power over the lives of others. And that, I have argued, is not the way our psychological revolution should proceed.

In my more optimistic moments, however, I recognize that you do not need complete authority over a social organization in order to reform it. The important thing is not to control the system, but to understand it. Someone who has a valid conception of the system as a whole can often introduce relatively minor changes that have extensive consequences throughout the entire organization. Lacking such a conception, worthwhile innovations may be total failures.

For example, if you institute a schedule of rewards and punishments in the psychiatric ward of a Veterans Hospital, you should not be indignant when the American Legion objects on the grounds that you cannot withhold food and clothing from veterans. If you had had a more adequate understanding of the hospital as a social system, you would have included the interests and influence of the American Legion in your diagnosis of the problem, and you would have formulated a plan to gain their endorsement as part of your task as a social engineer. You should not demand inordinate power just because you made an inadequate diagnosis of the problem. Understanding must come first.

In my optimistic moments I am able to convince myself that understanding is attainable and that social science is already at a stage where successful applications are possible. Careful diagnosis and astute planning based on what we already know can often resolve problems that at first glance seemed insurmountable. Many social, clinical, and industrial psychologists have already demonstrated the power of diagnosis and planning based on sound psychological principles.

Varela has illustrated such applications by his work in Uruguay. Diagnosis involves not only a detailed analysis of the social organization and of the perceptions and goals of all the people caught up in the problem, but also the description of their abilities and personalities. Planning involves the explicit formulation of a series of steps that will lead these people to consider the problem together and will help them to discover a solution that respects everyone's hopes and aspirations. If, in the course of this plan, it becomes necessary to persuade someone, this is not to be accomplished by coercion or by marshaling facts, but by a gradual, step-by-step process that enables him to reduce his reactance little by little as he convinces himself of the virtues of the alternative view and broadens his conception of the range of acceptable solutions (Zimbardo & Ebbeson 1969, pp. 114–121). This is not the place and I am not the person to describe the ingenuity with which Varela has constructed such plans and carried them out, but such applications give me some reason for optimism.

Diagnosing practical problems and developing detailed plans to deal with them may or may not be more difficult than solving scientific problems, but it is certainly different. Many psychologists, trained in an empiricist, experimental tradition, have tried to serve two masters at once. That is to say, they have tried to solve practical problems and simultaneously to collect data of scientific value on the effects of their interventions. Other fields, however, maintain a more equitable division of labor between scientist and engineer. Scientists are responsible for the validity of the principles; engineers accept them and try to use them to solve practical problems.

Although I recognize the importance of evaluating an engineer's product, in this domain it is no easy thing to do. Assessing social innovations is a whole art in itself, one that we are only beginning to develop. Economic considerations are relevant, of course, but we must also learn to evaluate the subtler psychological and social implications of our new solutions (Bauer 1966). Technological assessment in this sense will not be achieved by insisting that every reform should resemble a well-designed experiment. In particular, the need for assessment should not be allowed to discourage those who enjoy and have a talent for social engineering.

We are in serious need of many more psychological technologists who can apply our science to the personal and social problems of the general public, for it is through them that the public will eventually discover the new paradigm that psychologists are developing. That is to say, it is through the success of such practical applications that we have our best hope for revolutionizing public psychology.

Obviously, we must avoid the evils of superficiality; we must continue as scientists to refine, clarify, and integrate our new paradigm. Most importantly, we must self-consciously recognize that it *is* a new and revolutionary conception that we are working toward, so that isolated discoveries can be related to and evaluated in terms of that larger context. But all that would be futile, of course, if the general public did not accept it, or if public psychology were not altered by it.

There is no possibility of legislating the changes I have in mind. Passing laws that people must change their conceptions of themselves and others is precisely the opposite of what we need. Education would seem to be our only possibility. I do not mean only education in the schoolroom, although that is probably the best communication channel presently at our disposal. I have in mind a more ambitious program of educating the general public.

It is critically important to shape this education to fit the perceived needs of the people who receive it. Lectures suitable for graduate seminars are seldom suitable for laymen, and for a layman facing a concrete problem they are usually worse than useless. In order to get a factory supervisor or a ghetto mother involved, we must give them something they can use. Abstract theories, however elegant, or sensitivity training, however insightful, are too remote from the specific troubles they face. In order to get started, we must begin with people where they are, not assume we know where they should be. If a supervisor is having trouble with his men, perhaps we should teach him how to write a job description and how to evaluate the abilities and personalities of those who fill the job; perhaps we should teach him the art of persuasion, or the time and place for positive reinforcement. If a ghetto mother is not giving her children sufficient intellectual challenge, perhaps we should teach her how to encourage their motor, perceptual, and linguistic skills. The techniques involved are not some esoteric branch of witchcraft that must be reserved for those with Ph.D. degrees in psychology. When the ideas are made sufficiently concrete and explicit, the scientific foundations of psychology can be grasped by sixth-grade children.

There are many obvious and useful suggestions that we could make and that nonpsychologists could exploit. Not every psychological problem in human engineering has to be solved by a professional psychologist; engineers can rapidly assimilate psychological facts and theories that are relevant to their own work. Not every teaching program has to be written by a learning theorist; principles governing the design and evaluation of programmed materials can be learned by content specialists. Not every personnel decision has to be made by a psychometrician; not every interview has to be conducted by a clinical psychologist; not every problem has to be solved by a cognitive psychologist; not every reinforcement has to be supervised by a student of conditioning. Psychological principles and techniques can be usefully applied by everyone. If our suggestions actually work, people should be eager to learn more. If they do not work, we should improve them. But we should not try to give people something whose value they cannot recognize, then complain when they do not return for a second meeting.

Consider the teaching of reading, for example. Here is an obviously appropriate area for the application of psychological principles. So what do we do? We assemble experts who decide what words children know, and in what order they should learn to read them; then we write stories with those words and teachers make the children read them, or we use them in programmed instruction that exploits the principles of reinforcement. But all too often the children fail to recognize the value of learning these carefully constructed lessons.

Personally, I have been much impressed with the approach of Ashton-Warner (1963), who begins by asking a child what words he wants. Mummy, daddy, kiss, frightened, ghost, their own names—these are the words children ask for, words that are bound up with their own loves and fears. She writes each child's word on a large, tough card and gives it to him. If a child wants words like police, butcher, knife, kill, jail, and bomb, he gets them. And he learns to read them almost immediately. It is *his* word, and each morning he retrieves his own words from the pile collected each night by the teacher. These are not dead words of an expert's choosing, but words that live in a child's own experience. Given this start, children begin to write, using their own words, and from there the teaching of reading follows naturally. Under this regimen, a word is not an imposed task to be learned with reinforcements borrowed from some external source of motivation. Learning the word is itself reinforcing; it gives the child something he wants, a new way to cope with a desire or fear. Each child decides where he wants to start, and each child receives something whose value he can recognize.

Could we generalize this technique discovered by an inspired teacher in a small New Zealand school? In my own thinking I have linked it with something that White (1959) has called competence motivation. In order to tap this motivational system we must use psychology to give people skills that will satisfy their urge to feel more effective. Feeling effective is a very personal thing, for it must be a feeling of effectiveness in coping with personal problems in one's own life. From that beginning some might want to learn more about the science that helped them increase their competence, and then perhaps we could afford to be more abstract. But in the beginning we must try to diagnose and solve the problems people think they have, not the problems we experts think they ought to have, and we must learn to understand those problems in the social and institutional contexts that define them. With this approach we might do something practical for nurses, policemen, prison guards, salesmen—for people in many different walks of life. That, I believe, is what we should mean when we talk about applying psychology to the promotion of human welfare.

If you tell me that such a program is too ambitious or too foreign to our conception of ourselves as scientists and practitioners, I must agree that I do not know where to place our fulcrum to move the world. My goal is to persuade you that this is the problem we face, and that we dare not leave it for bureaucrats or businessmen to solve. We will have to cope with it however we can, and I hope that someone has better ideas than I about how to do it.

I can see some promise for innovations in particular subcultures. If we apply our new paradigm in particular institutions—in schools, hospitals, prisons, industries—we can perhaps test its validity and demonstrate its superiority. Many such social experiments are already in progress, of course. And much of the recent surge of interest in community psychology (Bennett 1966) has been stimulated by the realization that we really do have something to contribute to community life. Perhaps all this work will eventually have a cumulative effect.

One trouble, of course, is that we are trying to reverse the natural direction of influence. Ordinarily, an institution or a community models its own subculture more or less automatically after the larger culture in which it is embedded, and new members require little indoctrination in order to understand the tacit assumptions on which the institution is based. Whether the new paradigm will be powerful enough to reverse this direction is, I suppose, a matter for pure speculation at the present time. It seems unlikely that we will succeed, however, if each application of the new paradigm is viewed as unrelated to every other, and no attempt is made to integrate these experiments into a paradigm for society as a whole.

It is possible, however, that our society may not be quite as resistant as we anticipate. The demand for social relevance that we have been voicing as psychologists is only one aspect of a general dissatisfaction with the current state of our society. On every hand we hear complaints about the old paradigm. People are growing increasingly alienated from a society in which a few wise men behind closed doors decide what is good for everyone. Our system of justice based on punishment and retribution is not working. Even those most blessed by economic rewards are asking for something more satisfying to fill their lives. We desperately need techniques for resolving conflicts, and for preventing them from becoming public confrontations from which reasonable retreat is impossible. Anyone who reads the newspapers must realize that vast social changes are in the making, that they must occur if civilized society is to survive.

Vested interests will oppose these changes, of course, but as someone once said, vested interests, however powerful, cannot withstand the gradual encroachment of new ideas. If we psychologists are ready for it, we may be able to contribute a coherent and workable philosophy, based on the science of psychology, that will make this general agitation less negative, that will make it a positive search for something new.

I recognize that many of you will note these ambitions as little more than empty rhetoric. Psychologists will never be up to it, you will say. We should stay in our laboratories and do our own thing. The public will work out its own paradigms without us. Perhaps such skepticism is justified.

On the other hand, difficulty is no excuse for surrender. There is a sense in which the unattainable is the best goal to pursue. So let us continue our struggle to advance psychology as a means of promoting human welfare, each in our own way. For myself, however, I can imagine nothing we could do that would be more relevant to human welfare, and nothing that could pose a greater challenge to the next generation of psychologists, than to discover how best to give psychology away.

References

American Psychological Association. Bylaws of the American Psychological Association. *1968 Directory*. Washington, D.C.: Author, 1968.

Ashton-Warner, S. *Teacher*. New York: Simon & Schuster, 1963.

Bauer, R.A. (Ed.) *Social indicators*. Cambridge, Mass.: M.I.T. Press, 1966.

Bennett, C.C. *Community psychology*. Report of Boston Conference on the Education of Psychologists for Community Mental Health. Boston: Boston University, 1966.

Davis, K. The perilous promise of behavioral science. In *Research in the service of man: Biomedical knowledge, development, and use*. A conference sponsored by the Subcommittee on Government Research and the Frontiers of Science Foundation of Oklahoma for the Committee on Government, Operations of the U. S. Senate, October 1966. Washington, D.C.: U. S. Government Printing Office, 1967.

Deutsch, M. Reflections on some experimental studies of interpersonal conflict. Presidential address to the Eastern Psychological Association, New York, April 11, 1969.

Graziano, A.M. Clinical innovation and the mental health power structure: A social case history. *American Psychologist*, 1969, 24, 10–18.

Hofstadter, R. *Social Darwinism in American thought*. Philadelphia: University of Pennsylvania Press, 1944.

Kuhn, T. *The structure of scientific revolutions*. Chicago: University of Chicago Press, 1962.

Ladd, E.C., Jr. Professors and political petitions. *Science*, 1969, 163, 1425–1430.

McGregor, D. *The human side of enterprise*. New York: McGraw-Hill, 1960.

Sanford, F.H. Creative health and the principle of *habeas mentem*. *American Psychologist*, 1955, 10, 829–835.

Tyler, L. An approach to public affairs: Report of the ad hoc Committee on Public Affairs. *American Psychologist*, 1969, 24, 1–4.

Varela, J.A. *Introduction to social science technology*. New York: Academic Press, 1970.

White, R.W. Motivation reconsidered: The concept of competence. *Psychological Review*, 1959, 66, 297–333.

Zimbardo, P., & Ebbeson, E. *Influencing attitudes and changing behavior*. Reading, Mass.: Addison-Wesley, 1969.

Appendix B
Authors' Biographies

WILLAM BEVAN
William Preston Few Professor
Duke University
Academic Science and the Federal Government: Less Wed, More Locked

Dr. Bevan received his Ph.D. from Duke University in 1948. In addition to having served on the faculties of Heidelberg College and Emory University, he has been awarded several honorary doctorates. Between 1959 and 1970 he held a variety of professional and administrative positions at Kansas State University and The John Hopkins University. From 1970 to 1974 he served as the executive officer of the American Association for the Advancement of Science, and since that time he has been in the Department of Psychology at Duke. Dr. Bevan, who has served in a variety of consultant roles, also has more than 160 articles, chapters, and other publications to his credit, and belongs to numerous committees and boards of organizations such as the National Academy of Sciences-National Research Council, NIE, NIH and NIMH, and NSF.

JAMES S. JACKSON
Associate Professor
University of Michigan

Promoting Human Welfare Through Legislative Advocacy: A Proper Role for the Proper Science of Psychology?

Dr. Jackson was awarded his Ph.D. by Wayne State University in 1972. He joined the Psychology Department faculty of the University of Michigan in 1971, where he now also holds joint appointments as a faculty associate of the Institute of Gerontology and the Research Center for Group Dynamics with the Institute for Social Research. Dr. Jackson's current research concerns a "National Mental Health Survey of the Adult Black Population." Focused on health-seeking behaviors of minority group members, it represents an extension of his concern with methodological issues of large-scale surveys of minorities. He was a founding member of the Black Student Psychological Association in the late 1960s, which later became the Association of Black Psychologists, of which he remains a member. He became a member of the board of trustees of the Association for the Advancement of Psychology in 1974, serving as chairman of that board for 1978–1979.

SIGMUND KOCH
University Professor of Psychology and Philosophy
Boston University

Psychology and Its Human Clientele: Beneficiaries or Victims?

Dr. Koch received his Ph.D. from Duke University in 1942. Between 1942 and 1964 he was on the Duke University faculty, but also held a variety of positions at Clark University, University College (London), and Yale University. Since 1964 he has worked at The Ford Foundation, the University of Texas, and joined Boston University in 1971. Dr. Koch is perhaps most widely known for directing a multiyear study seeking assessment of the "methodological, theoretical, and empirical status" of psychology, which resulted in a six-volume work, *Psychology: A Study of a Science*. Author of articles and books, the main thread of his interest has been the analysis of psychological theories and studying problems at the borderline between psychology and philosophy.

GEORGE A. MILLER
Professor The Rockefeller University
Moderator/Discussant: Reactions

Dr. Miller was awarded his Ph.D. by Harvard University in 1946, where he stayed to continue his work in the Psycho-Acoustic Laboratory. Between 1948 and 1951 he was on the faculty at Harvard, moving to MIT for the period 1951–1955. In 1955 he returned to Harvard where he helped form the Center for Cognitive Studies in 1960. He was appointed a professor at The Rockefeller University in 1967, and in 1979 he accepted an appointment as professor of psychology at Princeton University, where he remains. Dr. Miller is a past president of both the Eastern Psychological Association and the American Psychological Association, having received the Distinguished Scientific Contribution Award from the APA in 1963 for his significant work in the study of language and communication—a field in which he remains a dominant force. His presidential address to the APA in late Summer 1969 ("Psychology as a Means of Promoting Human Welfare") is the focal point of this symposium.

MICHAEL SCRIVEN
Professor of Philosophy and Education
University of San Francisco
An Evaluation of Psychology

Dr. Scriven was awarded his D.Phil. by Oxford University. From 1952 to 1966 he held various faculty appointments in history, philosophy, or philosophy of science at the University of Minnesota, Swarthmore College, and Indiana University. In 1966 he became professor of philosophy at the University of California at Berkeley, where in 1975 he also accepted an appointment as professor of education. In 1976 he was a Fellow at the Institute of Higher Studies, University of California at Santa Barbara. In 1977 he became director of the Evaluation Institute at the University of San Francisco, where in 1978 he also became University Professor. Dr. Scriven has held a variety of visiting and summer appointments or fellowships at various institutions. He is the author of a number of books and about two hundred articles. Dr. Scriven is on the editorial

board of half a dozen journals and served as president of the American Educational Research Association in 1978–1979. His current areas of research interest include cognitive moral education, curriculum theory, practical logic and ethics, needs assessment models, and the philosophy of science.

SHELDON H. WHITE
Professor
Harvard University
Psychology in All Sorts of Places

Dr. White was granted his Ph.D. from the State University of Iowa in 1957 and was a member of the faculty at the University of Chicago from 1957 to 1963. After a year at the Center for Cognitive Studies at Harvard, he was on the faculty of the Graduate School of Education there from 1965 to 1973, becoming the Roy E. Larsen Professor. Since 1973 he has been professor with the Psychology Department, where he is chairman of the Division of Personality and Developmental Psychology. Dr. White is an active consultant to numerous agencies and organizations, including NIMH, OEO, OMB, Children's Television Workshop, and the Rand Corporation. He is a member of several major national advisory committees, and in 1972–1973 he conducted a major review of "Federal Programs for Young Children" for HEW. Dr. White's research interests focus on children's learning, which he has defined in different ways at different stages during his professional career.

E. BELVIN WILLIAMS
Senior Vice President, Program Areas
Educational Testing Service

Testing—The Limits of Social Responsibility

Dr. Williams was awarded his Ph.D. from Columbia University in 1962. Between 1962 and 1975 Dr. Williams held a variety of academic and administrative appointments in the Barnard, Columbia, and Teachers Colleges of Columbia University, in addition to directing the Computer Center at Columbia from 1964 to 1971. Since 1972 he has also served in a variety of administrative positions at the Educational Testing Service, assuming his current position in 1977. Member of a number of national organizations, Dr. Williams has also served as consultant to the Teacher Corps and the National Urban League, in addition to chairing the Review Committee on the Testing of Minorities for ETS.

Name Index

Aaron, H. J., 4–5
Abelson, P. H., 194
Abelson, R. P., 109
Albee, G. W., 150
Andrews, F. M., 151, 156
Angoff, W. H., 92
Ashton-Warner, S., 37, 41, 43, 266
Atkinson, R. C., 147, 150, 152, 153, 155, 163, 164

Bacon, F., 110, 111
Bales, R. F., 108–109
Bandura, A., 147, 150
Baratz, J. C., 15
Baratz, S. S., 15
Bartlett, T. A., 196
Bauer, R. A., 264
Beane, W. C., 107, 108
Beit-Hallahmi, B., 150
Bell, D., 90
Bennett, C. C., 267
Bennis, W. G., 109
Bergmann, G., 54
Bevan, A., 201
Bevan, W., 12, 18, 20, 136, 153, 154, 157, 164, 166, 167, 171, 176, 183, 184–217, 218–224, 225–227, 234, 235, 237, 238, 240, 241–242, 243–244, 270
Bissell, J. S., 15
Black, M., 240
Blanpied, W. A., 16–17
Bledstein, B. J., 112, 121
Blissett, M., 205, 207
Bonham, G. W., 194
Boring, E. G., 80, 81–82, 110, 111, 253
Bozeman, B., 198, 209
Brock, W., 204
Bronfenbrenner, U., 18

Bronowski, J., 207
Brown, M., 11
Bruner, J. S., 15, 18, 26, 240
Brunswik, E., 18, 19
Bush, V., 189
Buss, A. R., 153
Butler, N. M., 122

Caen, H., 70–71
Caldwell, B. M., 15
Califano, J. A., 88, 89, 204
Campbell, A., 151
Campbell, D. T., 11, 19, 74, 115, 150, 156, 157
Caplan, N., 153
Carter, J., 190, 193
Carter, L. F., 157
Carter, R., 191
Cassirer, E., 104–105
Cattell, J. M., 122
Cazden, C. B., 238
Chandler, A. D., Jr., 120–121, 125
Chomsky, N., 134
Churchman, C. W., 86, 87–88
Clark, K. B., 14
Clark, R. B., 13
Cohen, D. K., 17, 19, 20
Cohen, J. S., 236
Cohen, M., 94
Cole, M., 15, 18
Conant, J. B., 142
Converse, P. E., 151
Cronbach, L. J., 19, 91
Culliton, B. J., 198, 200
Cummings, N. A., 150
Cutter, W. B., 192, 193

Darlington, R. B., 93
Darwin, C., 112, 256
Davis, B., 76
Davis, K., 34, 254–255

Descartes, R., 111
Deutsch, M., 11, 14–15, 262–263
Diderich, P., 72
Dilthey, W., 128, 129
Dörken, H., 148, 153, 159
Doty, W. G., 107, 108
Dubos, R., 39
Dunphy, D. C., 108, 109

Ebbeson, E., 264
Ebert-Flattau, P., 197
Edsall, J. T., 16
Einstein, A., 13
Eliade, M., 107, 109
Engels, F., 112
Etheredge, L. S., 115

Fields, C. M., 199
Ford, G., 190, 201
Frank, L., 15
Frankfurter, F., 200
Fraser, D. M., 157
Freeman, H. E., 150, 152, 157
Freud, S., 13, 45, 64, 255, 257

Garet, M. S., 19
Garmezy, N., 187n
Garner, W. R., 153, 154, 155, 156, 157, 160
Gergen, K. J., 151
Goodwin, L., 148
Gordon, R., 187n
Gottlieb, D., 1, 2–5, 246n
Graziano, A. M., 262
Gross, A. L., 93
Gross, B. M., 149, 151
Gulliksen, H., 99
Guttentag, M., 15
Gwynne, P., 194

Haeberlin, H. K., 113
Hagen, E., 89, 91

Hall, G. S., 122
Harlow, H., 64
Harris, F., 28
Hartshorne, H., 64
Haskins, C. P., 10, 20
Heidbreder, E., 114
Heider, F., 18, 19
Hobbes, T., 111
Hodges, M. A., 129
Hofstadter, R., 112, 258
Holton, G., 7–8, 12, 16, 188, 235
Holtzman, W. A., 88, 89, 90
Horowitz, I. L., 148
Howard, G., 247n
Hull, C. L., 31
Hunter, W. S., 123

Jackson, J., 17–18, 144–162, 163–167, 169–171, 173–174, 176, 178, 180–182, 221, 223, 237, 238, 240, 271
Jackson, P., 246n
James, W., 123, 126
Jencks, C., 175
Jenkins, J. J., 243, 247n
Jensen, A. R., 65
Johnson, L. B., 174
Jones, W. T., 87

Kant, I., 87, 90, 113–114, 128
Karlesky, J. J., 194
Kasschau, R. A., 1, 6, 24, 86
Keller, F., 76
Keniston, K., 17
Kennedy, E. M., 182, 205
Kennedy, J. F., 3
Kessel, F. S., 7–23, 104, 234–247
Kieslar, S. B., 246n
King, J. A. S., 203

Klüver, H., 44
Koch, S., 10, 17, 27–53, 54–56, 57–60, 78, 142–143, 167–169, 170, 171, 177–180, 220, 221, 223, 237, 239–241, 242, 246–247n, 271
Kohlberg, L., 64
Kovach, J. K., 110
Kramer, J. R., 149
Krech, D., 13, 14
Kren, G., 150, 156
Kuhn, T., 17, 47, 140, 141–142, 260

LaBais, K., 84
Ladd, E. C., Jr., 250
Lance, B., 190
Lande, K. C., 151, 156
Lashley, K., 230
Lawrence, D. H., 30
Leacock, S., 179
Leavis, F. R., 30–31, 33
Leonard, J., 244–245
Lewin, K., 14, 19, 73, 238
Lippitt, R., 13
Lowman, R., 198

MacRae, D., 19
Makkreel, R. A., 129
Malinowski, B., 107
Marans, R., 151
Marx, K., 112
Matthews, T., 204
May, M. A., 64
Mayr, E., 141
McCarrell, N. S., 19
McElroy, W. D., 152, 154, 157
McGregor, D., 260, 261
McGuire, W. J., 14, 18
McKeachie, W. J., 150
Meehl, P. E., 17, 65, 92, 154
Melton, A., 26
Mill, J. S., 42
Miller, G. A., 3, 4, 7, 8–9, 10, 15, 24–27, 29, 31, 32, 33, 34, 35, 36–43, 53, 56–57, 58–60, 61, 74, 77–80, 83, 86–87, 90, 97, 98–101, 102, 105, 132, 135, 137, 140–141, 144, 148, 150, 151, 152, 153, 156, 157, 158, 160, 168, 171, 179–180, 182, 183, 184, 224–225, 227, 228, 229–233, 237, 239, 243–244, 246n, 247n, 249–268, 272
Minsky, M., 109
Mondale, W., 29
Moynihan, D. P., 4, 175, 200
Muller, S., 188, 203
Munitz, B., 2
Munsterberg, H., 114
Murchison, C., 114
Murphy, G., 110

Nelkin, D., 246n
Nelson, S. D., 153
Nightengale, F., 94
Nordhaus, W., 193
Novick, M. R., 93

Oppenheimer, J. R., 87
Orwell, G., 42
Owen, R., 40–41

Pavlov, I., 133
Pepper, C., 195
Perl, M., 16
Petersen, N. S., 93
Phillips, D. I., 190, 193
Piaget, J., 143
Pillemer, D., 109
Polyani, M., 198
Popper, K., 129
Portugal, F. H., 236
Pressey, S. L., 72
Price, D. K., 11–12, 147, 148, 152, 156, 158, 159
Price, D. J. de S., 192, 207, 209, 210
Proxmire, W., 66

Rappoport, L., 150, 151, 156
Raush, H. L., 154
Rawls, J. A., 94
Reagan, R., 165
Reich, C., 16
Rein, M., 125, 128
Rie, H. E., 148, 150, 151, 153, 155
Riecken, H., 187n
Rivlin, A., 175
Roark, A. C., 192, 202
Roback, H., 190, 193
Robinson, D. N., 111

Roberts, M. J., 148, 152, 153, 158
Rodgers, W. L., 151
Rogers, P., 202
Rogers, W. L., 151
Rosen, A., 92
Rosen, P. L., 246n
Rosenzweig, R. M., 200, 205
Rossi, P., 3, 4
Roszak, T., 16
Rovere, R., 204

Sagan, C., 246n
Saks, M. J., 242, 246n
Sanford, F. H., 258
Sanford, N., 14
Sarason, S. B., 151
Savoy, R., 116
Scarr, S., 247n
Schank, R. C., 109
Schroeer, D., 12
Scott, R. A., 200
Scribner, S., 18
Scriven, M., 17, 55, 61–77, 79n, 80–82, 171, 238, 239, 240, 241, 242, 272
Segall, M. H., 153, 157, 158
Seligman, J., 89, 90
Senn, M. J. E., 15
Shannon, J. A., 19
Shapley, W. H., 190, 193
Sheehan, M. R., 128
Shepard, H. A., 109
Sherwood, C. C., 150, 152, 157
Siegel, A. W., 109
Simon, H., 120
Skinner, B. F., 72
Smith, B. L. R., 194
Smith, B. M., 148, 150, 151, 153, 155, 158
Smith, M. S., 15
Smith, R. J., 192, 198
Spencer, H., 112
Stanley, J. C., 238, 246n
Stent, G. S., 246n
Stevenson, A. E., 205
Su, W., 93
Sullivan, W., 212

Thackray, A., 13, 16
Thorndike, E. B., 122
Thorndike, R. L., 88, 89, 90, 91, 92, 93

Titchener, E. B., 114
Toulmin, S., 235, 239
Truman, H. S., 189
Tu, J., 148
Tussman, J., 208
Tyack, D. B., 121
Tyler, L. A., 152, 154, 157, 251

Vallance, T. R., 152, 153, 156, 157, 158
Varela, J. A., 9, 37–41, 150, 151, 152, 157, 160, 249n, 260–261, 264
Verbrugge, R. R., 19

Walcott, J., 204
Walker, E. L., 10–11, 13
Wallach, M. A., 238
Walsh, J., 207
Warren, E., 214
Wartofsky, M., 17
Watson, J. B., 31, 33, 36, 246n
Weber, M., 74
Weinberg, A., 207
Weiss, J. A., 20
White, R. W., 232, 266
White, S. H., 18, 41, 53–54, 102–131, 132–136, 137–142, 165–166, 168, 169, 174–176, 178–179, 222–223, 237, 238, 240, 242, 246n, 273
Williams, E. B., 18, 83–97, 98–101, 134, 136, 143, 163, 164, 165, 168, 170–173, 178, 217–218, 219, 221, 222, 223, 239, 247n, 274
Williams, R., 42
Withey, S. B., 151, 156
Woodworth, R. S., 114, 128
Wundt, W., 110, 113, 114, 128, 240

Yarmolinsky, A., 203, 208

Zamoro, R., 18
Zimbardo, P., 264
Zonana, V. F., 89, 90
Zuniga, B., 151, 153, 160

SUBJECT INDEX

Academic science, 202–205
  basic research, 189–193
  enrollment, 196–197
  and government, future relationship of, 208–210
  retirement and tenure, 195–196
Accountability, 198
Action research, 14
Activist/collaborator model, 159
Advocacy, 157–159, 179–183
  and professional science, 212–213
  as role for psychology, 147–162
American Psychological Association:
  role of, 250–253
  and social concerns, 17–18, 25–26
Association for the Advancement of Psychology (AAP), 148, 159, 166, 169, 180, 237
Atomic bomb, 13

Bakke discrimination case, 4
Basic research:
  as consumption or investment good, 193
  failing equipment and facilities, 193–195
  future of, 195–198
Behavior control, 8–9, 256–259
  and public psychology, 258
Behaviorism, 31
Black Americans, and graduate study, 145
Brown desegregation case, 14–15

Children, categorizing of, 125–126
Committee on Scientific Freedom and Responsibility (AAAS), 16
Communication, constraints on, 51
Community psychology, 267
Competence motivation, 41–43, 266
Compliance, costs of, 199
Conflict, 255
  inevitability of, 37, 39
Contract teaching, 41–43

Control, as goal of psychology, 34, 35–36
Cost analysis, 75
Culture, concept of, 263
Culture of professionalism, 121
Cumulativeness, of knowledge, 47–48

Decision demand, 91
Definition:
  as perception training, 45–46
  perceptual theory of, 49–51
Dehumanization, by science, 33–34
Diagnosis, 264
Division of labor, and teaching, 118–119
Dream time, of psychology, 109, 110–115

Education, occupational groups in, 122
Educational Testing Service, 100–101
Ethics:
  of experimentation, 75
  and recombinant DNA, 235–236
Evaluator model, 157–158
Evaluation movement, 11
Existential psychology, 114
Experimentation, neo-Wundtian, 58
Expert witness model, 157

Fact-value distinction, 74, 75
Falsification, and science, 129
Federation of Atomic Scientists, 13
Folk psychology, 113
Freudian psychology, 255–256
Functionalism, 114

Giving away of psychology, 9, 120–127, 127–129, 237–240, 262–268
Government, federal:
  and academic science, 187–217
  control by, 181
  idealism in, 139
  and psychology, 103–104
  regulation tendency, 198–202
  and research funding, 11–12, 67, 135–136, 163–164, 170–171, 189–193

Great Society programs, 173–174

Headstart program, 103
Health Professions Educational Assistance Amendment (1965), 201–202
HEW (Department of Health, Education and Welfare), 204–205
Human welfare:
  defining, 150–151, 251–252
  and psychology, 249–268
Humanism, 58–59
  methods of, 47–48
  and motivation, 38

Images, as organizers, 108–109
Individual differences, 38, 93–94, 261
Integrated Queue model, 72, 238
Intelligence tests (IQ), 72–73
Intrinsic content validity, 99
Intrinsic motivation, 42

Keller plan teaching, 76

Language:
  lexical units, 45
  and psychologists, 47
Learning theory, 114–115
Legislation, and social problems, 148–150
Legislative advocacy (see Advocacy)

Man, as object, 34, 43
Measurement, 86–97
  preoccupation with, 51
Medical schools, and federal regulation, 201–202
Mental health, 155–156
Metaphor, 46
Miller's "Law of Seven", 183
Morality, 86
Motivation, 139–140
  competence, 41–43
  intrinsic, 42
  of regulation, 199
Myths, 141
  as organizers, 124–125

National Academy of Science, 206
National Health Planning and Resource